Surge

STORY BY KYLE GREEN, AR[illegible] KOSARU
LETTERS BY LAILA REIMOZ, EDITED BY XAVIERA PALLARS

Surge EPILOGUE

STORY BY KYLE GREEN, ART BY RHEA SILVAN
LETTERS BY LAILA REIMOZ, EDITED BY XAVIERA PALLARS

~ We also Present Two Short Bonus Stories ~

Obsessive Compulsive Desire

STORY AND ART BY LAILA REIMOZ
EDITED BY XAVIERA PALLARS

schoolboy crush

STORY BY YAMILA ABRAHAM, ART BY STUDIO KOSARU
LETTERS BY LAILA REIMOZ, EDITED BY XAVIERA PALLARS

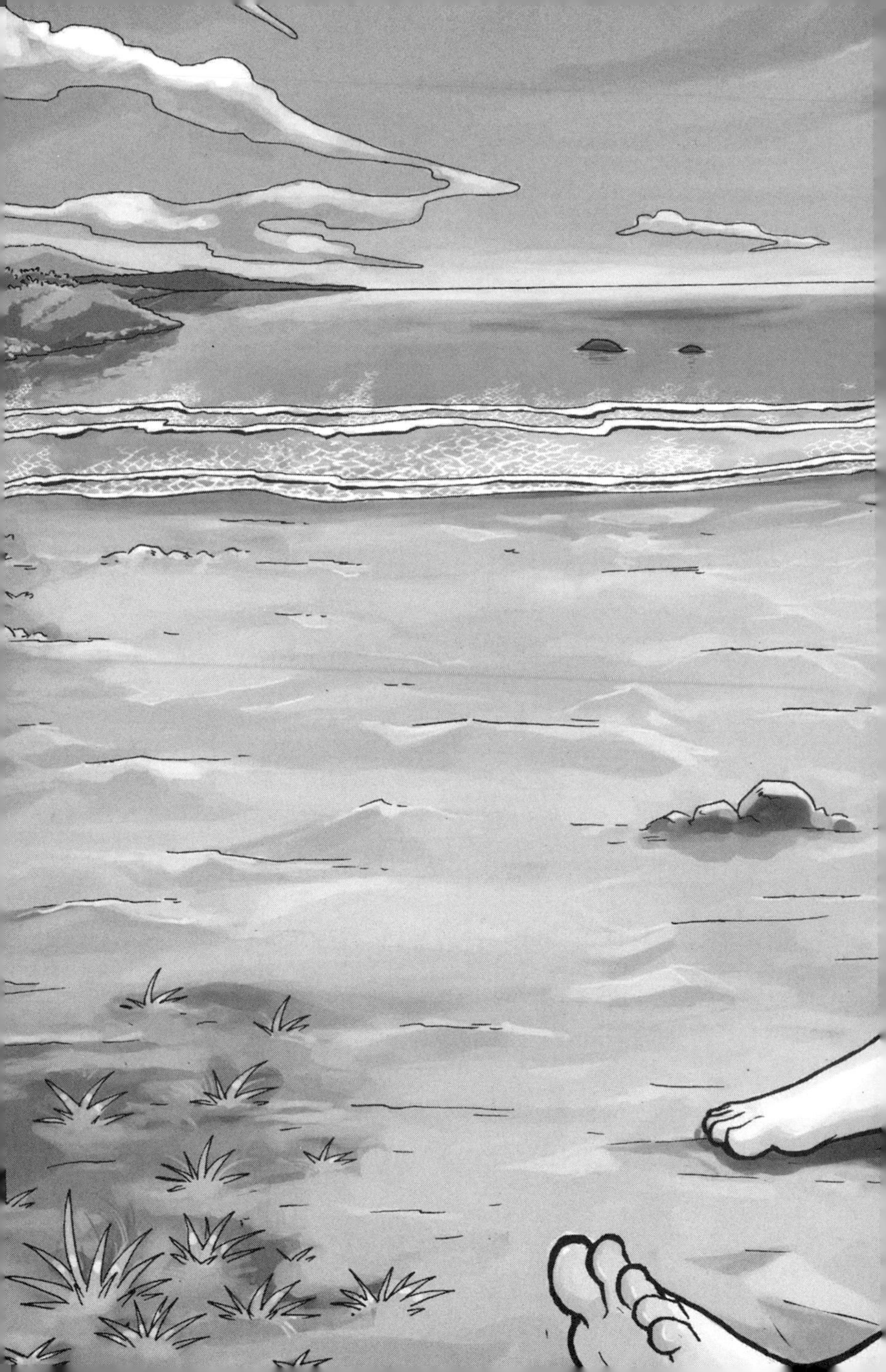

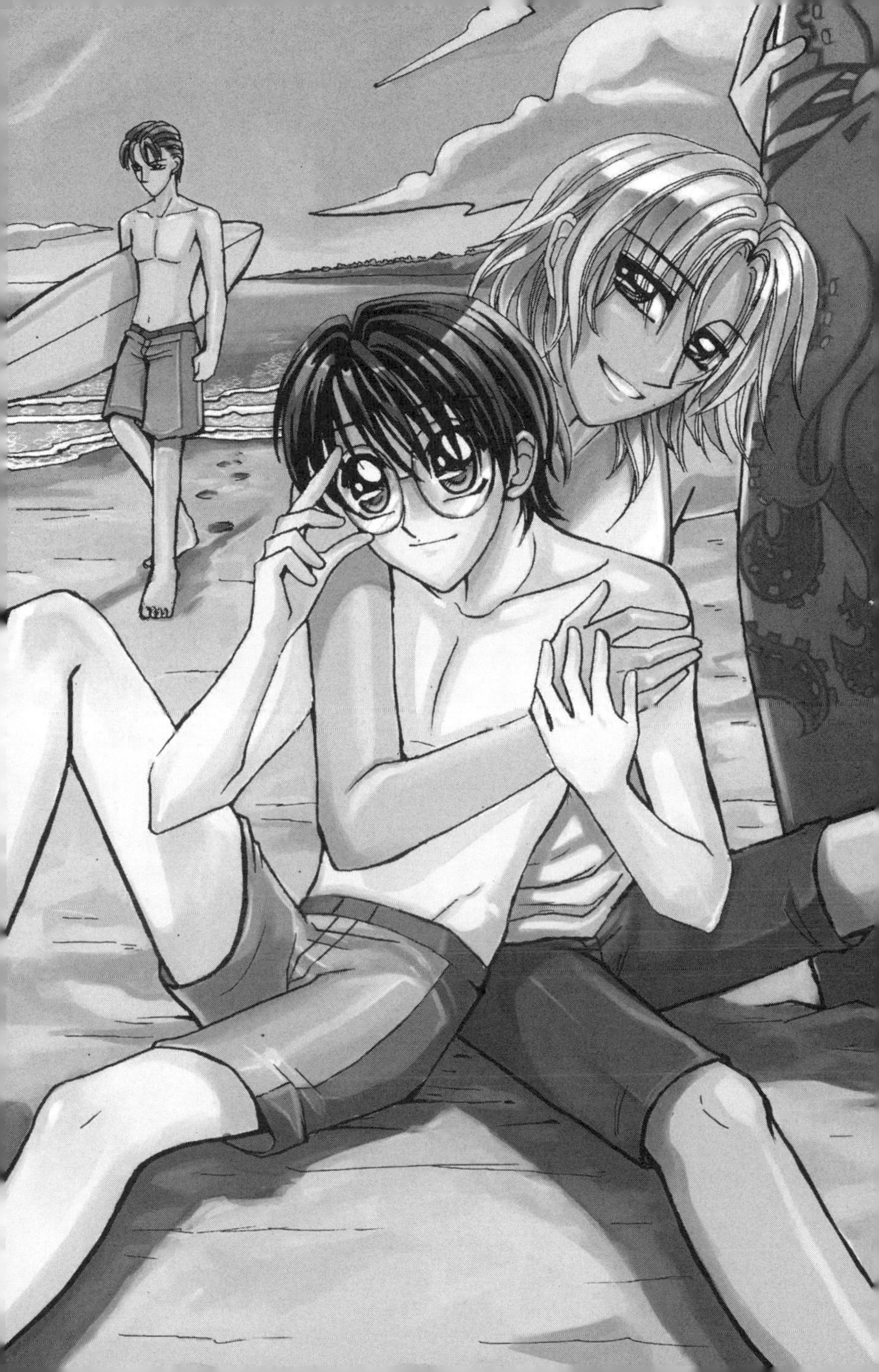

Available Now!

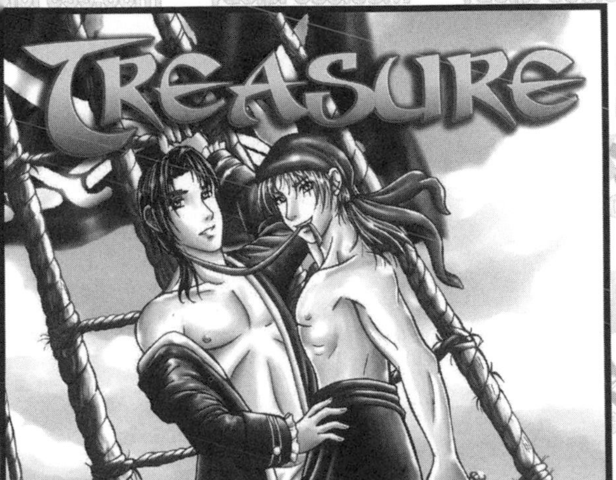
TREASURE
STUDIO KAWAII

Treasure

by Studio Kawaii

Two navy sailors have their romance shattered when one is abducted by pirates and forced to become a pirate himself. Now they must face each other again, but this time as enemies. An exciting yaoi romance on the high seas!

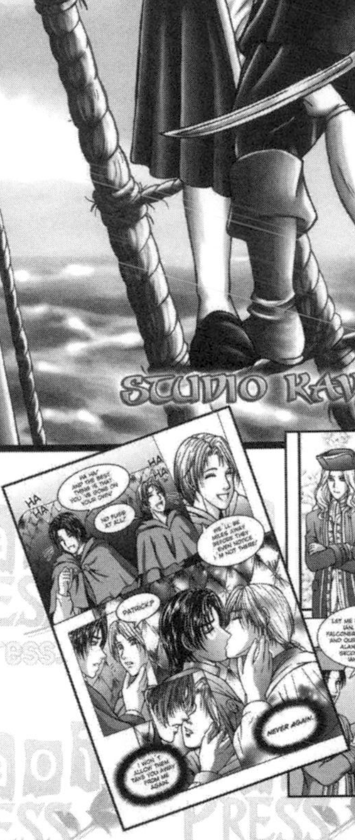
PATRICK?
NEVER AGAIN!

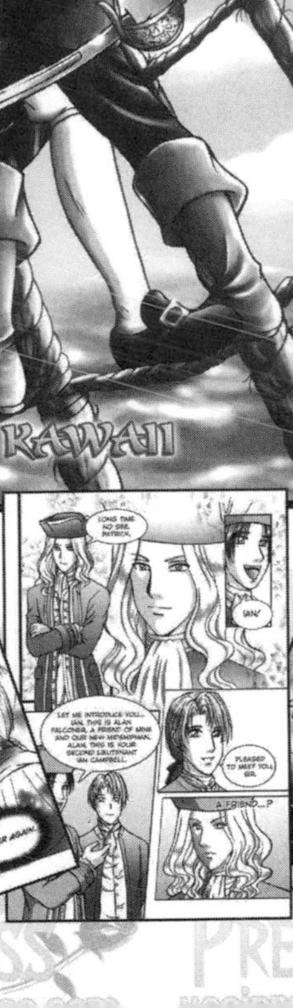
LONG TIME NO SEE, PATRICK.
IAN!
PLEASED TO MEET YOU, SIR.
A FRIEND...?

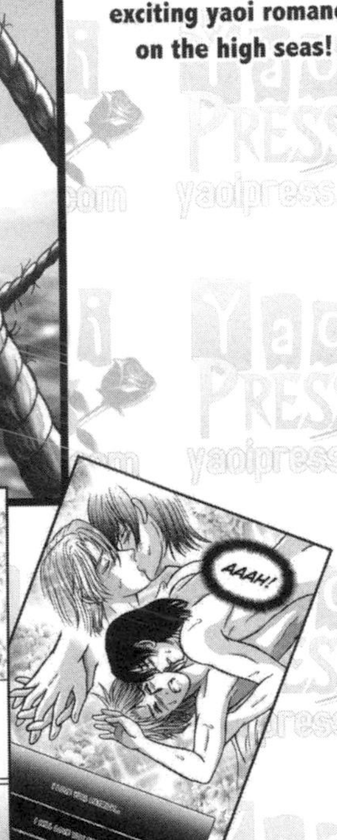
AAAH!

Surge
Story and Cover Color by Kyle Greene, Art by Studio Kosaru,
Letters by Laila Reimoz, Edited by Xaviera Pallars

Surge Epilogue
Story by Kyle Greene, Art by Rhea Silvan, Letters by Laila Reimoz,
Edited by Xaviera Pallars

Obsessive Compulsive Desire
Story, art, and letters by Laila Reimoz, Edited by Xaviera Pallars

Schoolboy Crush
Story by Yamila Abraham, Art by Studio Kosaru,
Letters by Laila Reimoz, Edited by Xaviera Pallars

Printed in the United States of America

ISBN: 1-933664-07-X
ISBN 13: 978-1-933664-07-1

www.yaoipress.com

10 9 8 7 6 5 4 3 2 1

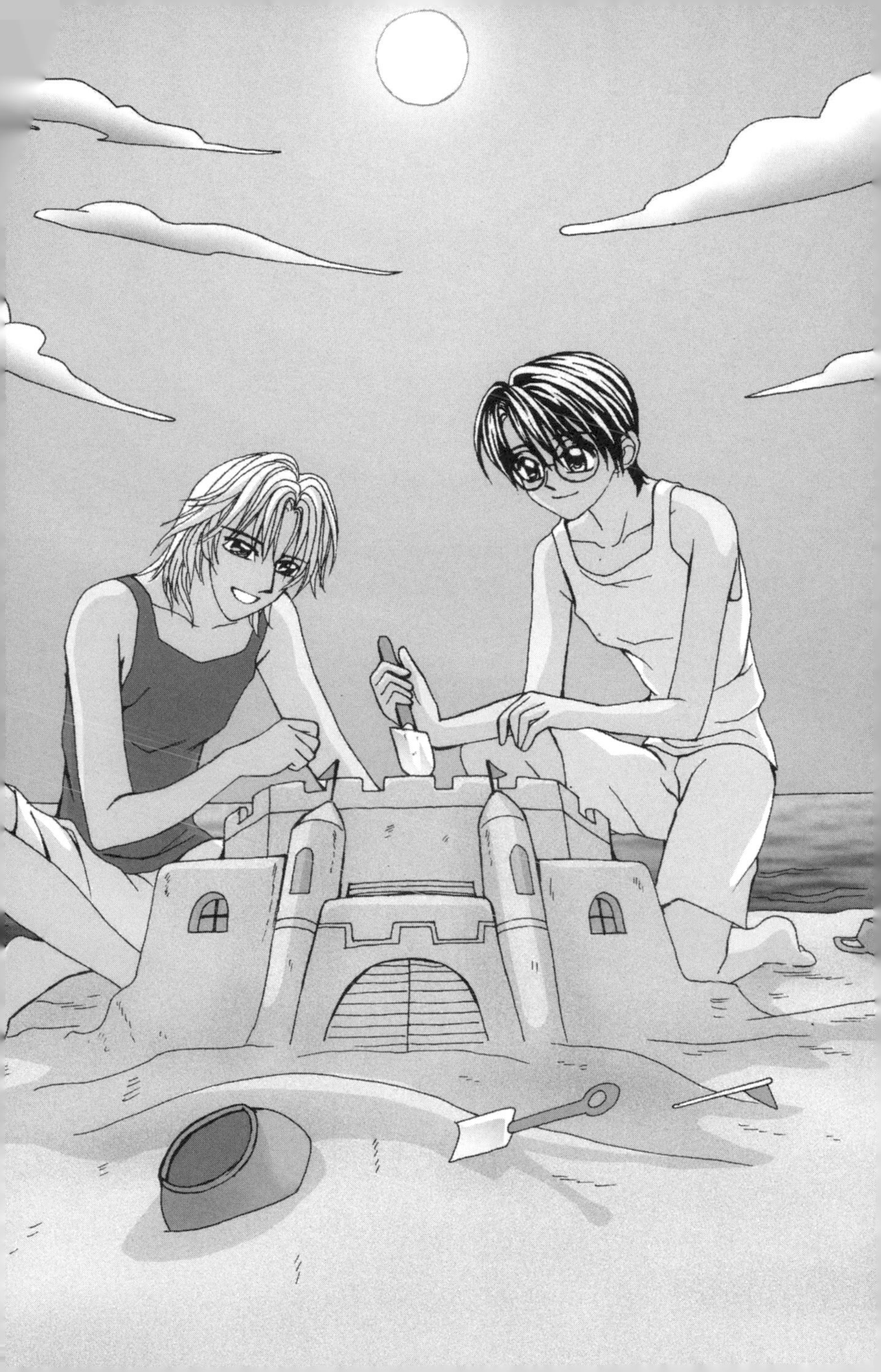

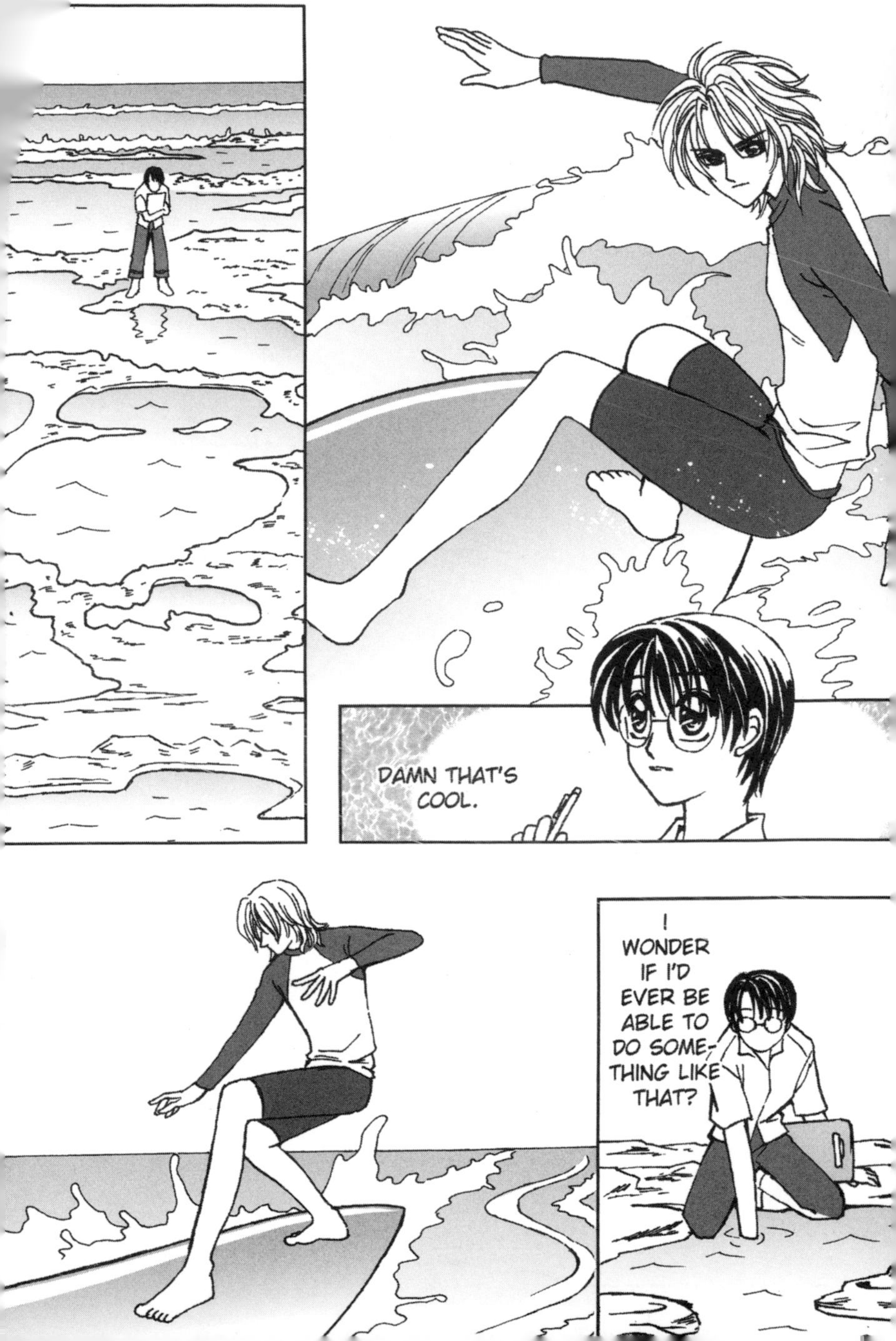
DAMN THAT'S COOL.
I WONDER IF I'D EVER BE ABLE TO DO SOME-THING LIKE THAT?

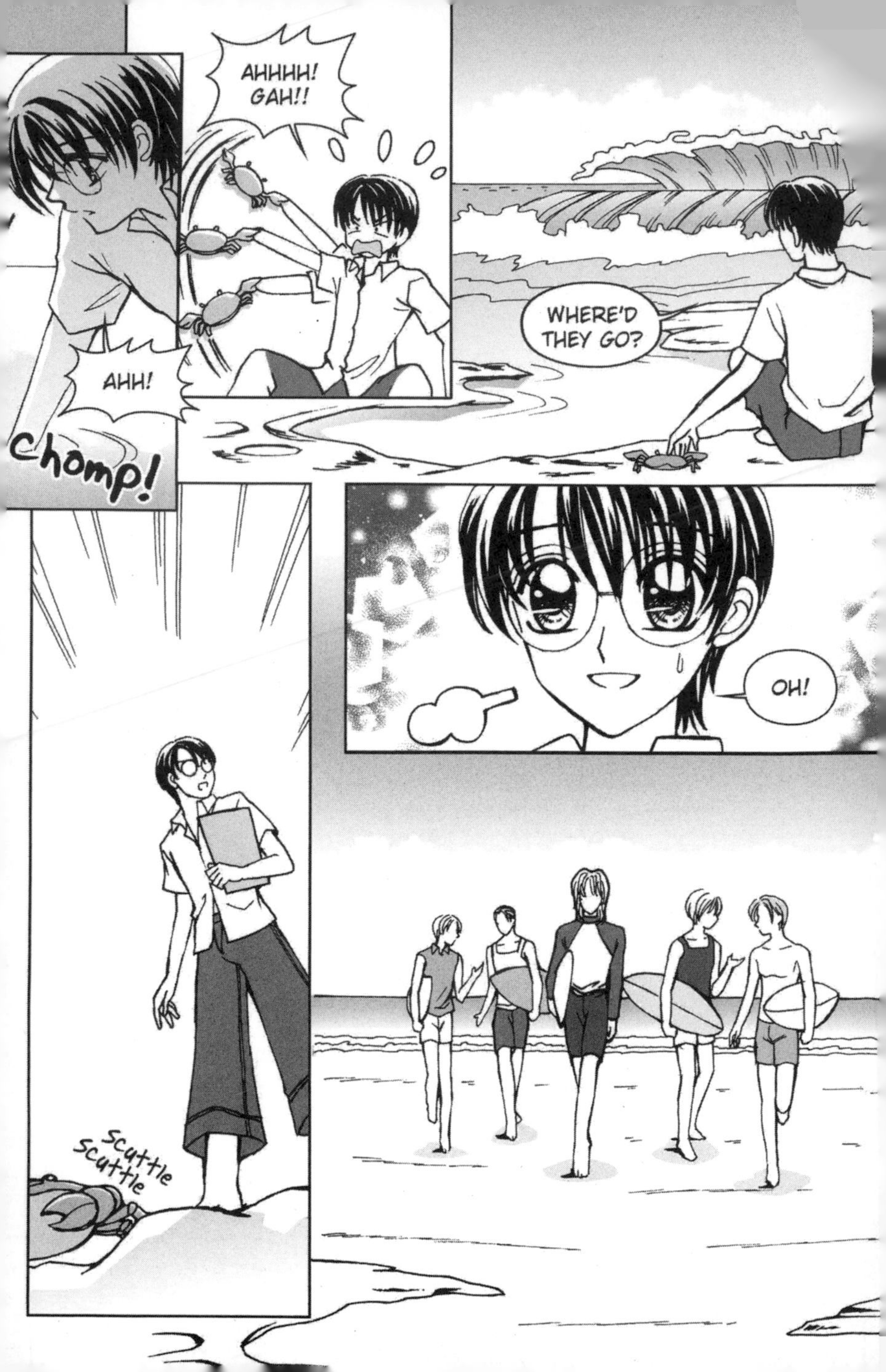
AHHHH! GAH!!
AHH!
Chomp!
WHERE'D THEY GO?
OH!
Scuttle scuttle

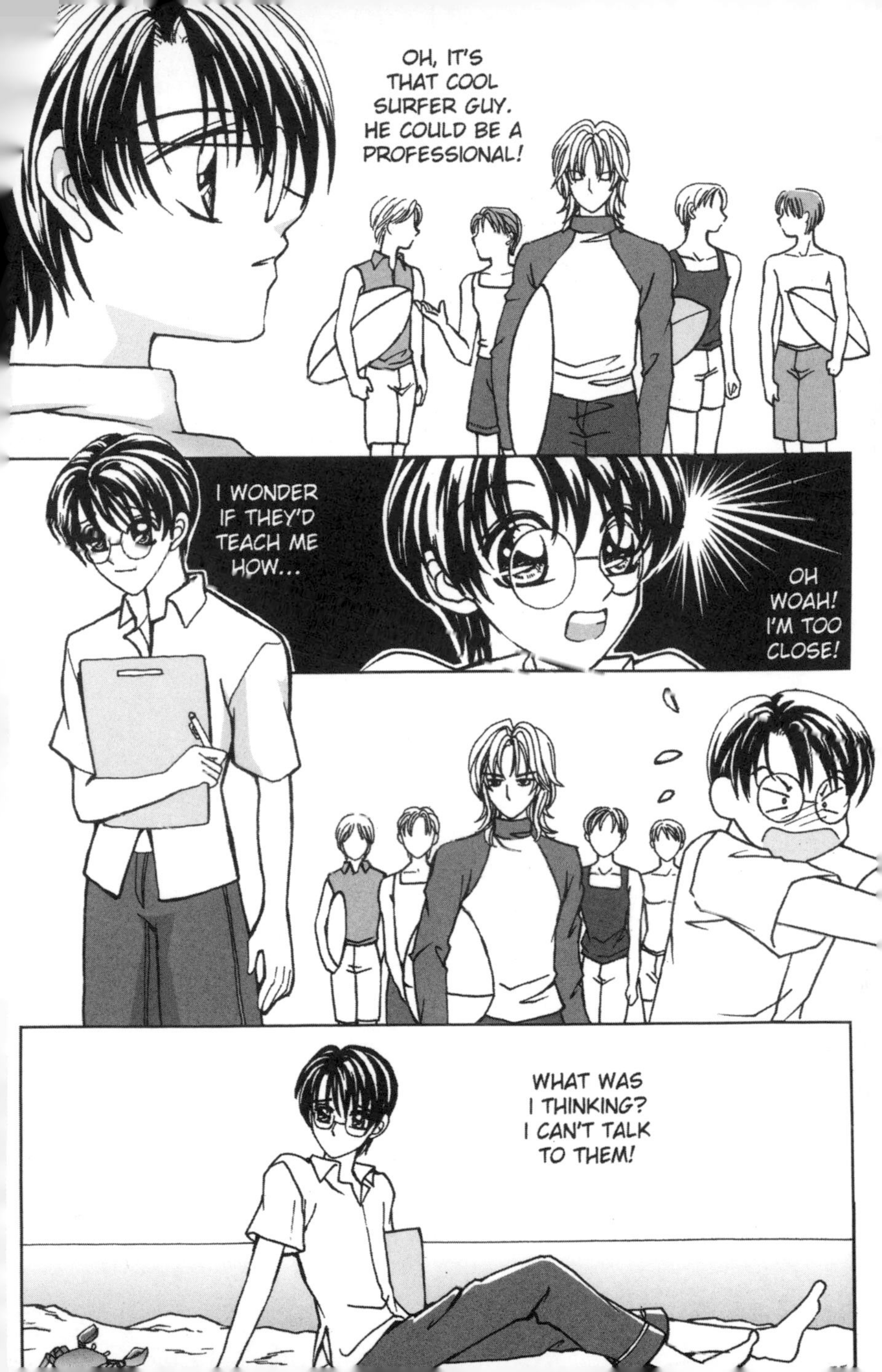
OH, IT'S THAT COOL SURFER GUY. HE COULD BE A PROFESSIONAL!
I WONDER IF THEY'D TEACH ME HOW...
OH WOAH! I'M TOO CLOSE!
WHAT WAS I THINKING? I CAN'T TALK TO THEM!

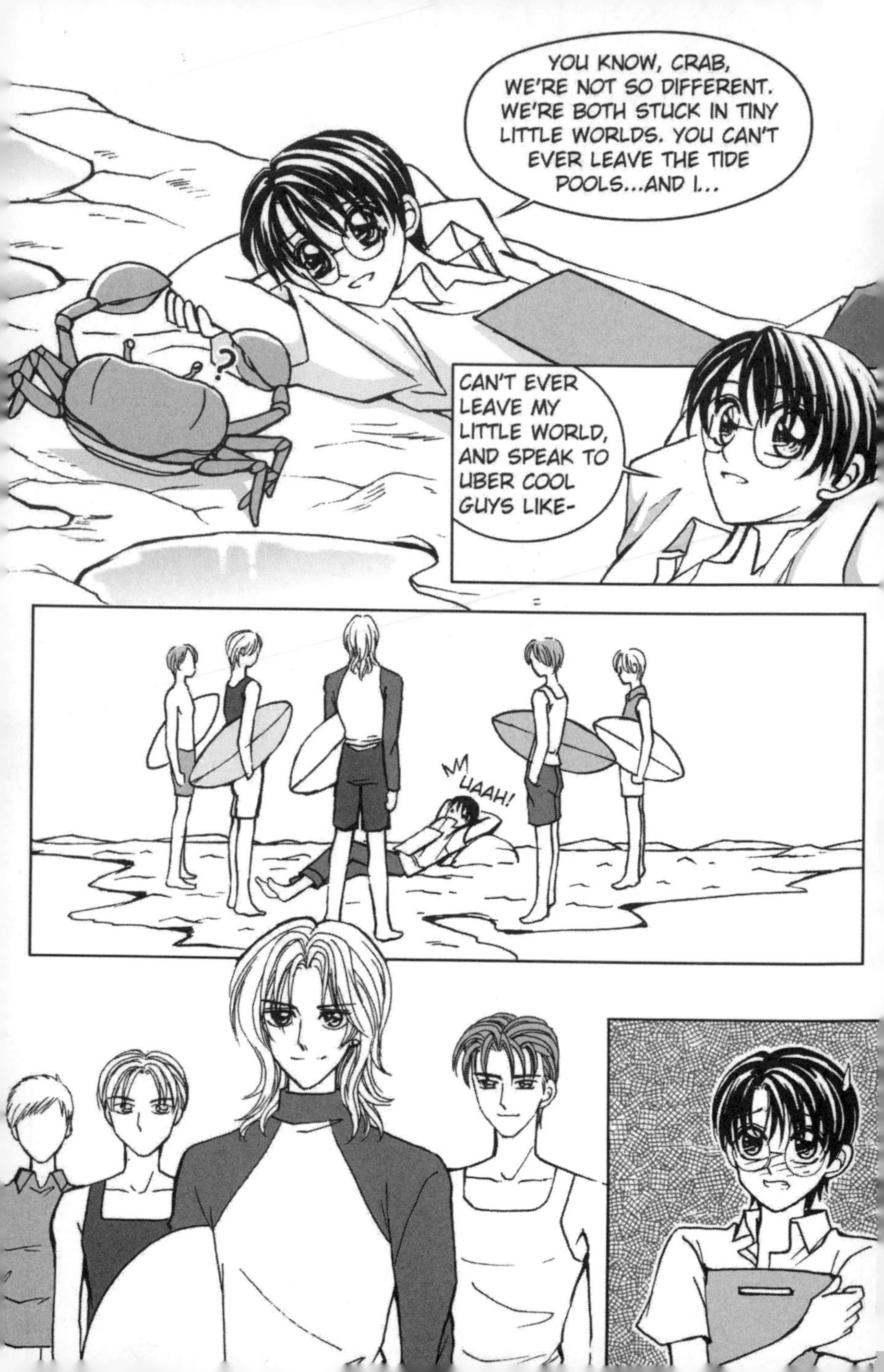
YOU KNOW, CRAB, WE'RE NOT SO DIFFERENT. WE'RE BOTH STUCK IN TINY LITTLE WORLDS. YOU CAN'T EVER LEAVE THE TIDE POOLS...AND I...
?
CAN'T EVER LEAVE MY LITTLE WORLD, AND SPEAK TO UBER COOL GUYS LIKE-
UAAH!

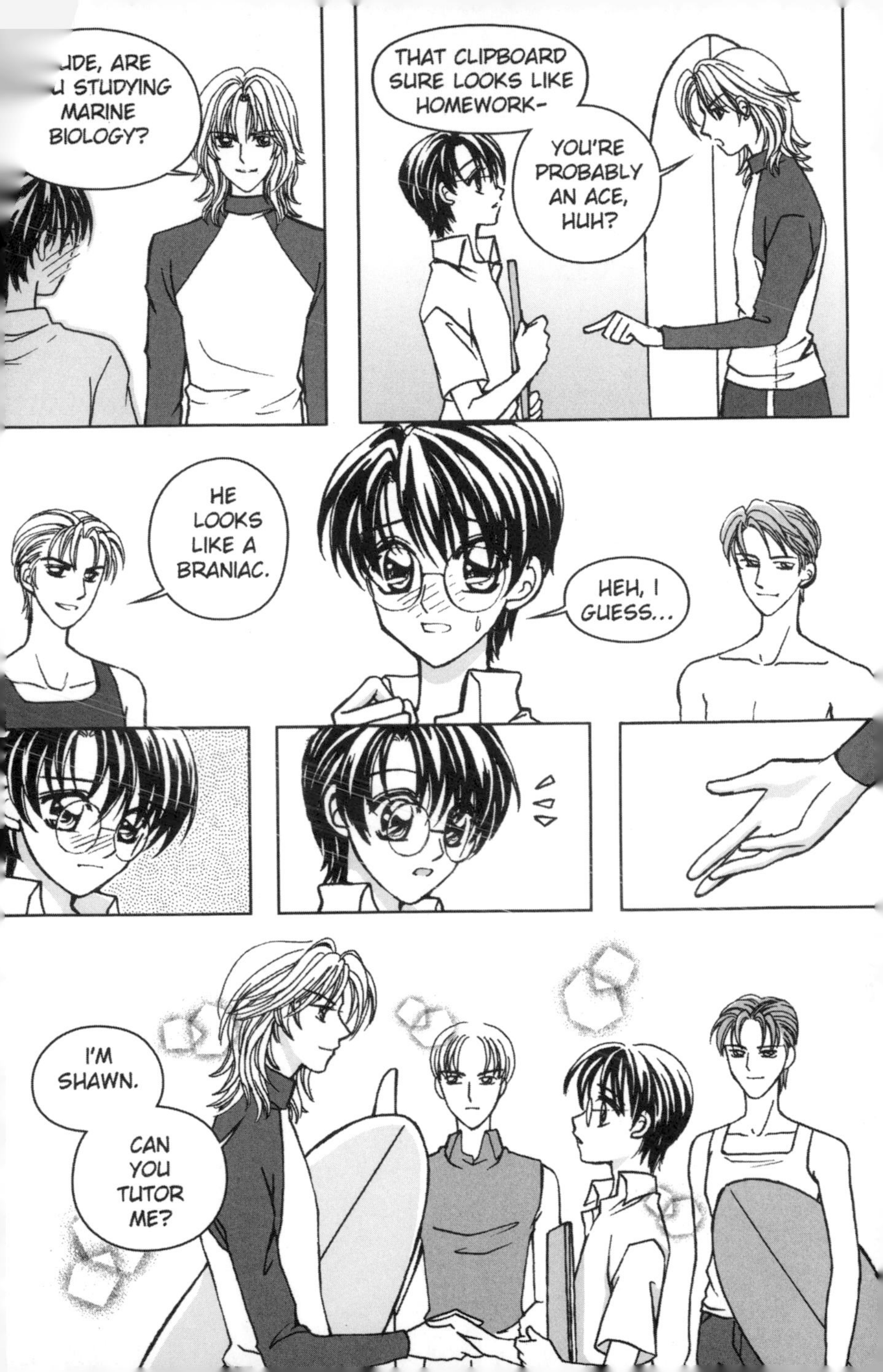
UDE, ARE
U STUDYING
MARINE
BIOLOGY?
THAT CLIPBOARD
SURE LOOKS LIKE
HOMEWORK-
YOU'RE
PROBABLY
AN ACE,
HUH?
HE
LOOKS
LIKE A
BRANIAC.
HEH, I
GUESS...
I'M
SHAWN.
CAN
YOU
TUTOR
ME?

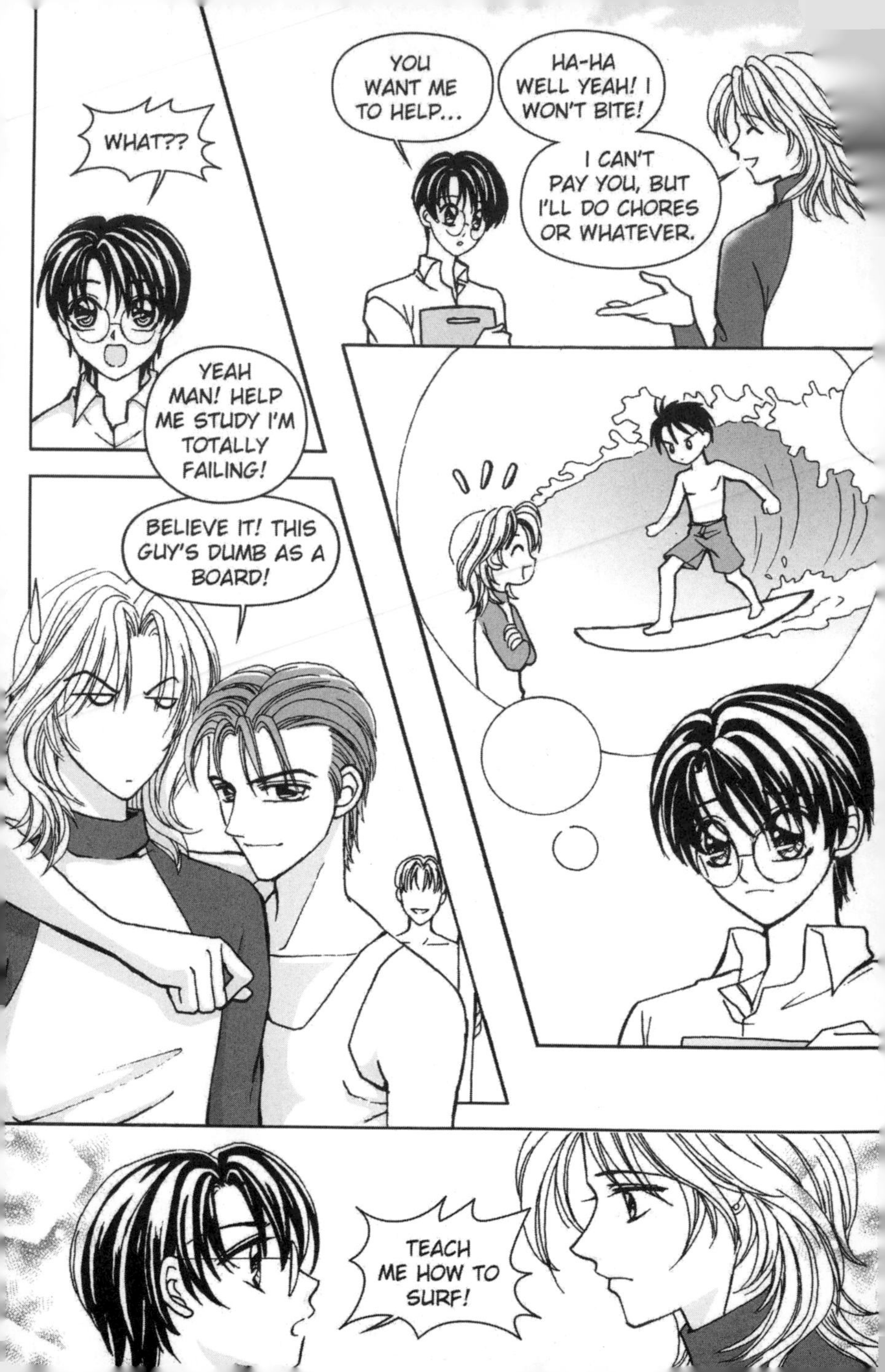

WHAT??
YEAH MAN! HELP ME STUDY I'M TOTALLY FAILING!
BELIEVE IT! THIS GUY'S DUMB AS A BOARD!
YOU WANT ME TO HELP...
HA-HA WELL YEAH! I WON'T BITE!
I CAN'T PAY YOU, BUT I'LL DO CHORES OR WHATEVER.
TEACH ME HOW TO SURF!

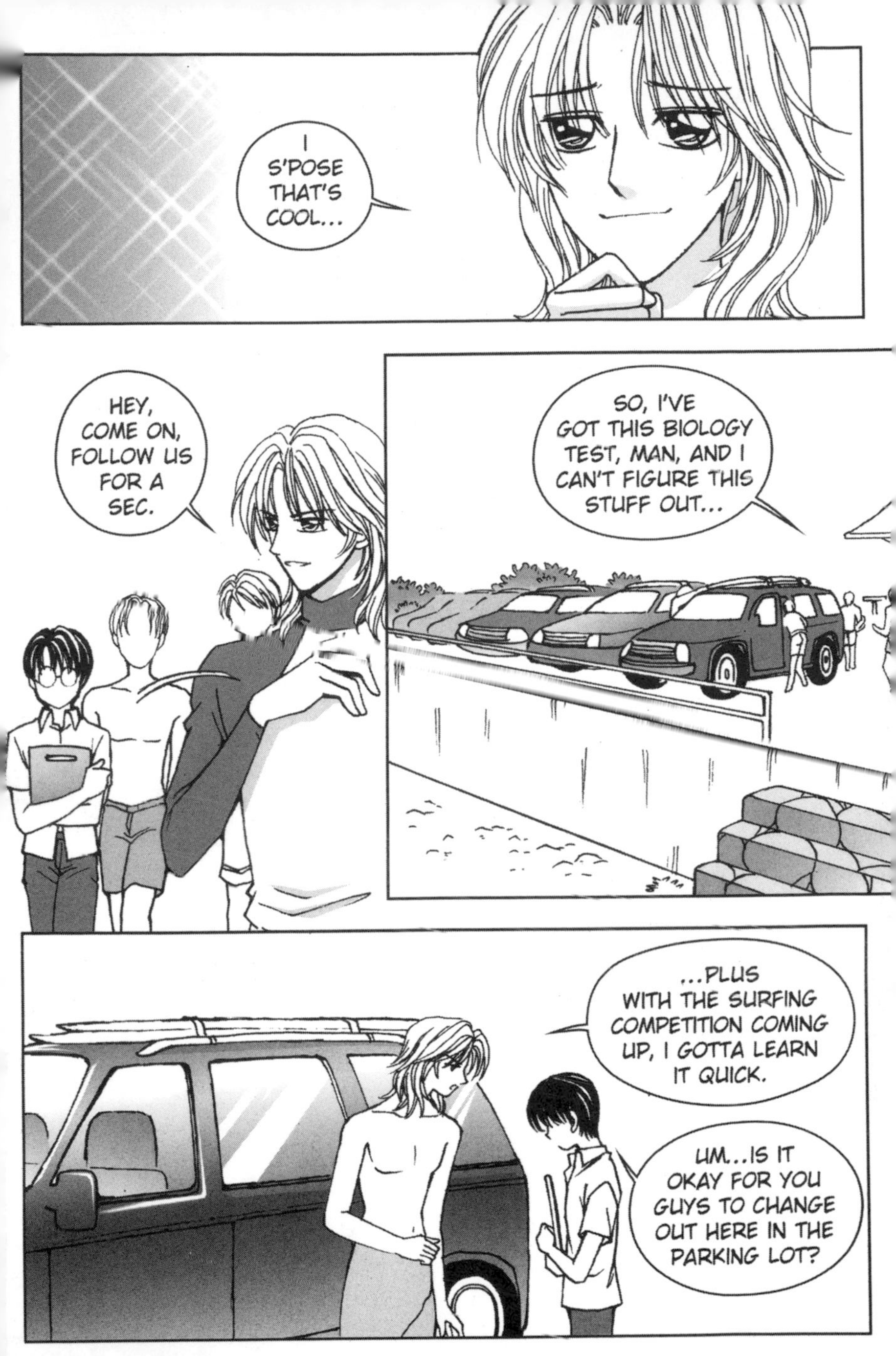
I S'POSE THAT'S COOL...
HEY, COME ON, FOLLOW US FOR A SEC.
SO, I'VE GOT THIS BIOLOGY TEST, MAN, AND I CAN'T FIGURE THIS STUFF OUT...
...PLUS WITH THE SURFING COMPETITION COMING UP, I GOTTA LEARN IT QUICK.
UM...IS IT OKAY FOR YOU GUYS TO CHANGE OUT HERE IN THE PARKING LOT?

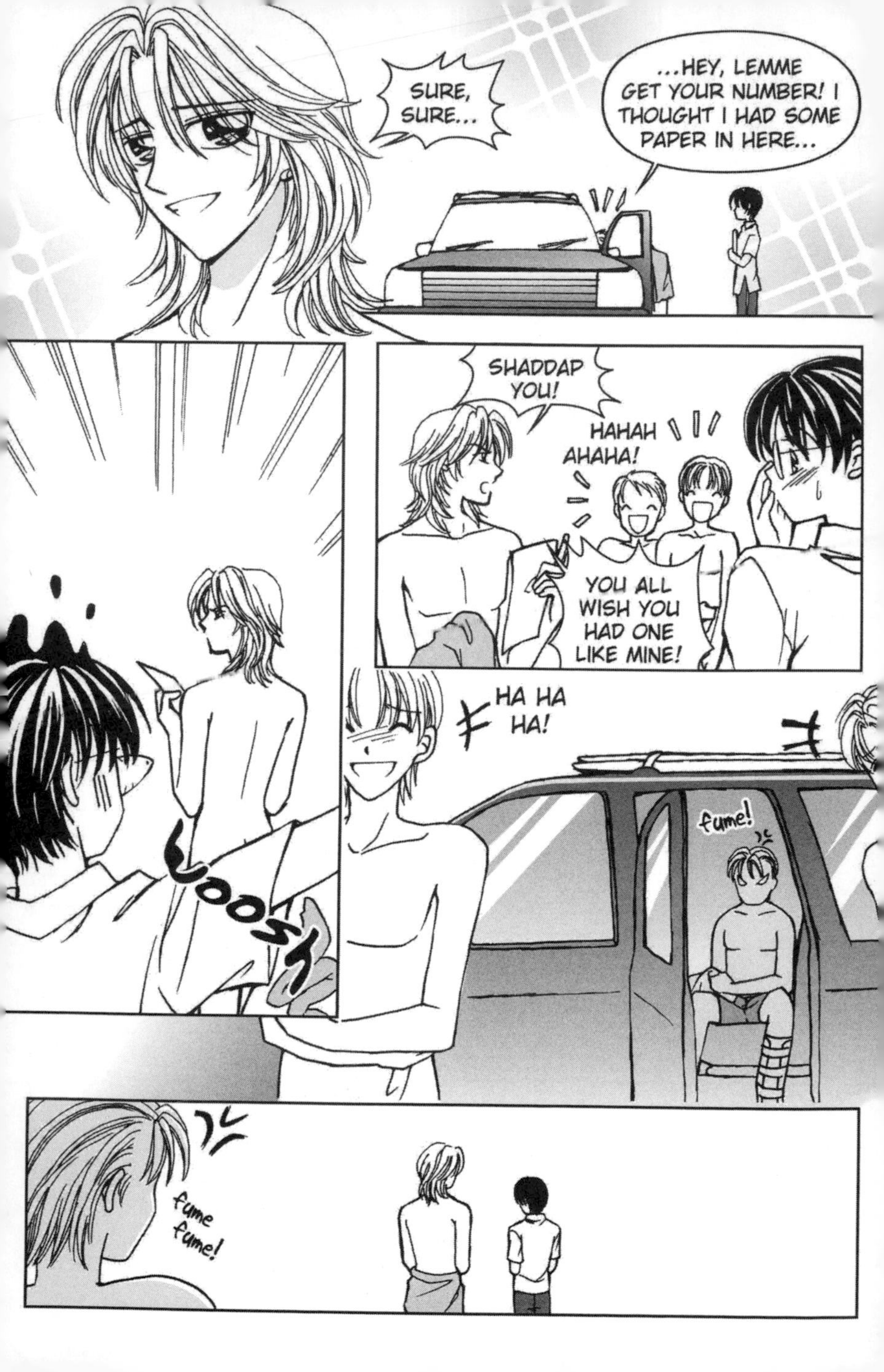
SURE, SURE...
...HEY, LEMME GET YOUR NUMBER! I THOUGHT I HAD SOME PAPER IN HERE...
SHADDAP YOU!
HAHAH AHAHA!
YOU ALL WISH YOU HAD ONE LIKE MINE!
WOOSH
HA HA HA!
fume!
fume fume!

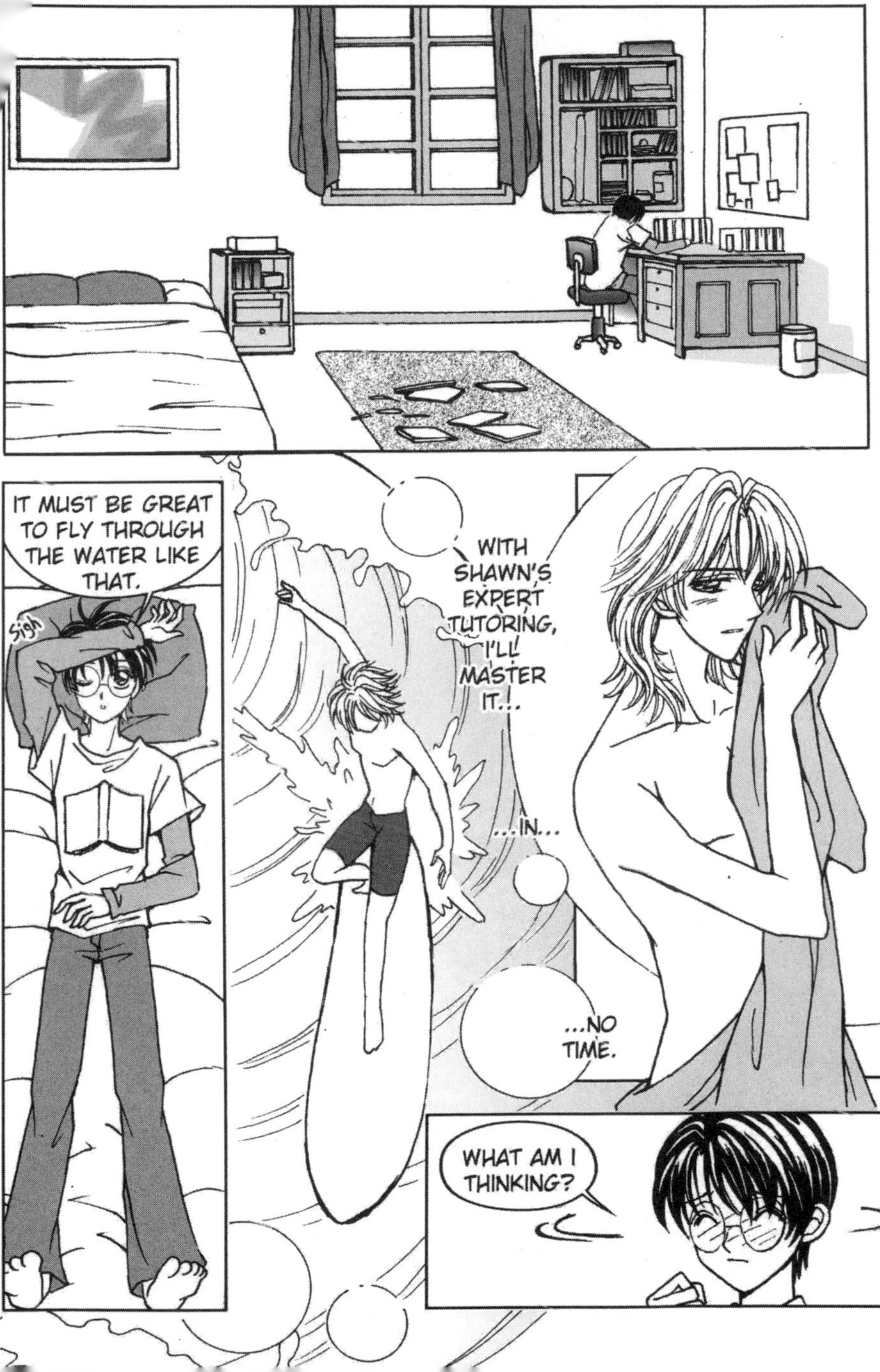

IT MUST BE GREAT TO FLY THROUGH THE WATER LIKE THAT.
Sigh
WITH SHAWN'S EXPERT TUTORING, I'LL MASTER IT...
...IN...
...NO TIME.
WHAT AM I THINKING?

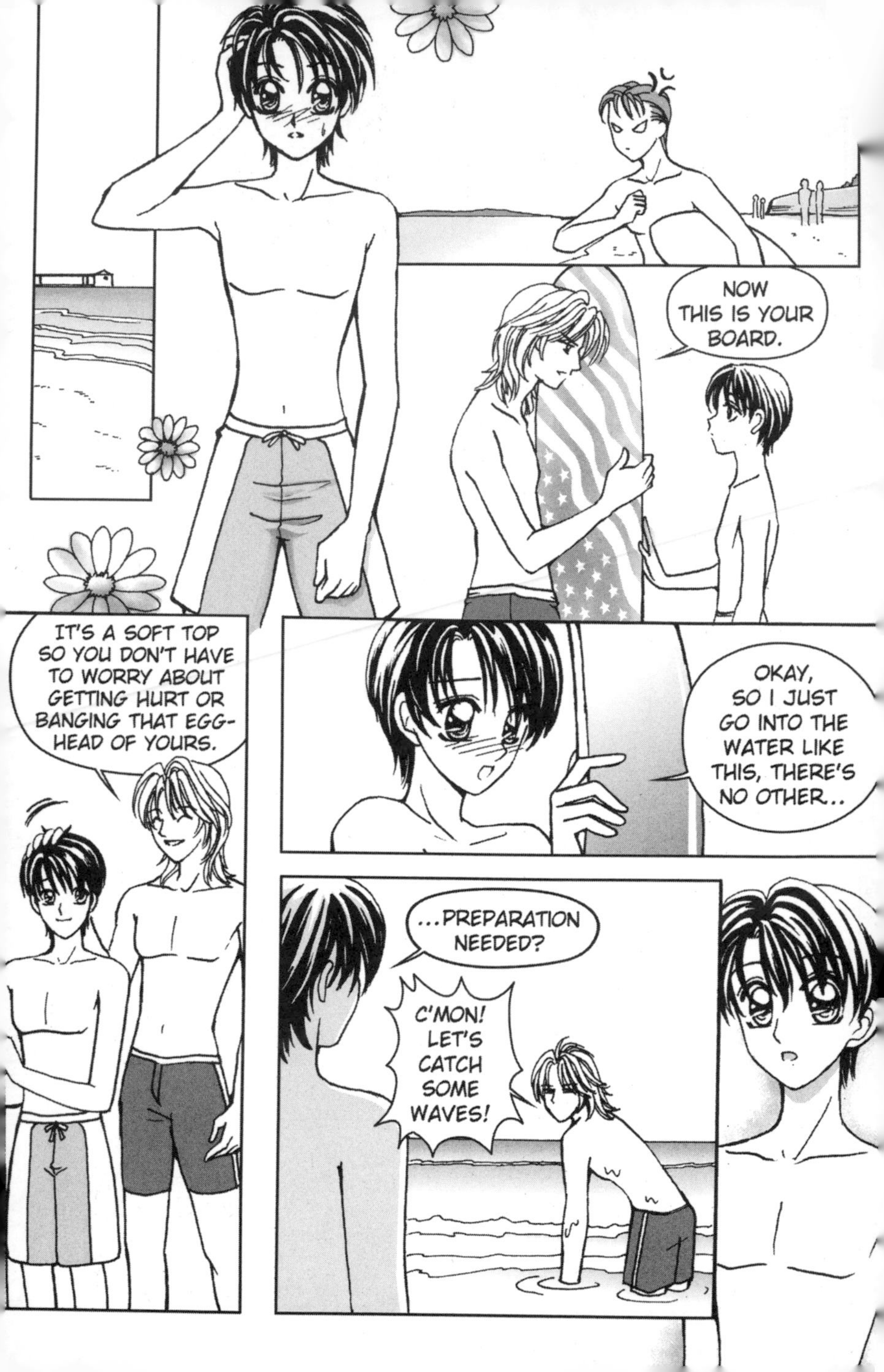
NOW THIS IS YOUR BOARD.
IT'S A SOFT TOP SO YOU DON'T HAVE TO WORRY ABOUT GETTING HURT OR BANGING THAT EGG-HEAD OF YOURS.
OKAY, SO I JUST GO INTO THE WATER LIKE THIS, THERE'S NO OTHER...
...PREPARATION NEEDED?
C'MON! LET'S CATCH SOME WAVES!

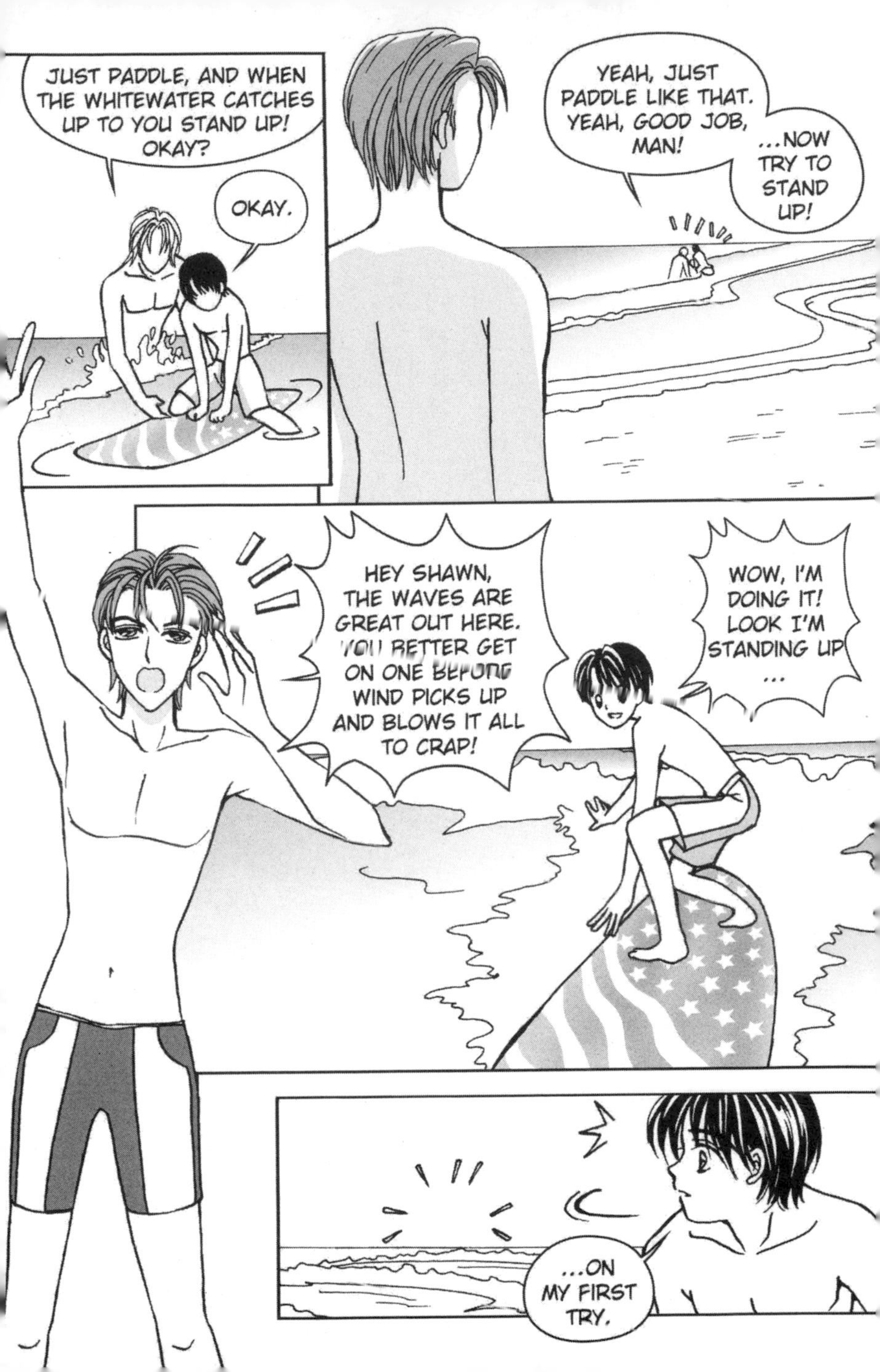
JUST PADDLE, AND WHEN THE WHITEWATER CATCHES UP TO YOU STAND UP! OKAY?
OKAY.
YEAH, JUST PADDLE LIKE THAT. YEAH, GOOD JOB, MAN!
...NOW TRY TO STAND UP!
HEY SHAWN, THE WAVES ARE GREAT OUT HERE. YOU BETTER GET ON ONE BEFORE WIND PICKS UP AND BLOWS IT ALL TO CRAP!
WOW, I'M DOING IT! LOOK I'M STANDING UP ...
...ON MY FIRST TRY.

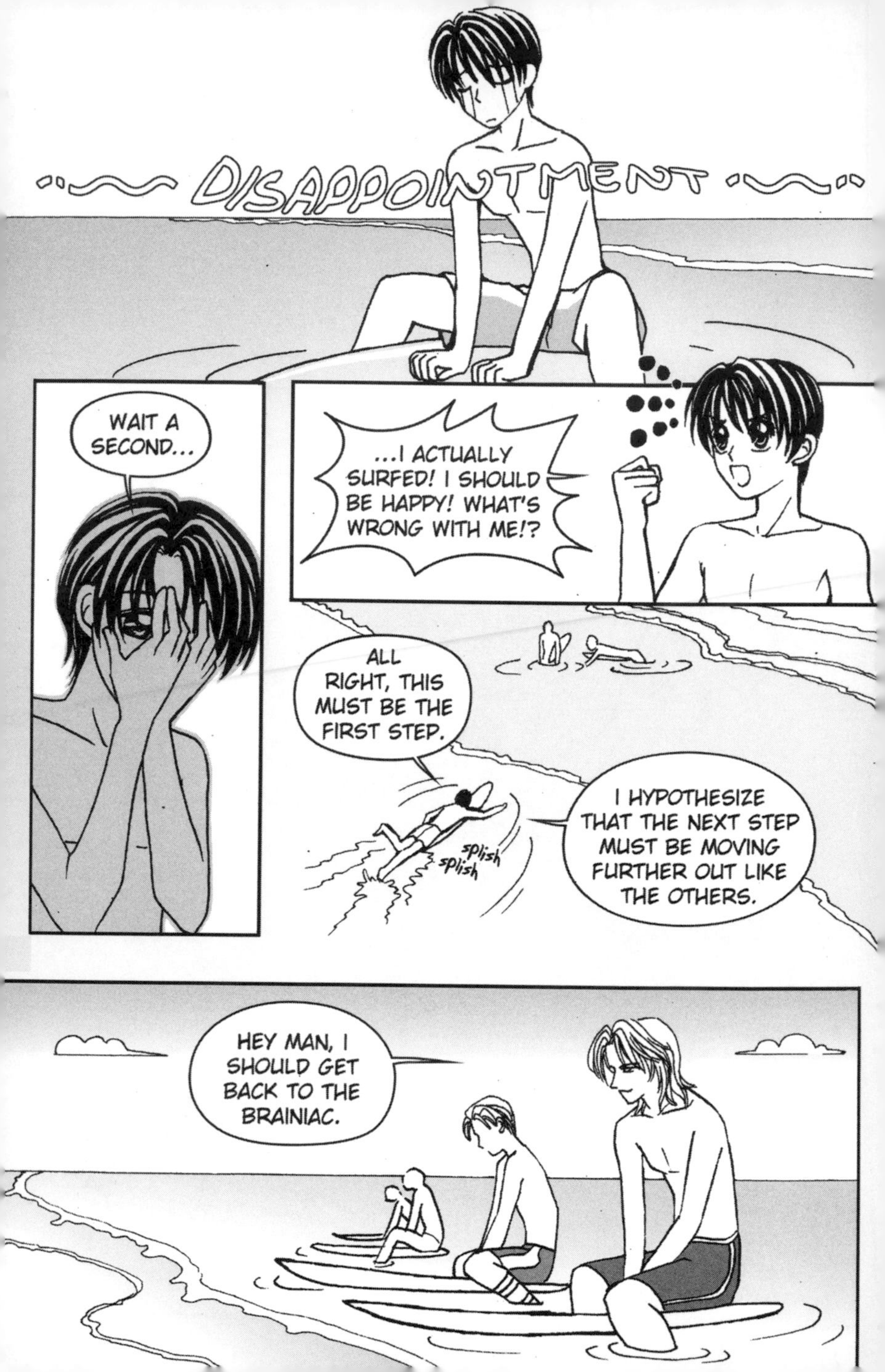
DISAPPOINTMENT
WAIT A SECOND...
...I ACTUALLY SURFED! I SHOULD BE HAPPY! WHAT'S WRONG WITH ME!?
ALL RIGHT, THIS MUST BE THE FIRST STEP.
splish splish
I HYPOTHESIZE THAT THE NEXT STEP MUST BE MOVING FURTHER OUT LIKE THE OTHERS.
HEY MAN, I SHOULD GET BACK TO THE BRAINIAC.

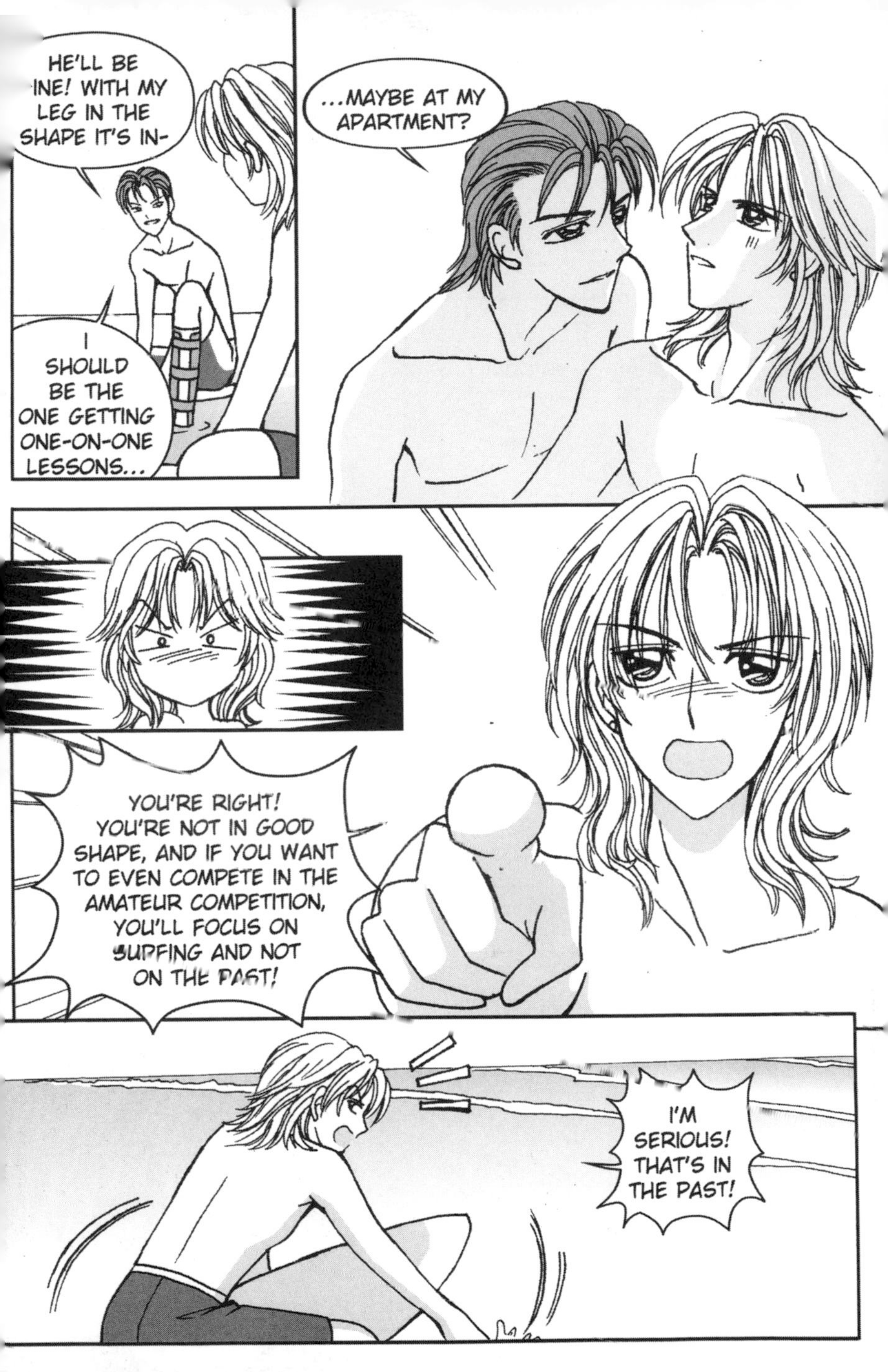
HE'LL BE
INE! WITH MY LEG IN THE SHAPE IT'S IN-
I SHOULD BE THE ONE GETTING ONE-ON-ONE LESSONS...
...MAYBE AT MY APARTMENT?
YOU'RE RIGHT! YOU'RE NOT IN GOOD SHAPE, AND IF YOU WANT TO EVEN COMPETE IN THE AMATEUR COMPETITION, YOU'LL FOCUS ON SURFING AND NOT ON THE PAST!
I'M SERIOUS! THAT'S IN THE PAST!

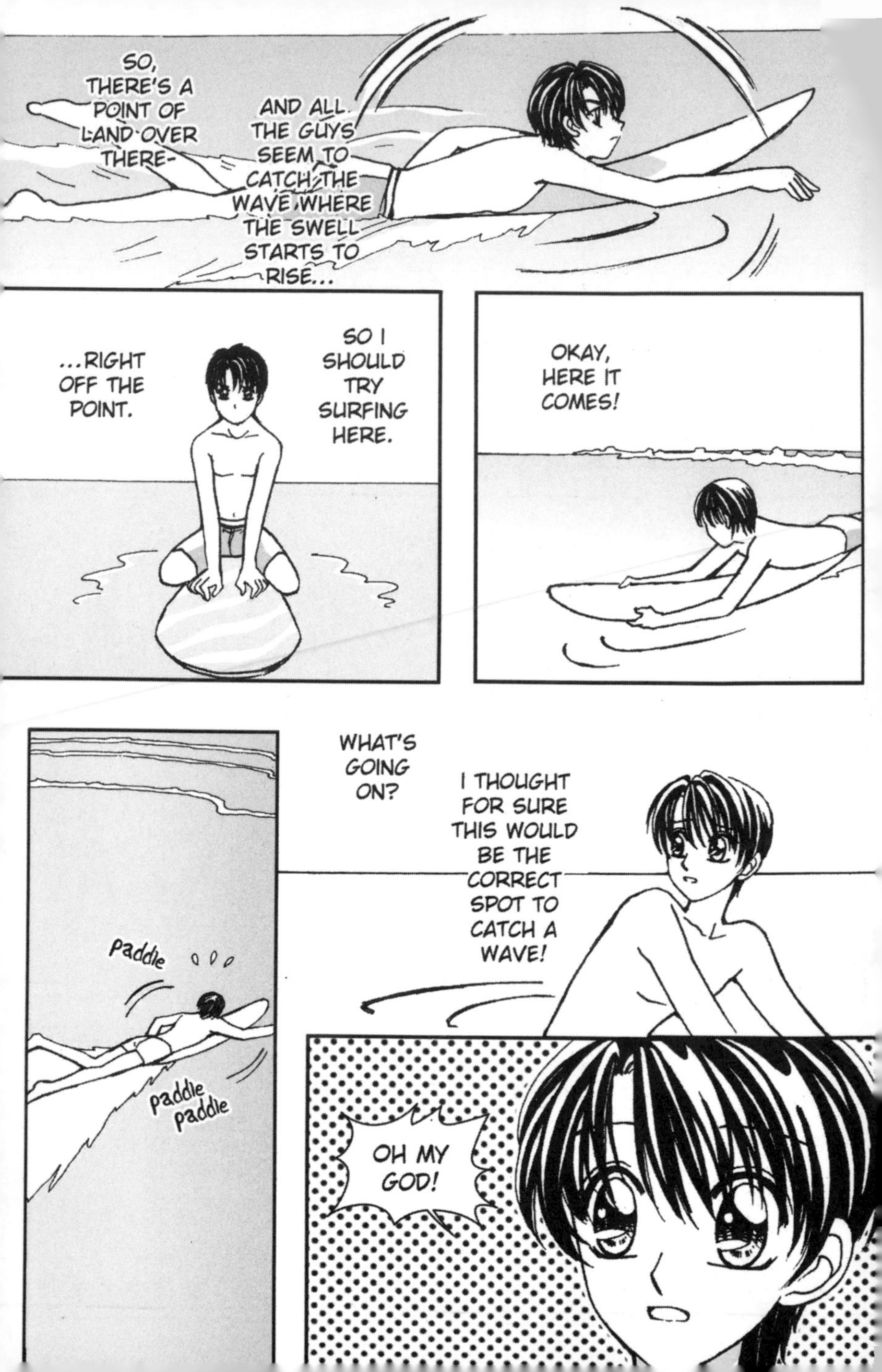
SO, THERE'S A POINT OF LAND OVER THERE-
AND ALL THE GUYS SEEM TO CATCH THE WAVE WHERE THE SWELL STARTS TO RISE...
...RIGHT OFF THE POINT.
SO I SHOULD TRY SURFING HERE.
OKAY, HERE IT COMES!
paddle
paddle paddle
WHAT'S GOING ON?
I THOUGHT FOR SURE THIS WOULD BE THE CORRECT SPOT TO CATCH A WAVE!
OH MY GOD!

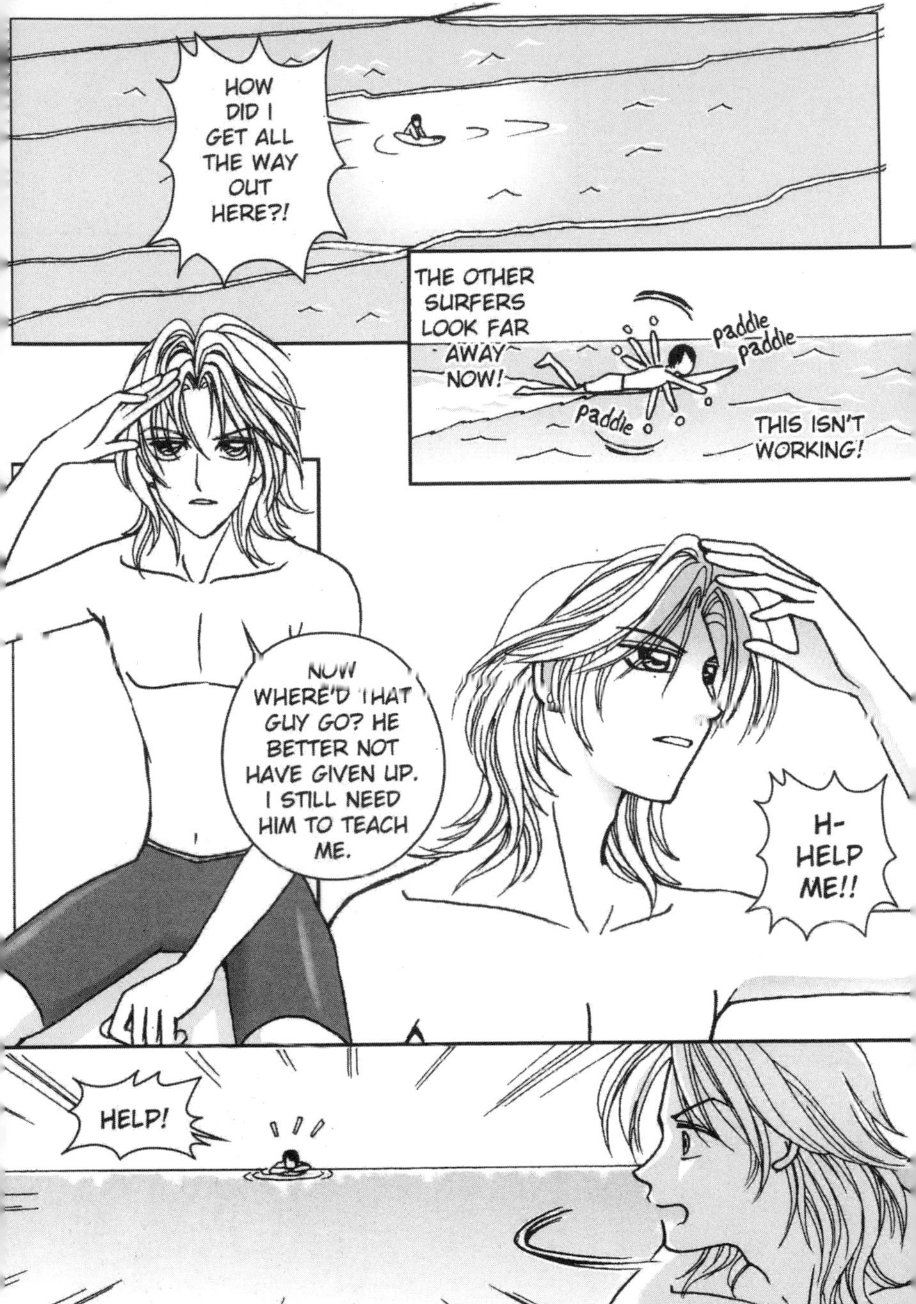
HOW DID I GET ALL THE WAY OUT HERE?!
THE OTHER SURFERS LOOK FAR AWAY NOW!
paddle paddle
paddle
THIS ISN'T WORKING!
NOW WHERE'D THAT GUY GO? HE BETTER NOT HAVE GIVEN UP. I STILL NEED HIM TO TEACH ME.
H-HELP ME!!
HELP!

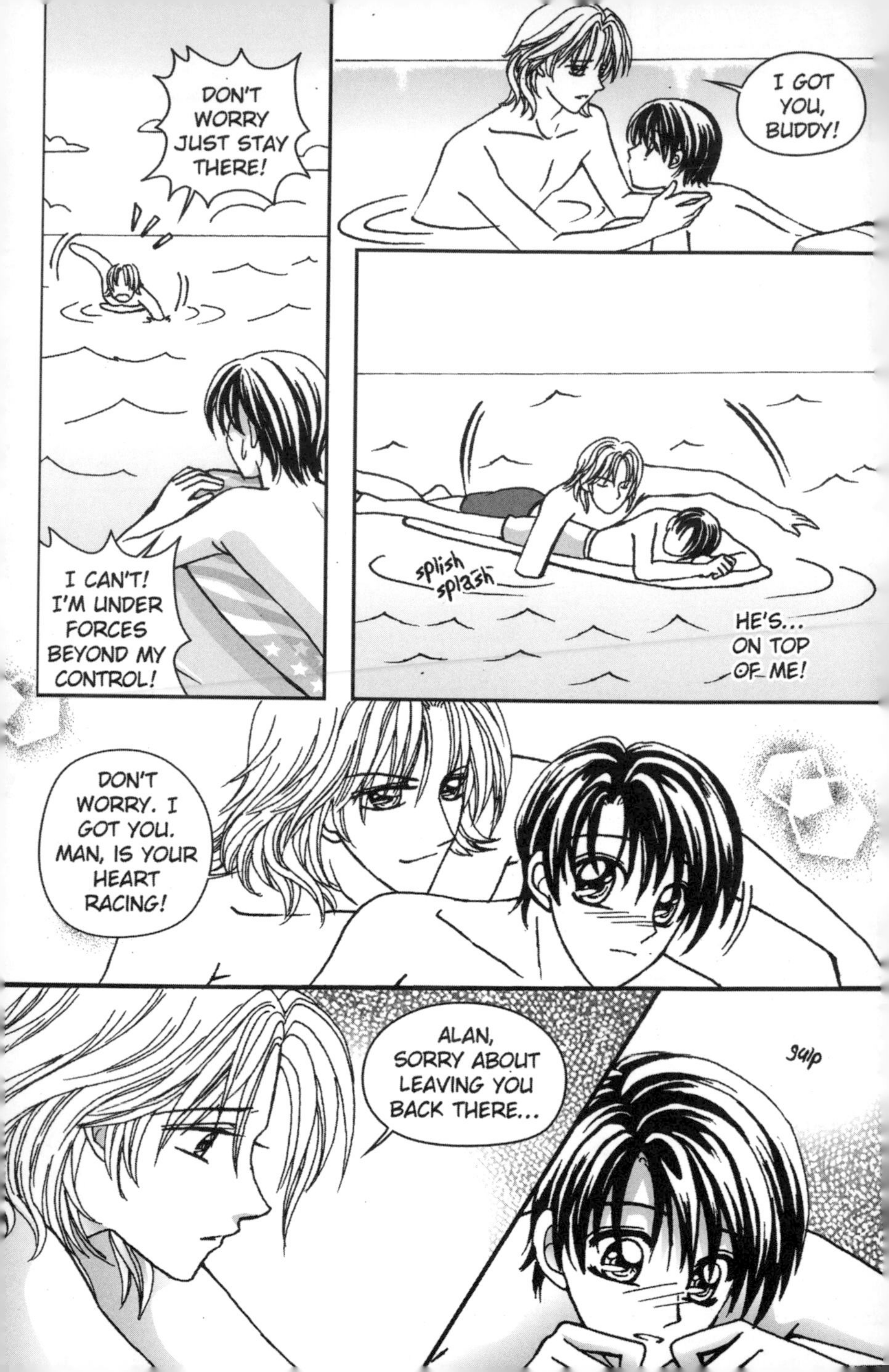
DON'T WORRY JUST STAY THERE!
I GOT YOU, BUDDY!
I CAN'T! I'M UNDER FORCES BEYOND MY CONTROL!
splish splash
HE'S... ON TOP OF ME!
DON'T WORRY. I GOT YOU. MAN, IS YOUR HEART RACING!
ALAN, SORRY ABOUT LEAVING YOU BACK THERE...
gulp

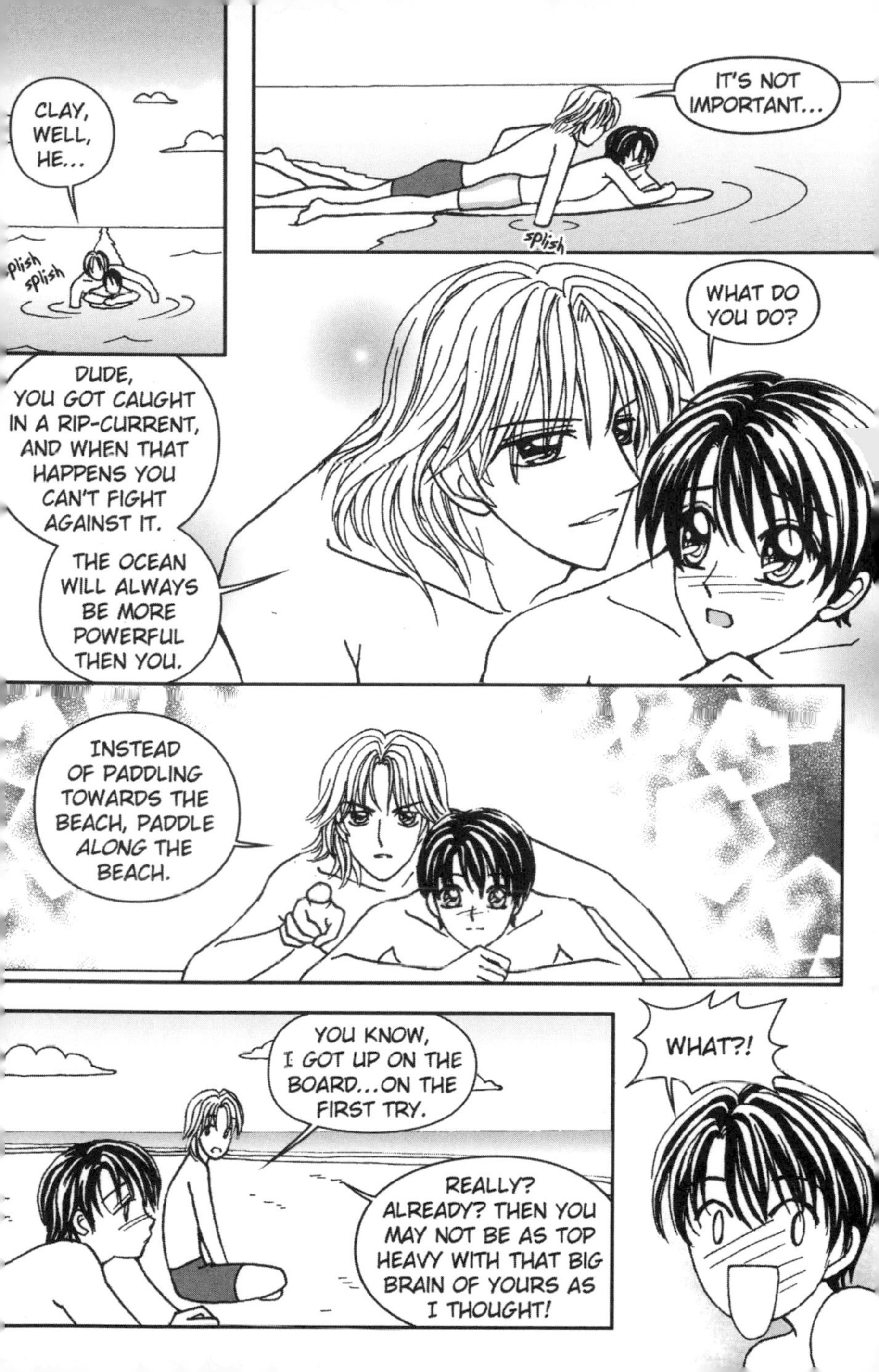
CLAY, WELL, HE...
splish splish
IT'S NOT IMPORTANT...
splish
WHAT DO YOU DO?
DUDE, YOU GOT CAUGHT IN A RIP-CURRENT, AND WHEN THAT HAPPENS YOU CAN'T FIGHT AGAINST IT.
THE OCEAN WILL ALWAYS BE MORE POWERFUL THEN YOU.
INSTEAD OF PADDLING TOWARDS THE BEACH, PADDLE ALONG THE BEACH.
YOU KNOW, I GOT UP ON THE BOARD...ON THE FIRST TRY.
REALLY? ALREADY? THEN YOU MAY NOT BE AS TOP HEAVY WITH THAT BIG BRAIN OF YOURS AS I THOUGHT!
WHAT?!

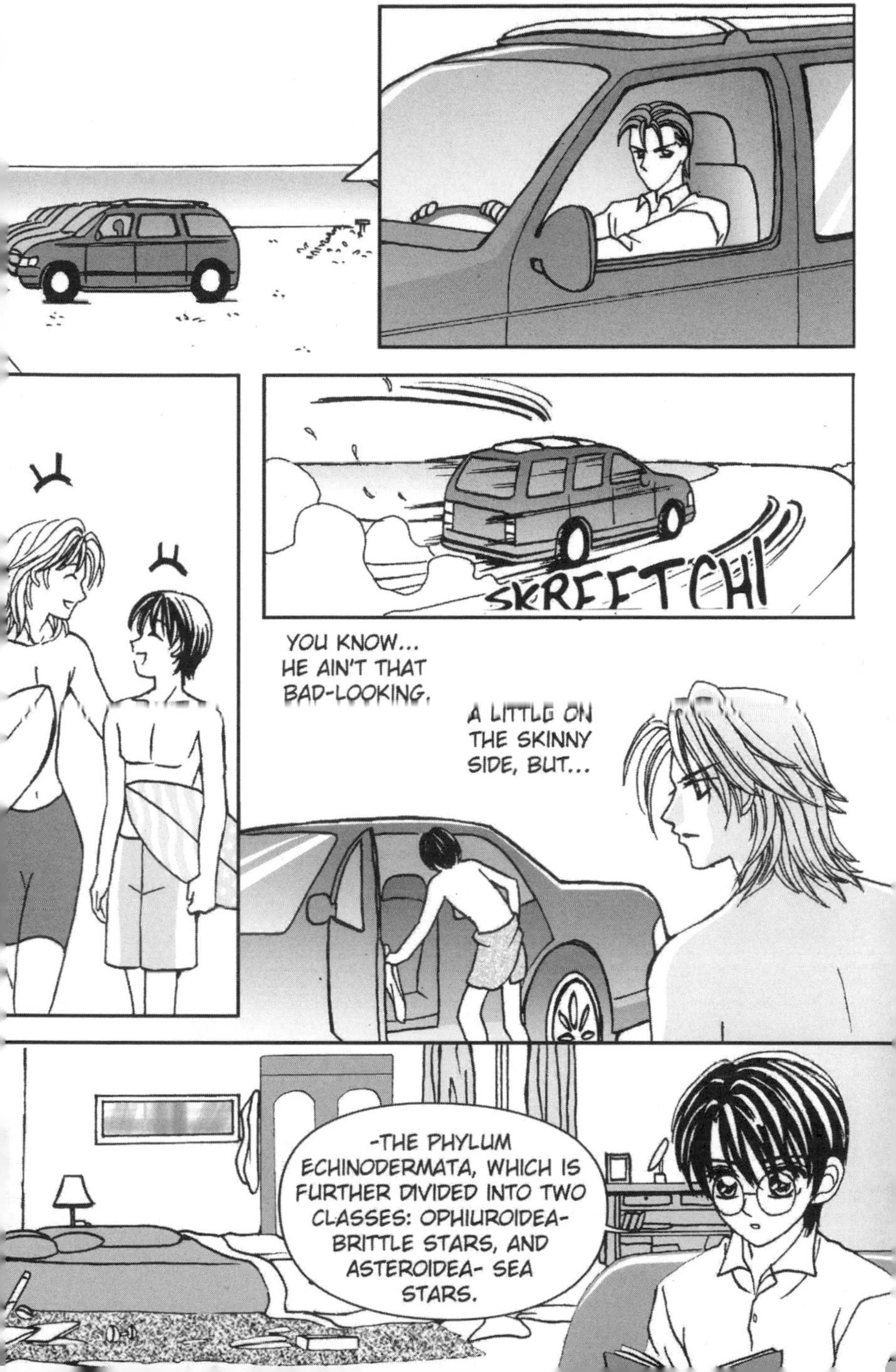
SKREETCH!
YOU KNOW... HE AIN'T THAT BAD-LOOKING.
A LITTLE ON THE SKINNY SIDE, BUT...
-THE PHYLUM ECHINODERMATA, WHICH IS FURTHER DIVIDED INTO TWO CLASSES: OPHIUROIDEA- BRITTLE STARS, AND ASTEROIDEA- SEA STARS.

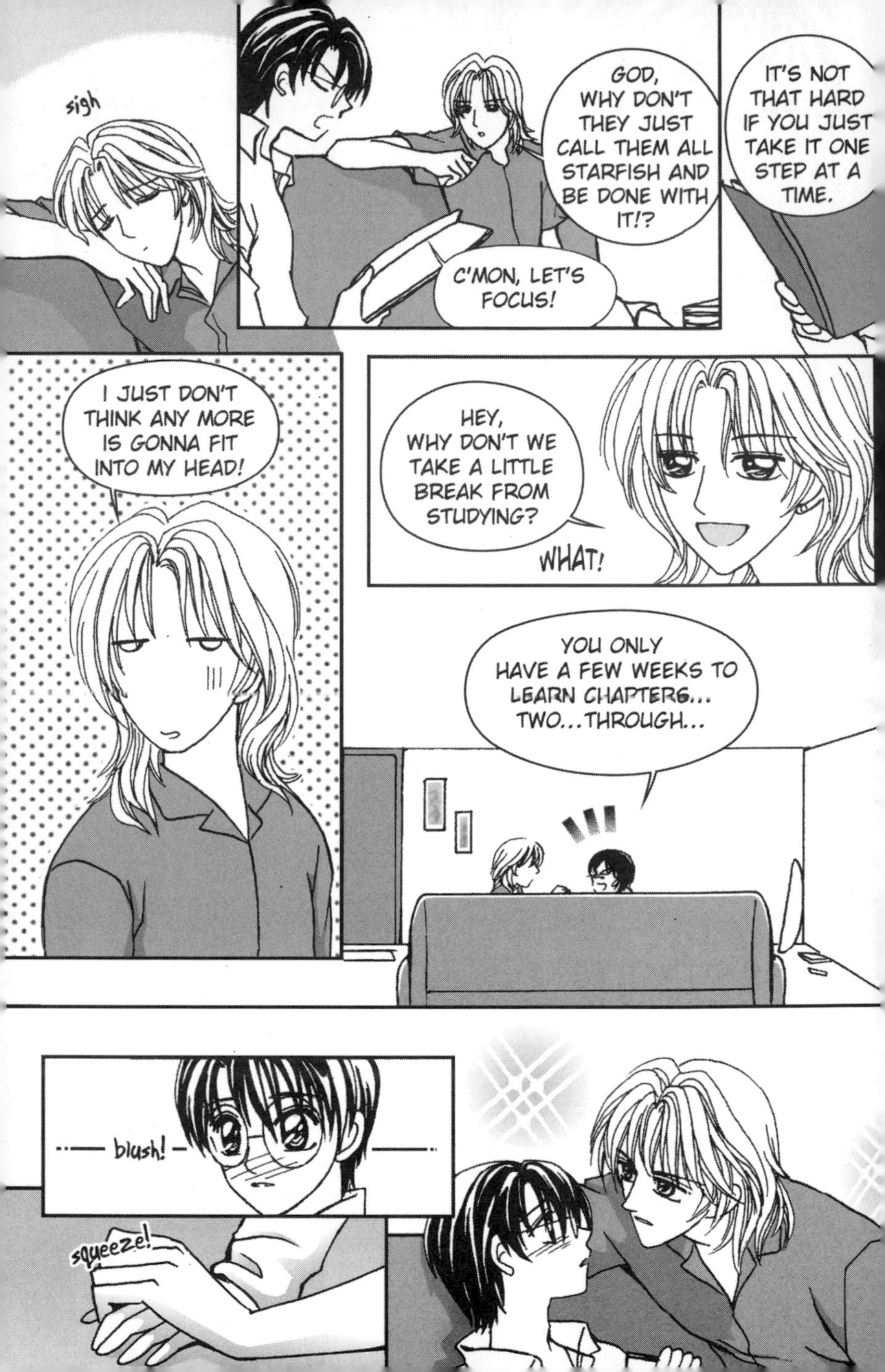

sigh
GOD, WHY DON'T THEY JUST CALL THEM ALL STARFISH AND BE DONE WITH IT!?
C'MON, LET'S FOCUS!
IT'S NOT THAT HARD IF YOU JUST TAKE IT ONE STEP AT A TIME.
I JUST DON'T THINK ANY MORE IS GONNA FIT INTO MY HEAD!
HEY, WHY DON'T WE TAKE A LITTLE BREAK FROM STUDYING?
WHAT!
YOU ONLY HAVE A FEW WEEKS TO LEARN CHAPTERS... TWO...THROUGH...
blush!
squeeze!

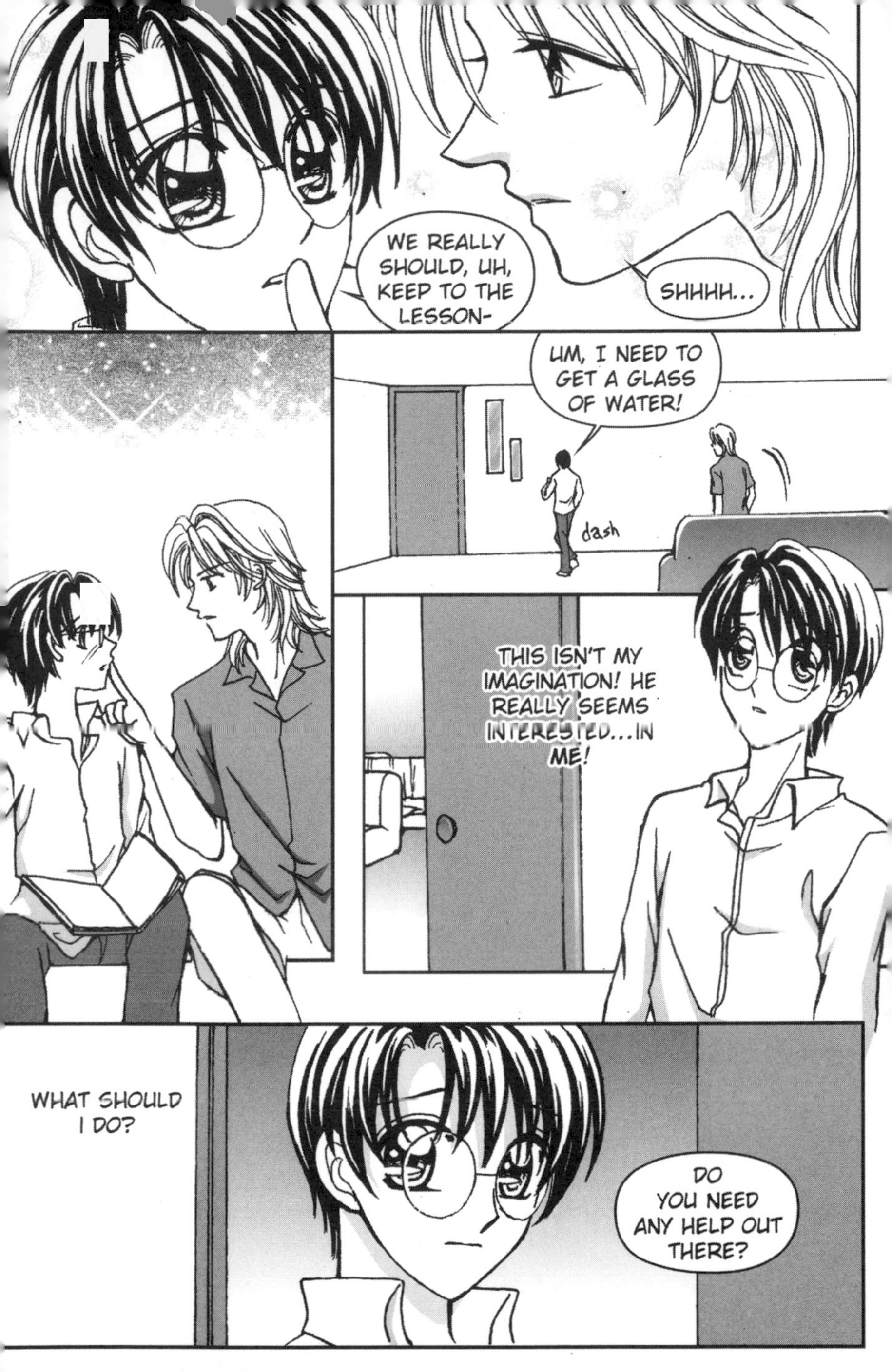
WE REALLY SHOULD, UH, KEEP TO THE LESSON-
SHHHH...
UM, I NEED TO GET A GLASS OF WATER!
dash
THIS ISN'T MY IMAGINATION! HE REALLY SEEMS INTERESTED...IN ME!
WHAT SHOULD I DO?
DO YOU NEED ANY HELP OUT THERE?

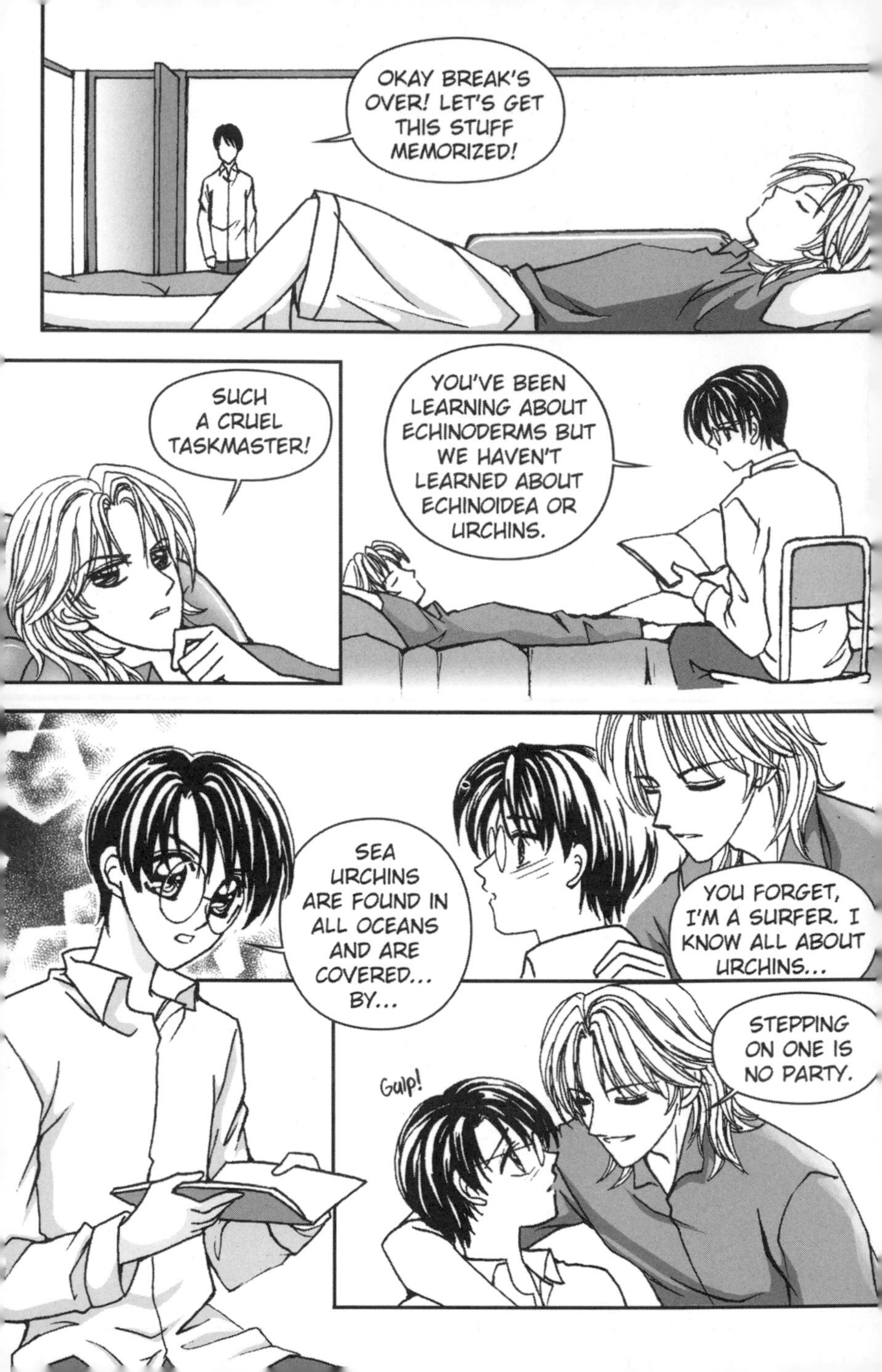
OKAY BREAK'S OVER! LET'S GET THIS STUFF MEMORIZED!
SUCH A CRUEL TASKMASTER!
YOU'VE BEEN LEARNING ABOUT ECHINODERMS BUT WE HAVEN'T LEARNED ABOUT ECHINOIDEA OR URCHINS.
SEA URCHINS ARE FOUND IN ALL OCEANS AND ARE COVERED... BY...
YOU FORGET, I'M A SURFER. I KNOW ALL ABOUT URCHINS...
STEPPING ON ONE IS NO PARTY.
Gulp!

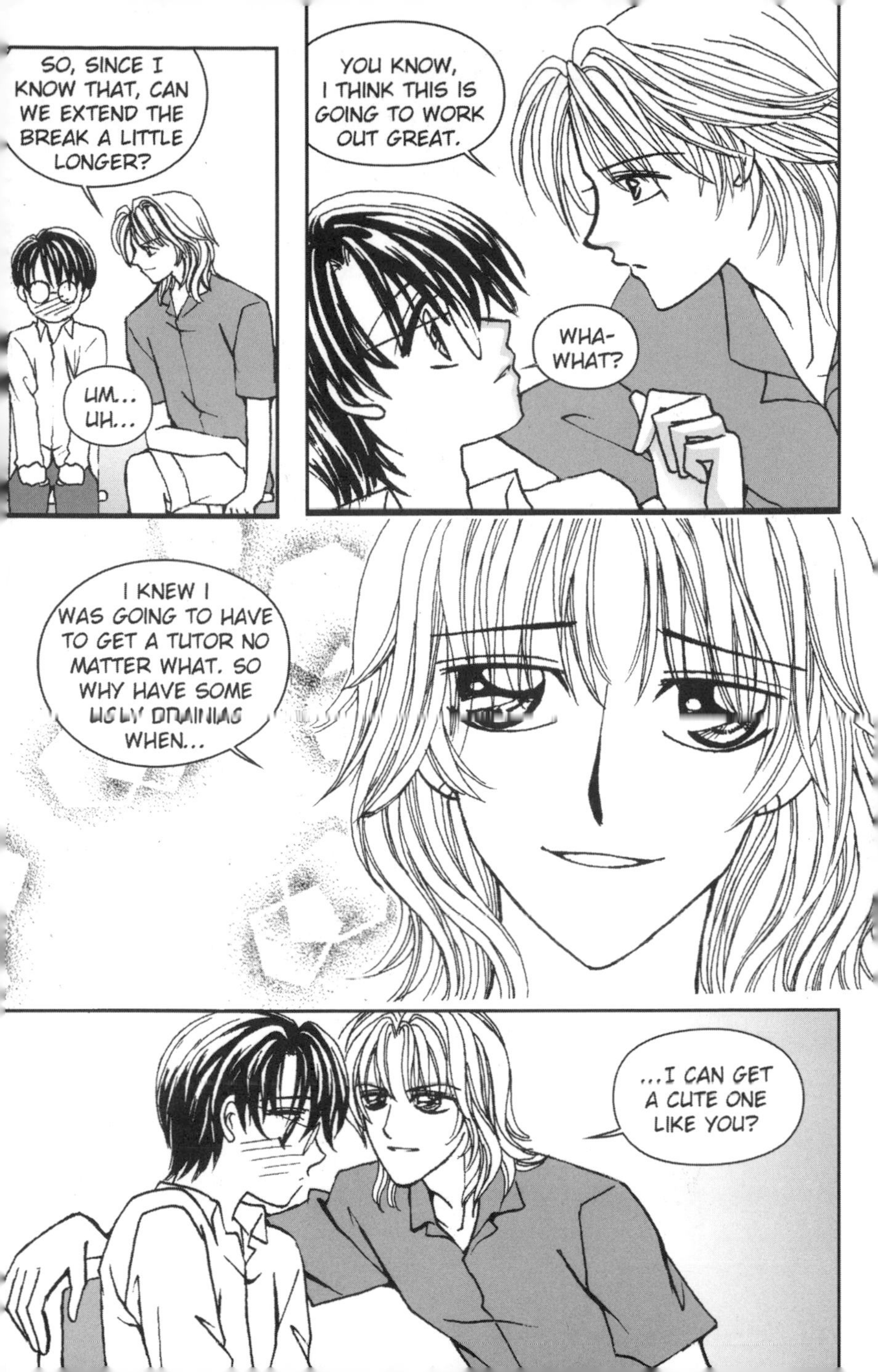
SO, SINCE I KNOW THAT, CAN WE EXTEND THE BREAK A LITTLE LONGER?
UM... UH...
YOU KNOW, I THINK THIS IS GOING TO WORK OUT GREAT.
WHA-WHAT?
I KNEW I WAS GOING TO HAVE TO GET A TUTOR NO MATTER WHAT. SO WHY HAVE SOME
WHEN...
...I CAN GET A CUTE ONE LIKE YOU?

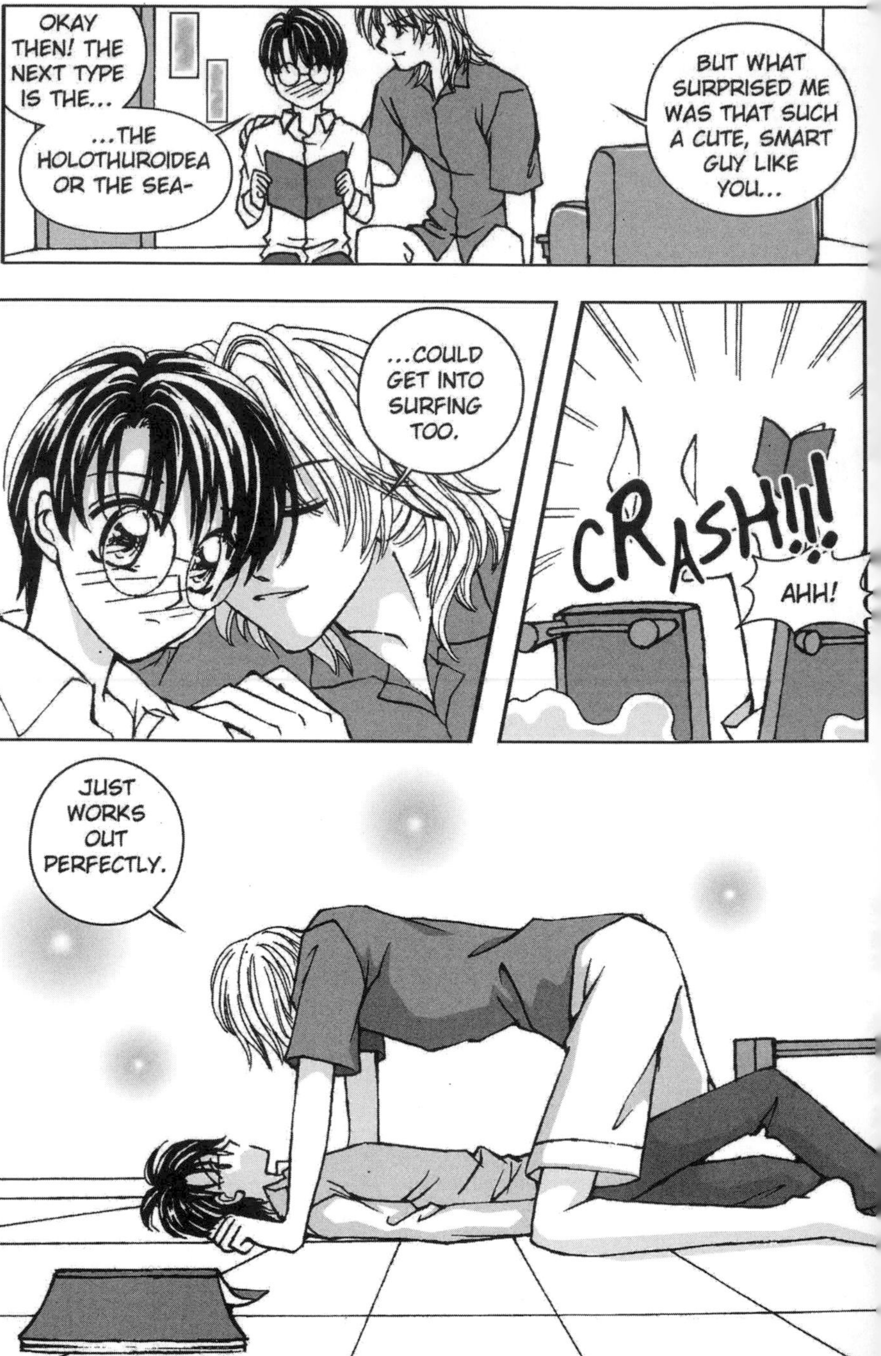
OKAY THEN! THE NEXT TYPE IS THE...
...THE HOLOTHUROIDEA OR THE SEA-
BUT WHAT SURPRISED ME WAS THAT SUCH A CUTE, SMART GUY LIKE YOU...
...COULD GET INTO SURFING TOO.
CRASH!!!
AHH!
JUST WORKS OUT PERFECTLY.

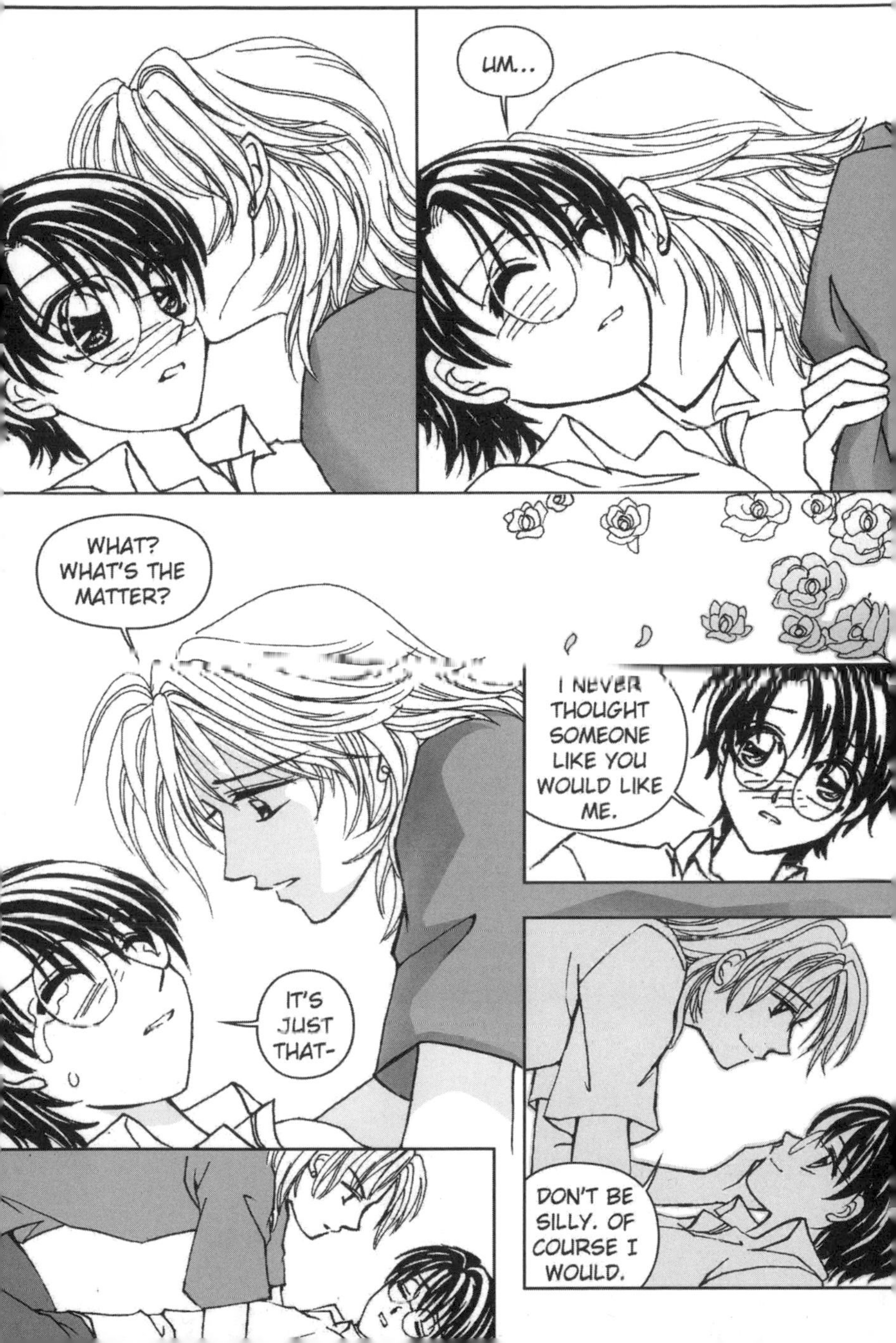
UM...
WHAT? WHAT'S THE MATTER?
I NEVER THOUGHT SOMEONE LIKE YOU WOULD LIKE ME.
IT'S JUST THAT-
DON'T BE SILLY. OF COURSE I WOULD.

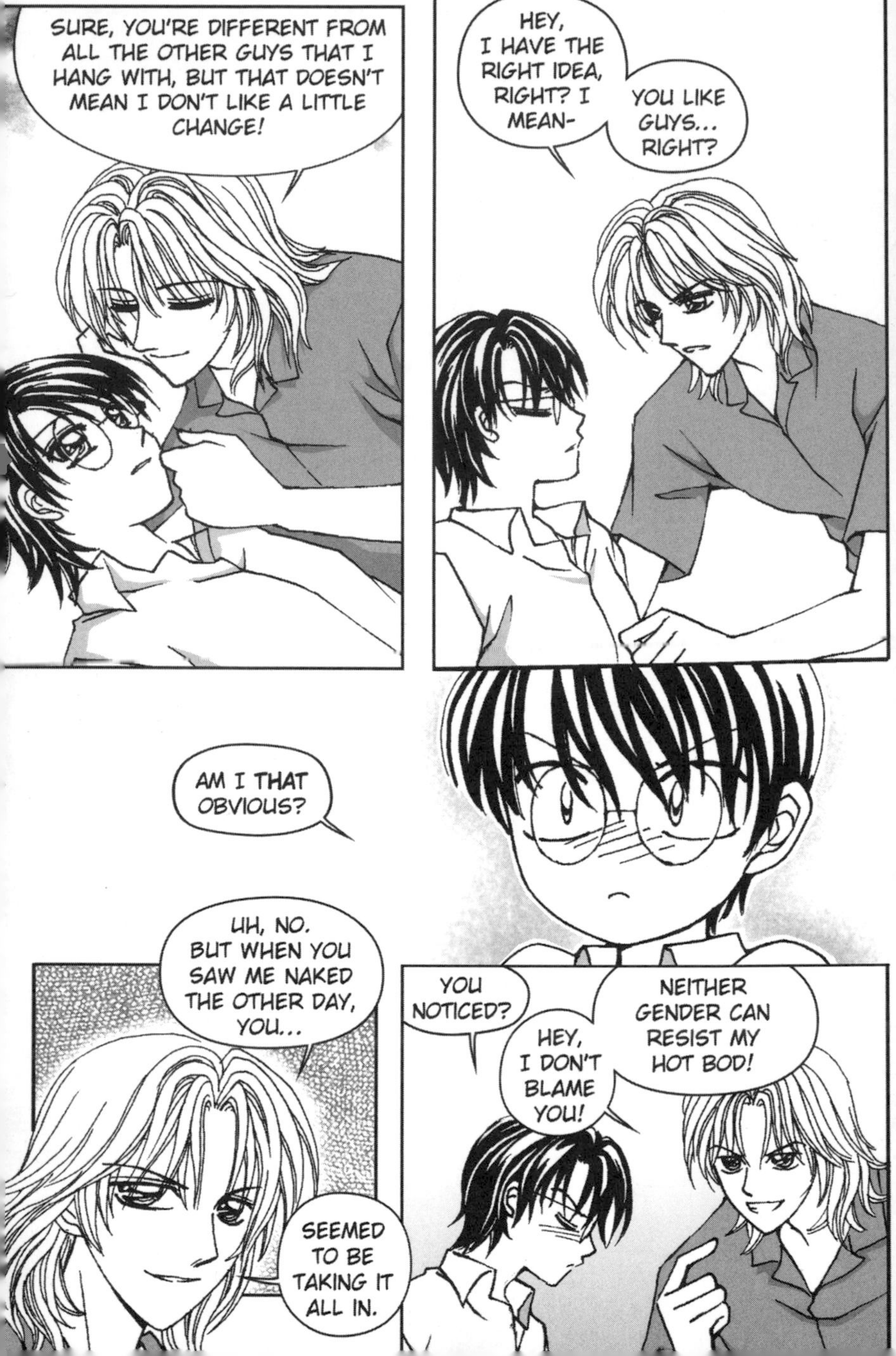
SURE, YOU'RE DIFFERENT FROM ALL THE OTHER GUYS THAT I HANG WITH, BUT THAT DOESN'T MEAN I DON'T LIKE A LITTLE CHANGE!
HEY, I HAVE THE RIGHT IDEA, RIGHT? I MEAN-
YOU LIKE GUYS... RIGHT?
AM I THAT OBVIOUS?
UH, NO. BUT WHEN YOU SAW ME NAKED THE OTHER DAY, YOU...
SEEMED TO BE TAKING IT ALL IN.
YOU NOTICED?
HEY, I DON'T BLAME YOU!
NEITHER GENDER CAN RESIST MY HOT BOD!

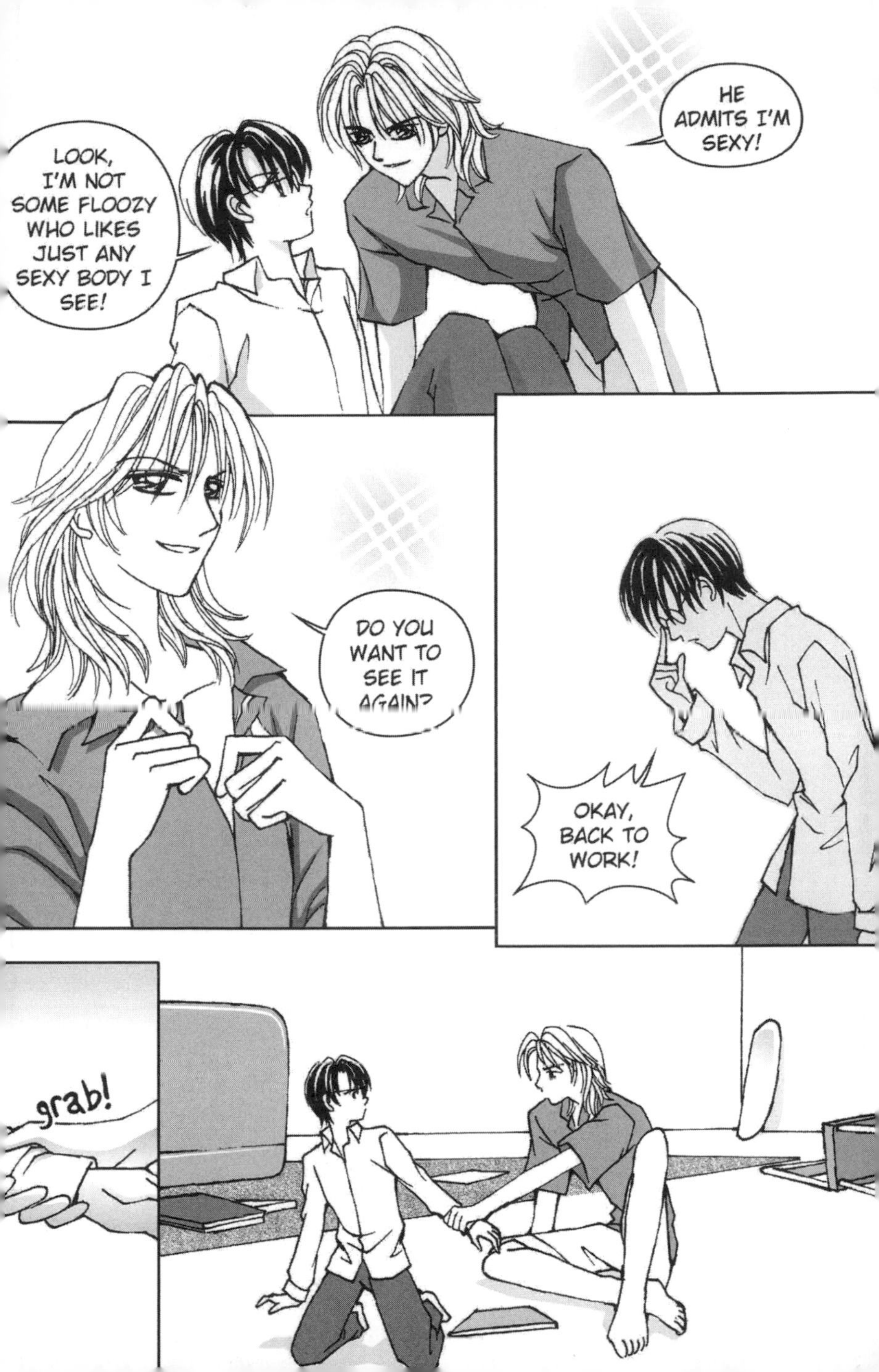
HE ADMITS I'M SEXY!
LOOK, I'M NOT SOME FLOOZY WHO LIKES JUST ANY SEXY BODY I SEE!
DO YOU WANT TO SEE IT AGAIN?
OKAY, BACK TO WORK!
grab!

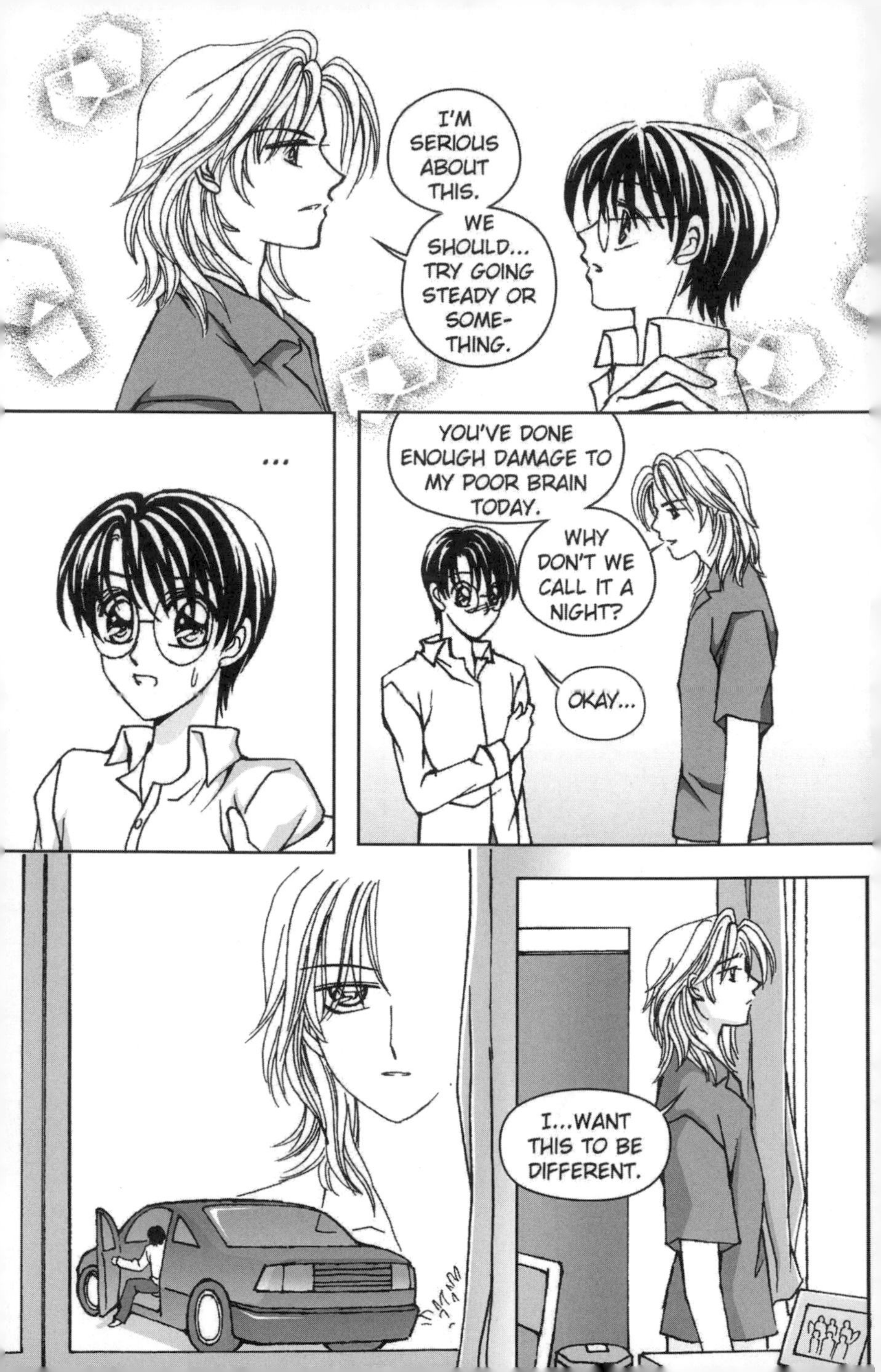
I'M SERIOUS ABOUT THIS.
WE SHOULD... TRY GOING STEADY OR SOME-THING.
...
YOU'VE DONE ENOUGH DAMAGE TO MY POOR BRAIN TODAY.
WHY DON'T WE CALL IT A NIGHT?
OKAY...
I...WANT THIS TO BE DIFFERENT.

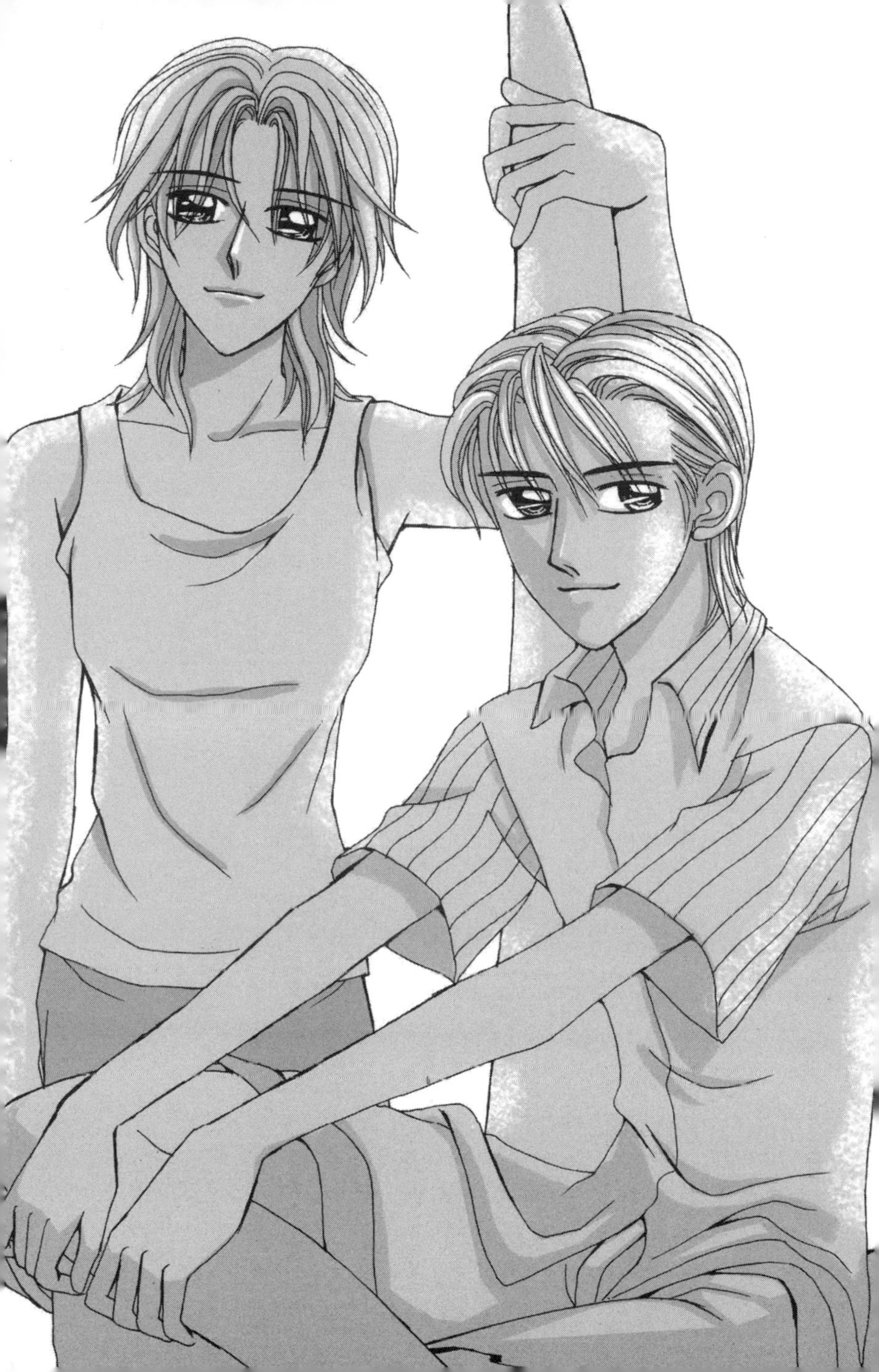

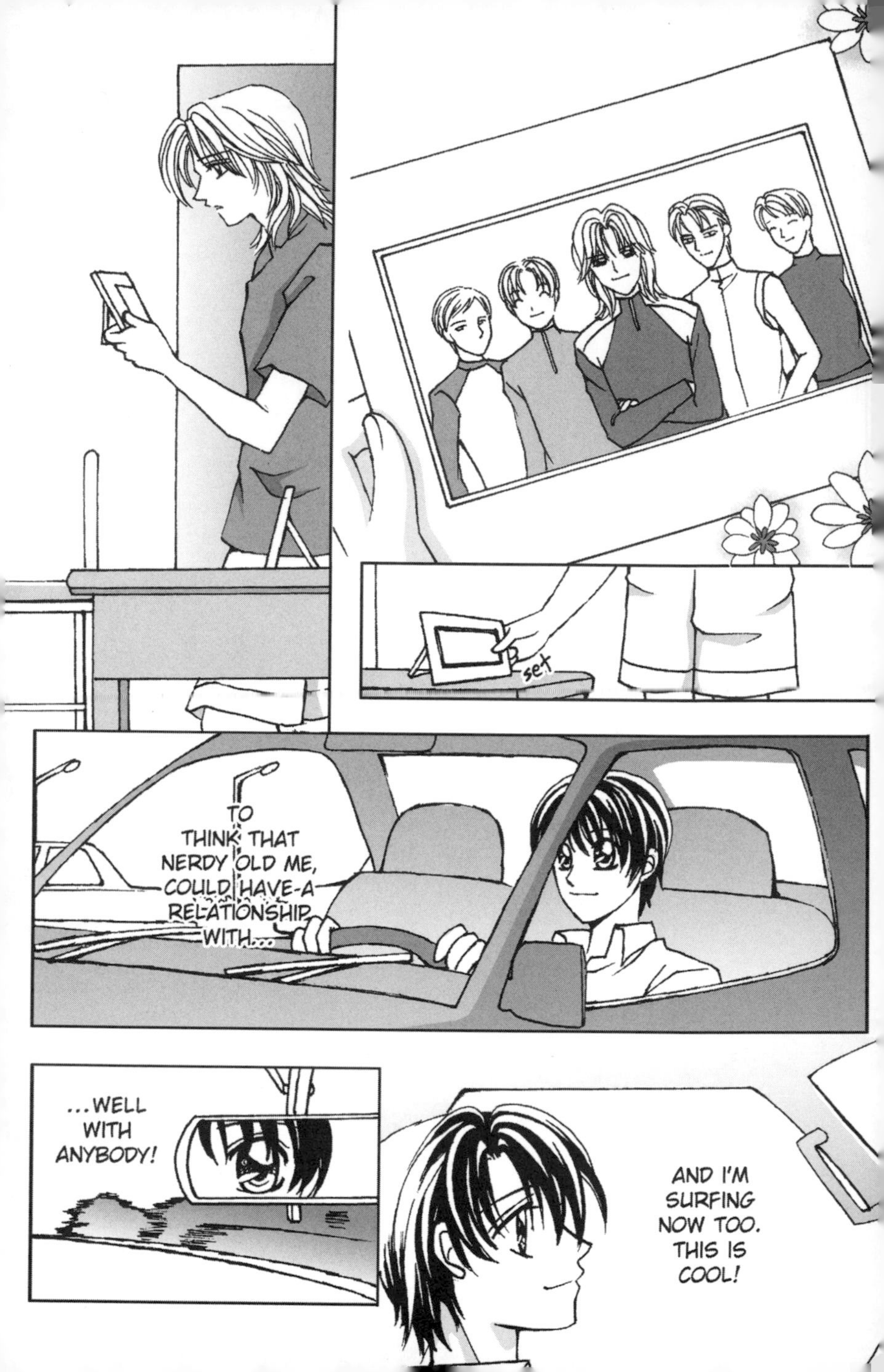
set
TO THINK THAT NERDY OLD ME, COULD HAVE A RELATIONSHIP WITH...
...WELL WITH ANYBODY!
AND I'M SURFING NOW TOO. THIS IS COOL!

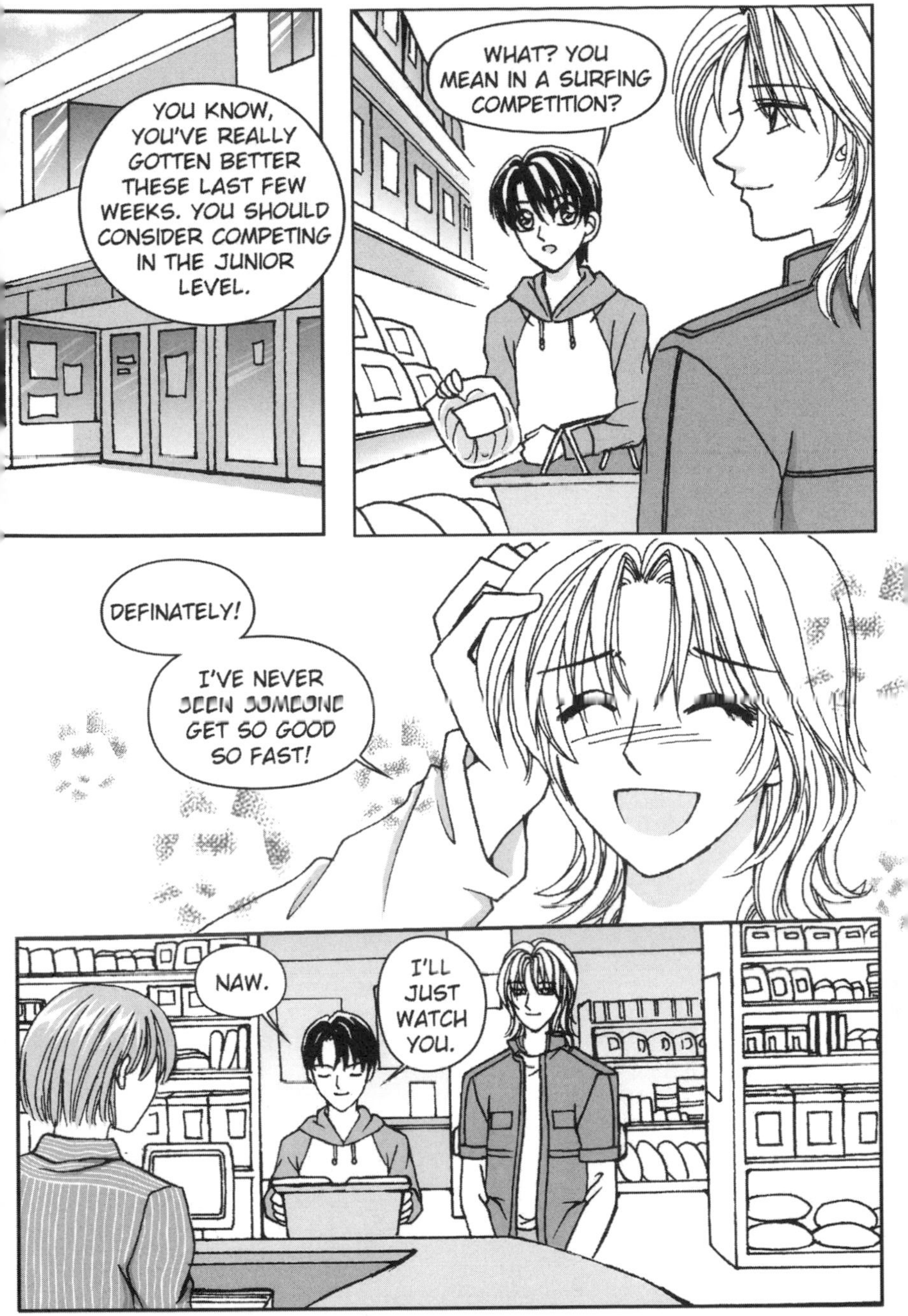
YOU KNOW, YOU'VE REALLY GOTTEN BETTER THESE LAST FEW WEEKS. YOU SHOULD CONSIDER COMPETING IN THE JUNIOR LEVEL.
WHAT? YOU MEAN IN A SURFING COMPETITION?
DEFINATELY!
I'VE NEVER SEEN SOMEONE GET SO GOOD SO FAST!
NAW.
I'LL JUST WATCH YOU.

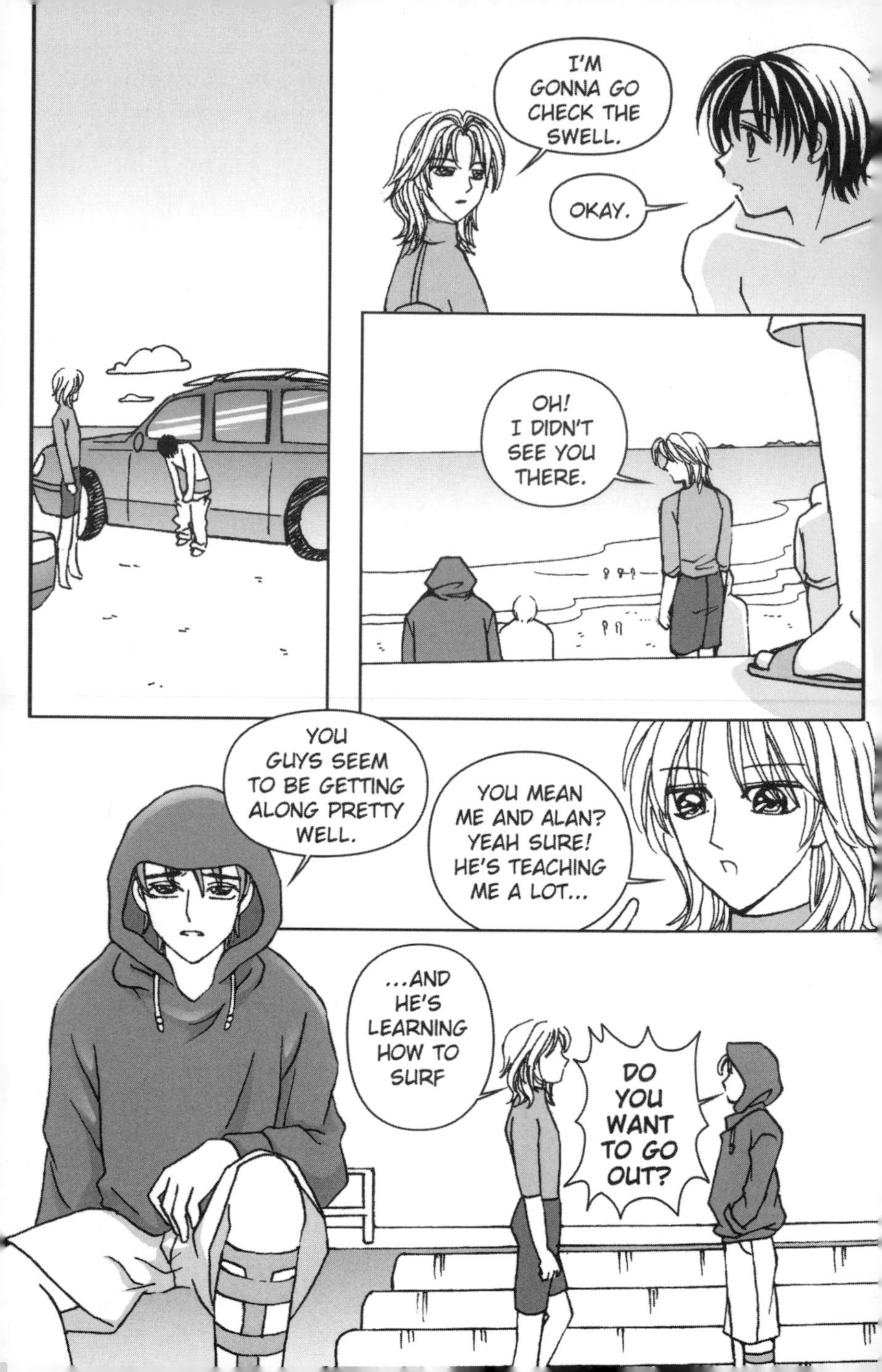
I'M GONNA GO CHECK THE SWELL.
OKAY.
OH! I DIDN'T SEE YOU THERE.
YOU GUYS SEEM TO BE GETTING ALONG PRETTY WELL.
YOU MEAN ME AND ALAN? YEAH SURE! HE'S TEACHING ME A LOT...
...AND HE'S LEARNING HOW TO SURF
DO YOU WANT TO GO OUT?

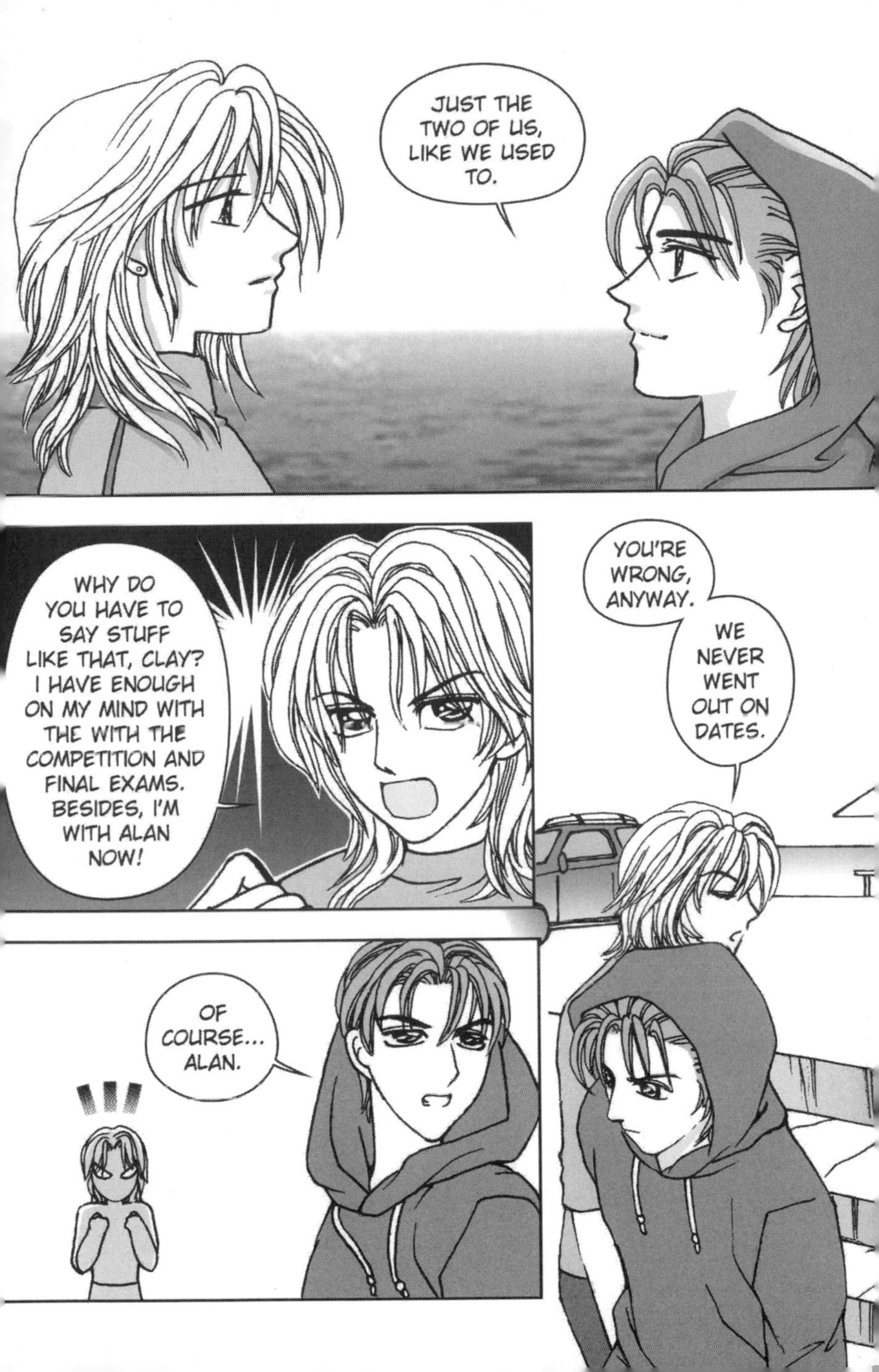
JUST THE TWO OF US, LIKE WE USED TO.
WHY DO YOU HAVE TO SAY STUFF LIKE THAT, CLAY? I HAVE ENOUGH ON MY MIND WITH THE WITH THE COMPETITION AND FINAL EXAMS. BESIDES, I'M WITH ALAN NOW!
YOU'RE WRONG, ANYWAY.
WE NEVER WENT OUT ON DATES.
OF COURSE... ALAN.

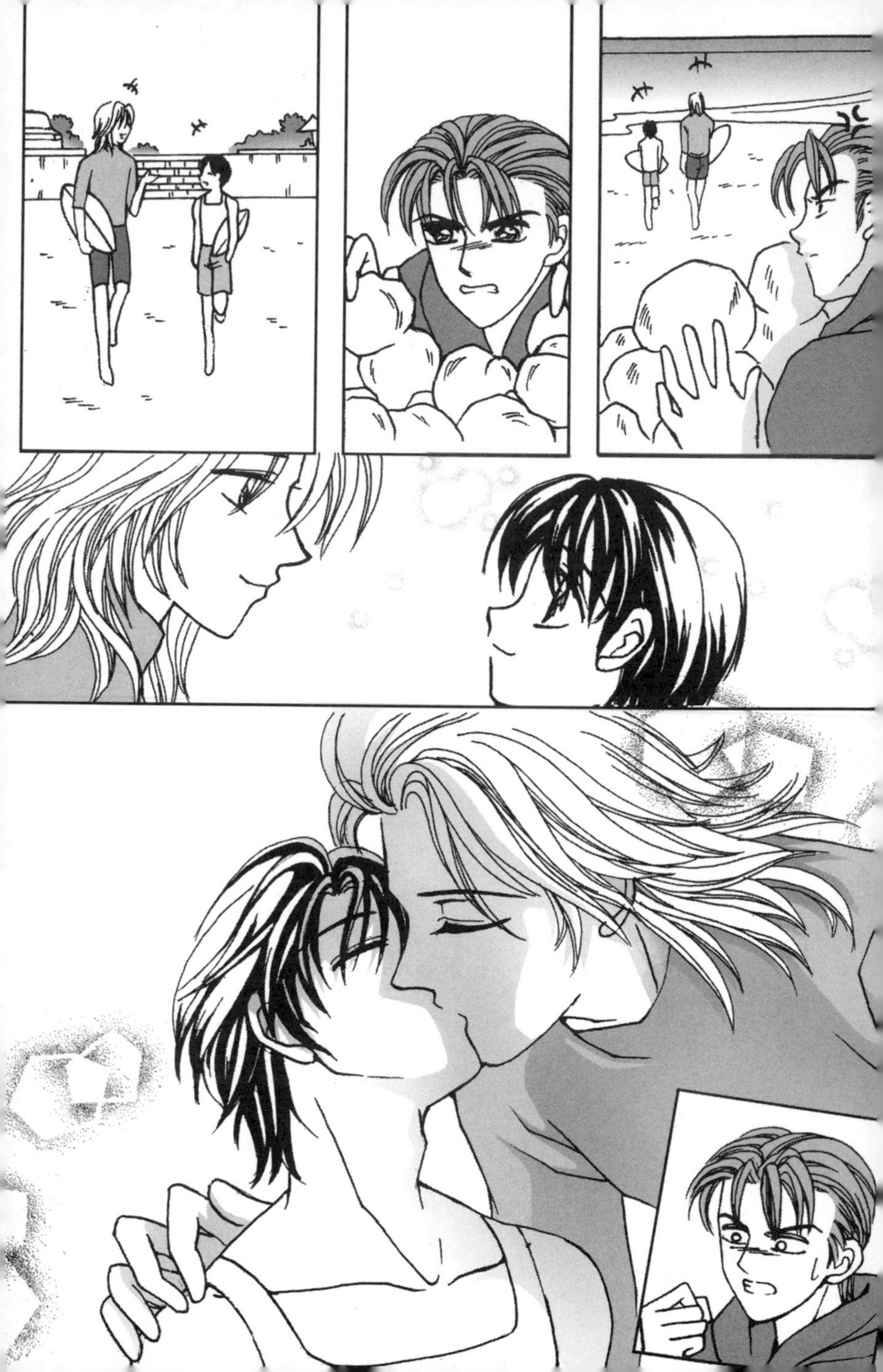

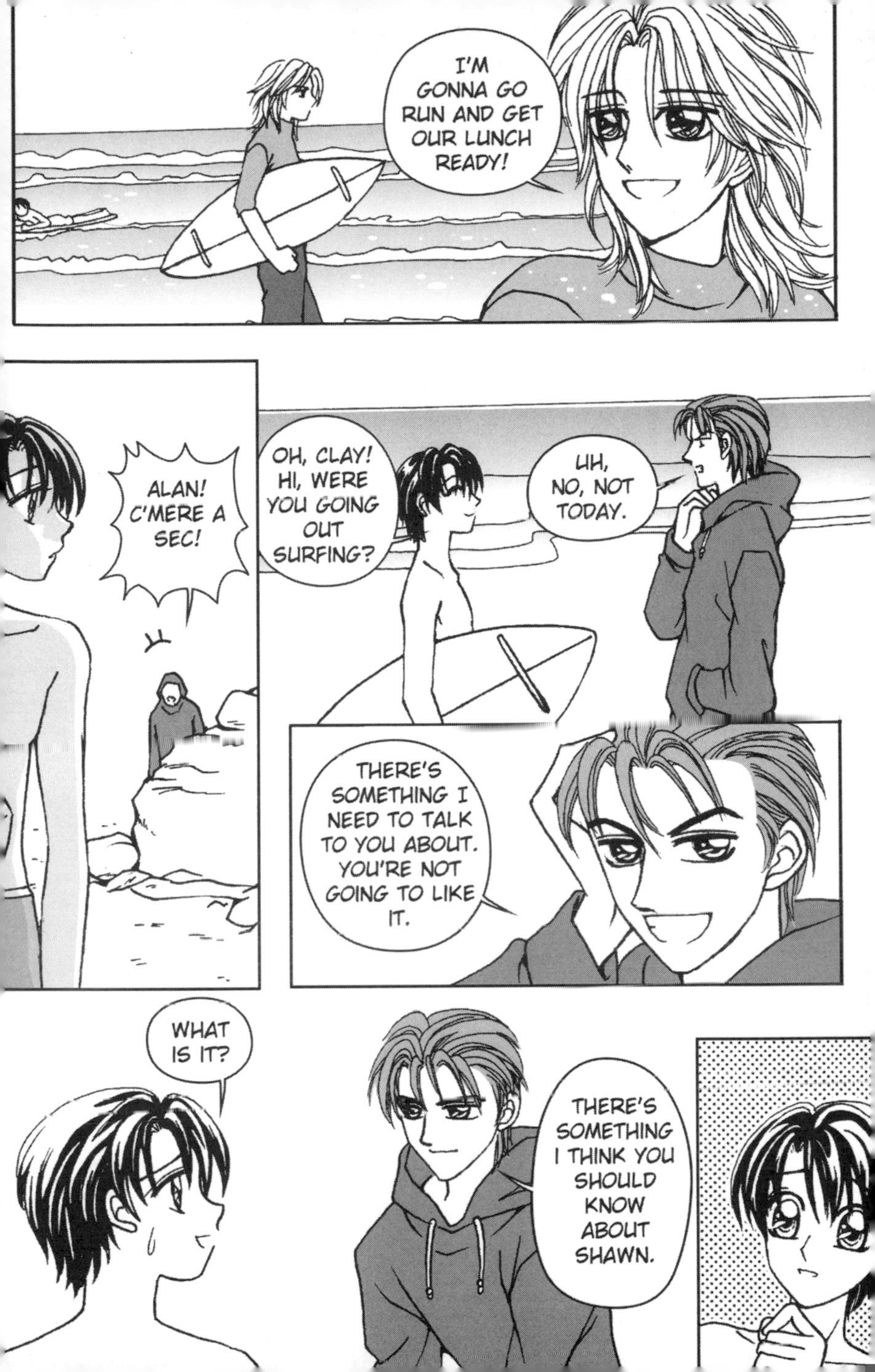
I'M GONNA GO RUN AND GET OUR LUNCH READY!
ALAN! C'MERE A SEC!
OH, CLAY! HI, WERE YOU GOING OUT SURFING?
UH, NO, NOT TODAY.
THERE'S SOMETHING I NEED TO TALK TO YOU ABOUT. YOU'RE NOT GOING TO LIKE IT.
WHAT IS IT?
THERE'S SOMETHING I THINK YOU SHOULD KNOW ABOUT SHAWN.

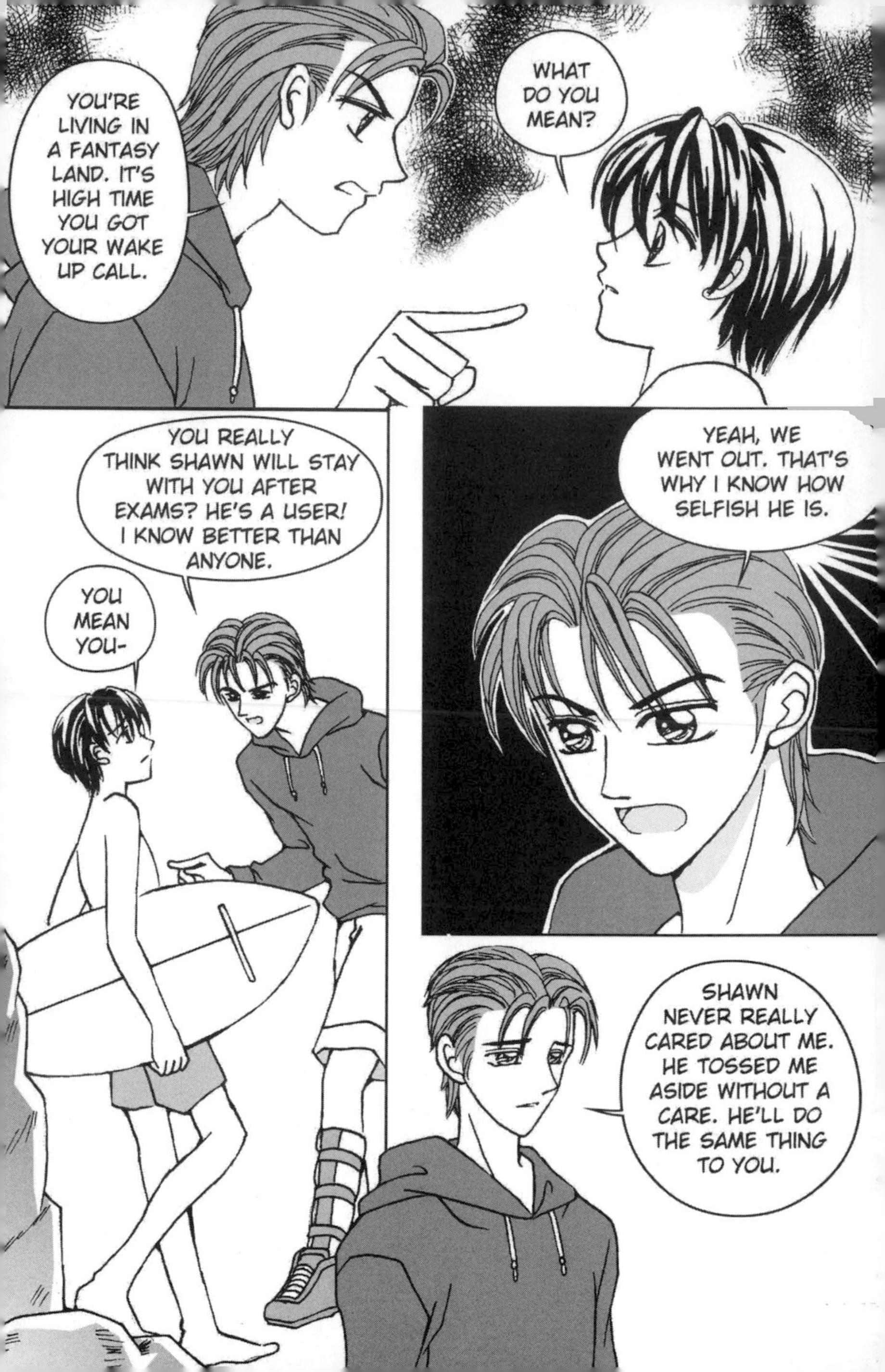
YOU'RE LIVING IN A FANTASY LAND. IT'S HIGH TIME YOU GOT YOUR WAKE UP CALL.
WHAT DO YOU MEAN?
YOU REALLY THINK SHAWN WILL STAY WITH YOU AFTER EXAMS? HE'S A USER! I KNOW BETTER THAN ANYONE.
YOU MEAN YOU-
YEAH, WE WENT OUT. THAT'S WHY I KNOW HOW SELFISH HE IS.
SHAWN NEVER REALLY CARED ABOUT ME. HE TOSSED ME ASIDE WITHOUT A CARE. HE'LL DO THE SAME THING TO YOU.

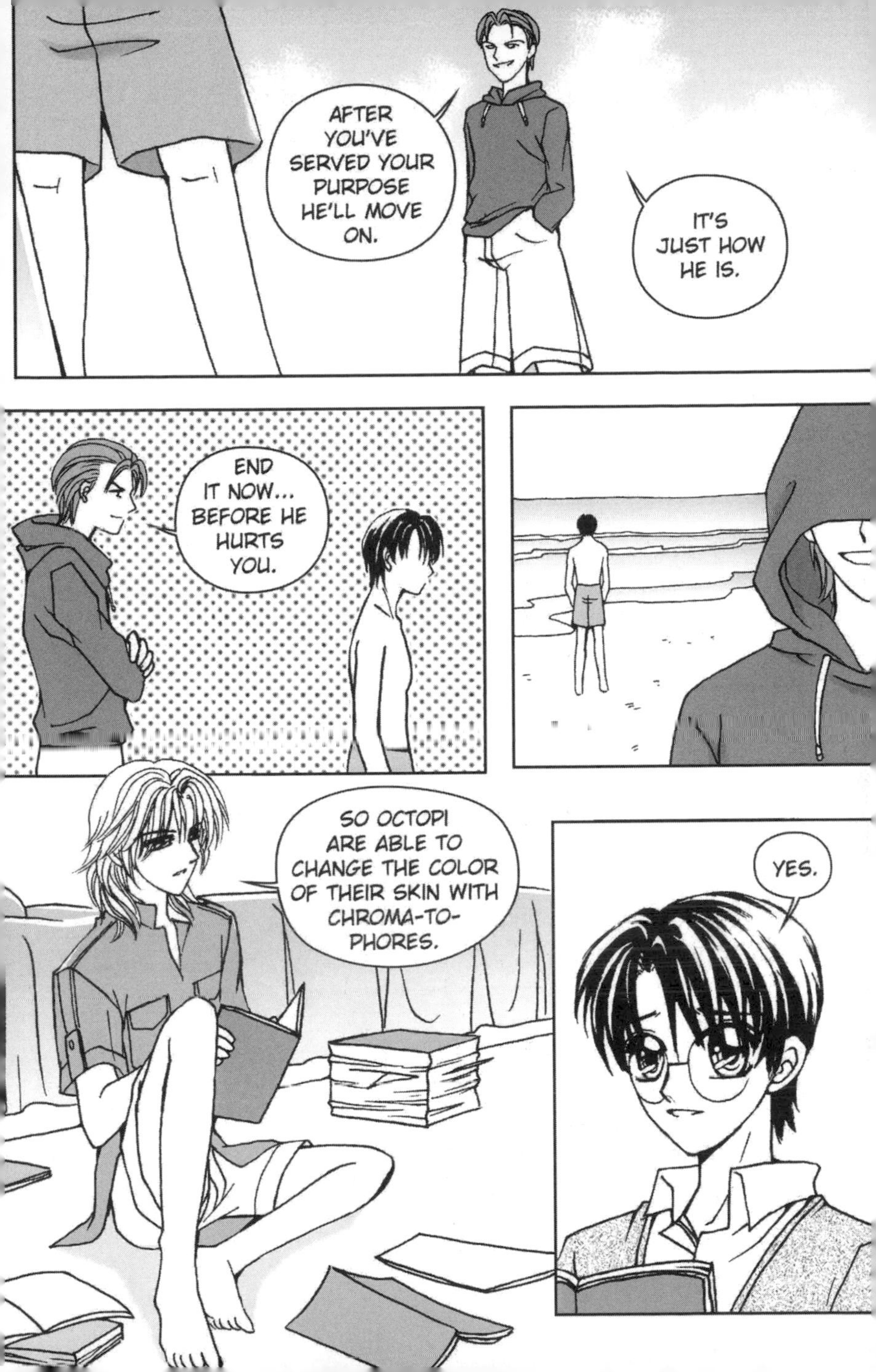
AFTER YOU'VE SERVED YOUR PURPOSE HE'LL MOVE ON.
IT'S JUST HOW HE IS.
END IT NOW... BEFORE HE HURTS YOU.
SO OCTOPI ARE ABLE TO CHANGE THE COLOR OF THEIR SKIN WITH CHROMA-TO-PHORES.
YES.

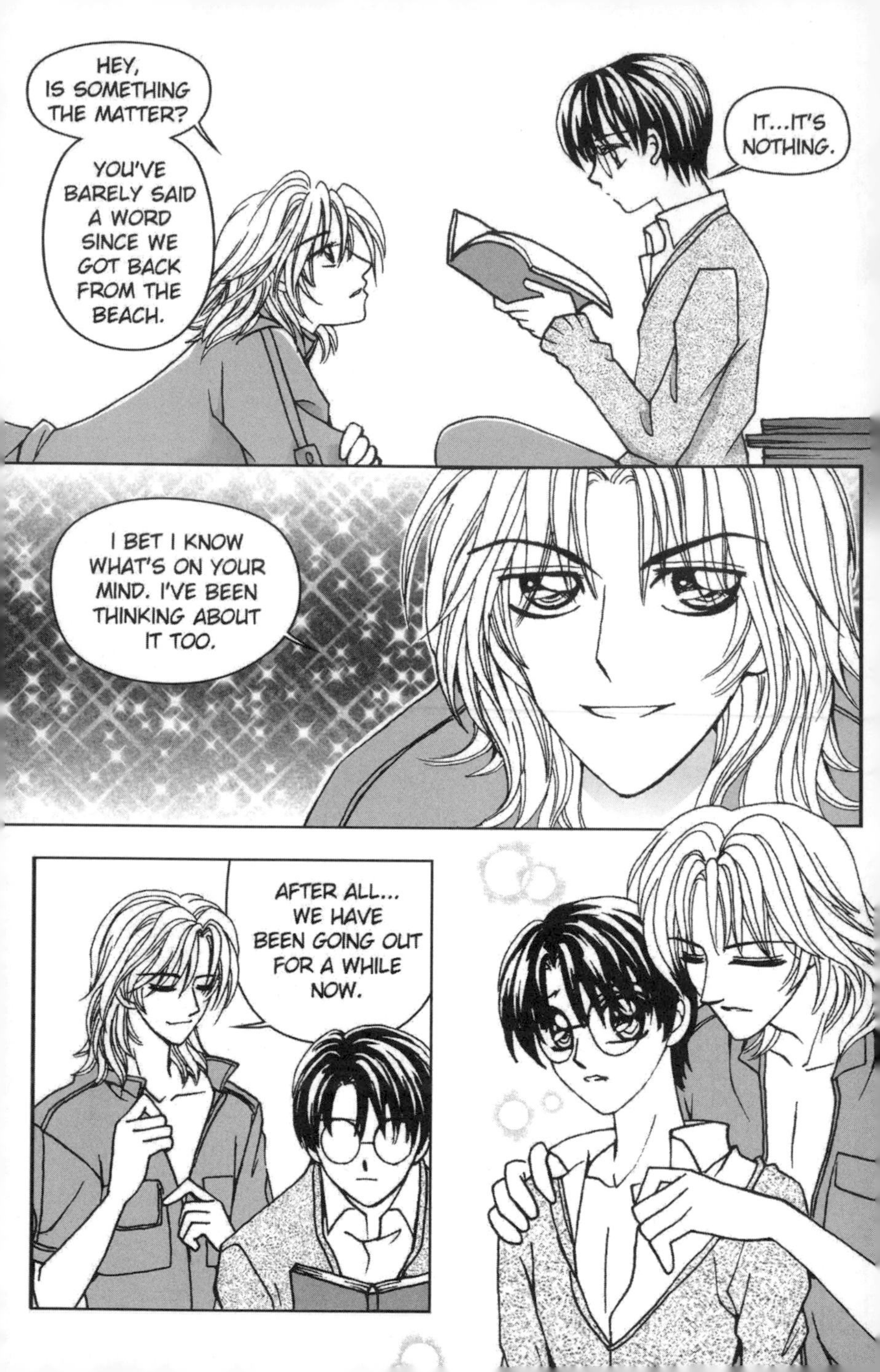
HEY, IS SOMETHING THE MATTER?
YOU'VE BARELY SAID A WORD SINCE WE GOT BACK FROM THE BEACH.
IT...IT'S NOTHING.
I BET I KNOW WHAT'S ON YOUR MIND. I'VE BEEN THINKING ABOUT IT TOO.
AFTER ALL... WE HAVE BEEN GOING OUT FOR A WHILE NOW.

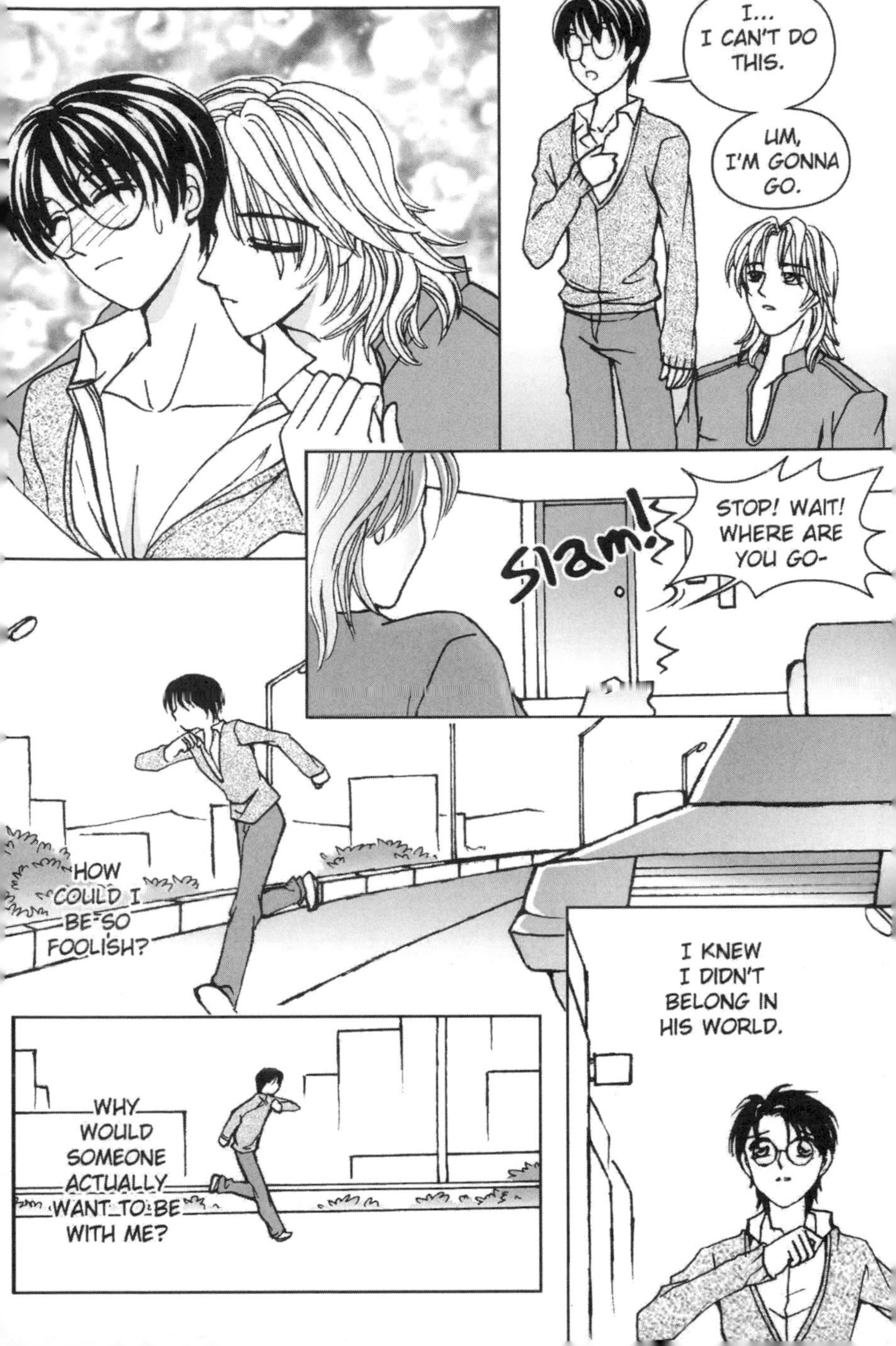
I...
I CAN'T DO THIS.
UM, I'M GONNA GO.
STOP! WAIT! WHERE ARE YOU GO-
SLAM!
HOW COULD I BE SO FOOLISH?
I KNEW I DIDN'T BELONG IN HIS WORLD.
WHY WOULD SOMEONE ACTUALLY WANT TO BE WITH ME?

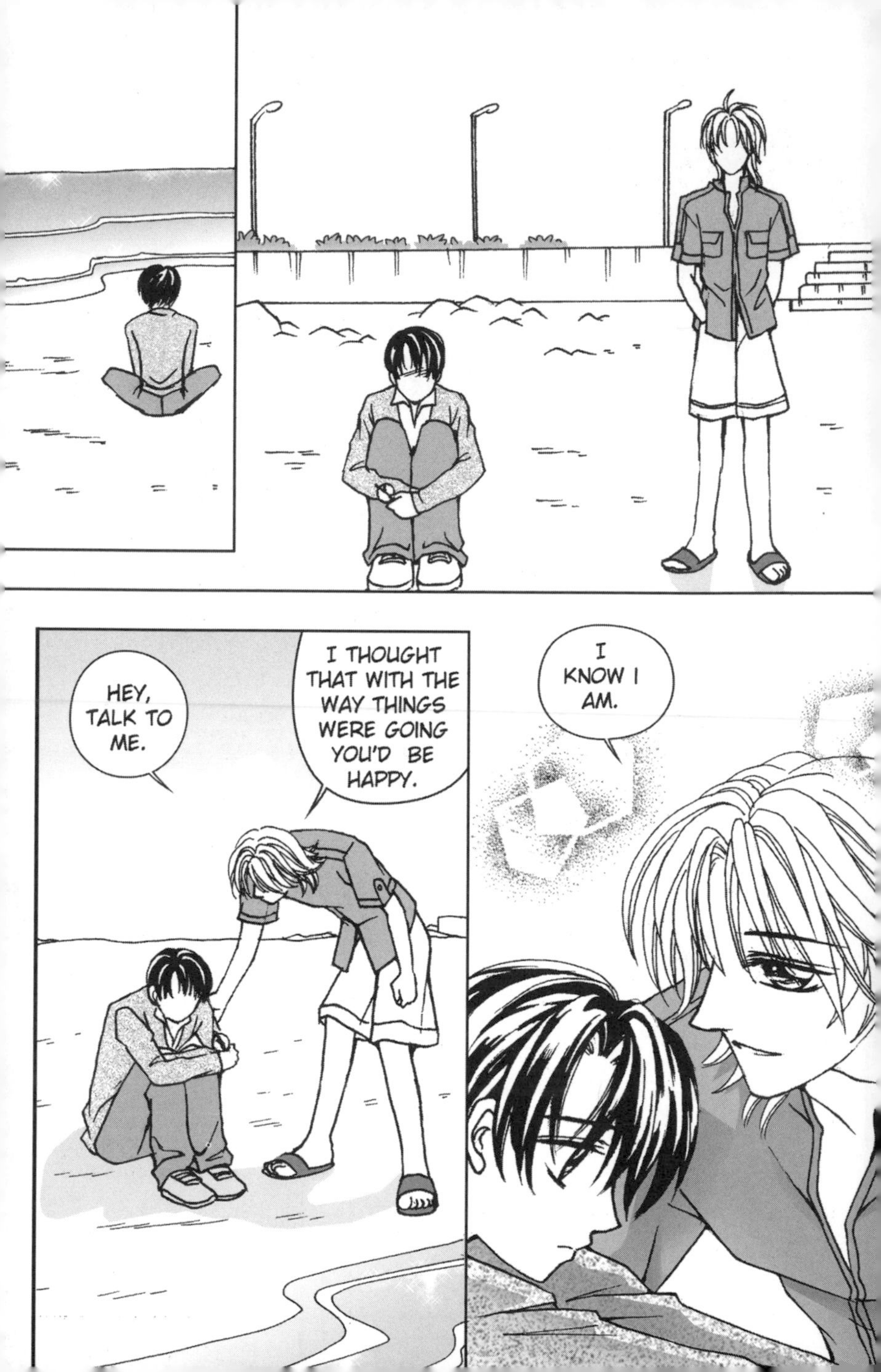

I KNOW I AM.
I THOUGHT THAT WITH THE WAY THINGS WERE GOING YOU'D BE HAPPY.
HEY, TALK TO ME.

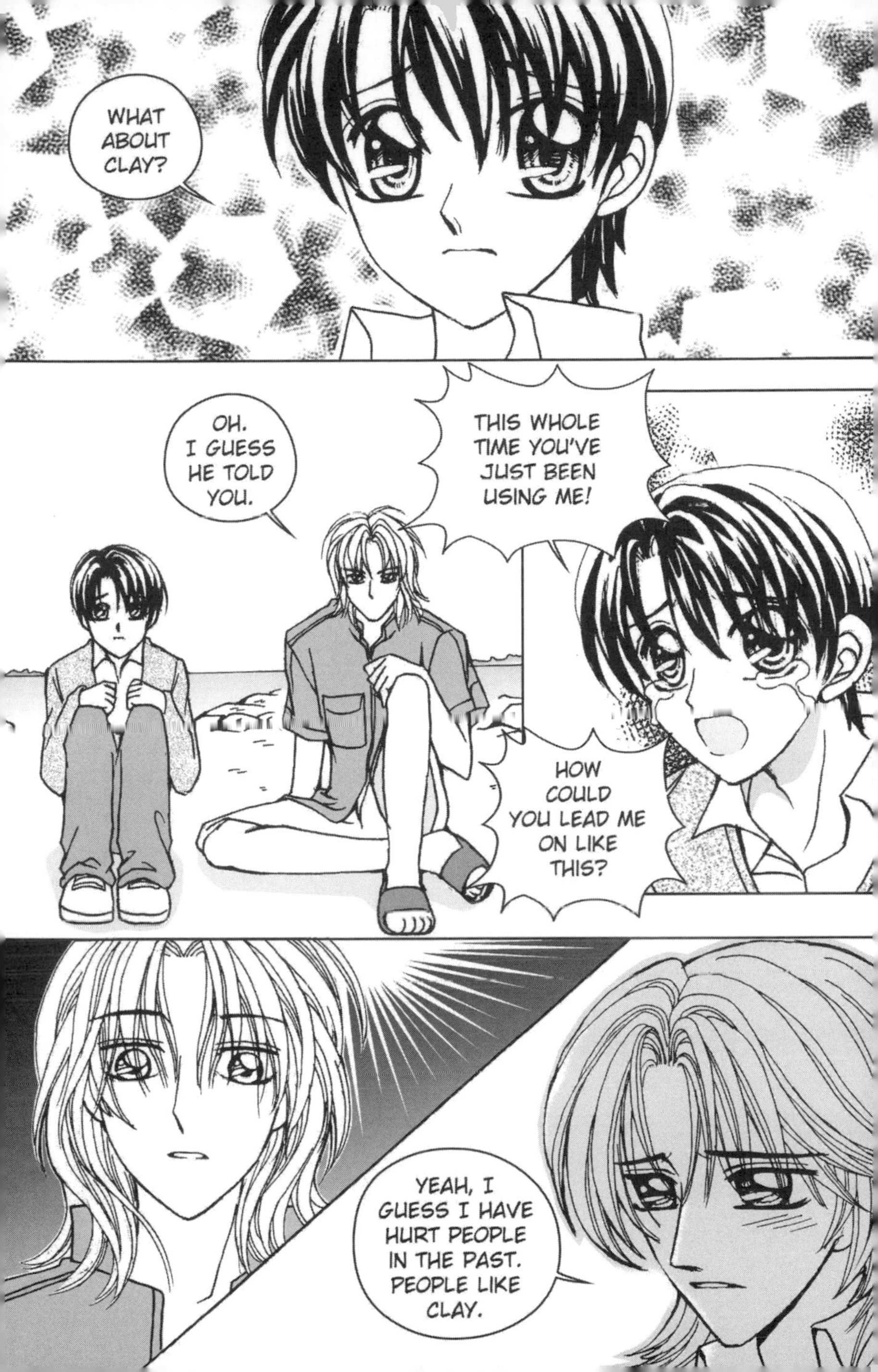
WHAT ABOUT CLAY?
OH. I GUESS HE TOLD YOU.
THIS WHOLE TIME YOU'VE JUST BEEN USING ME!
HOW COULD YOU LEAD ME ON LIKE THIS?
YEAH, I GUESS I HAVE HURT PEOPLE IN THE PAST. PEOPLE LIKE CLAY.

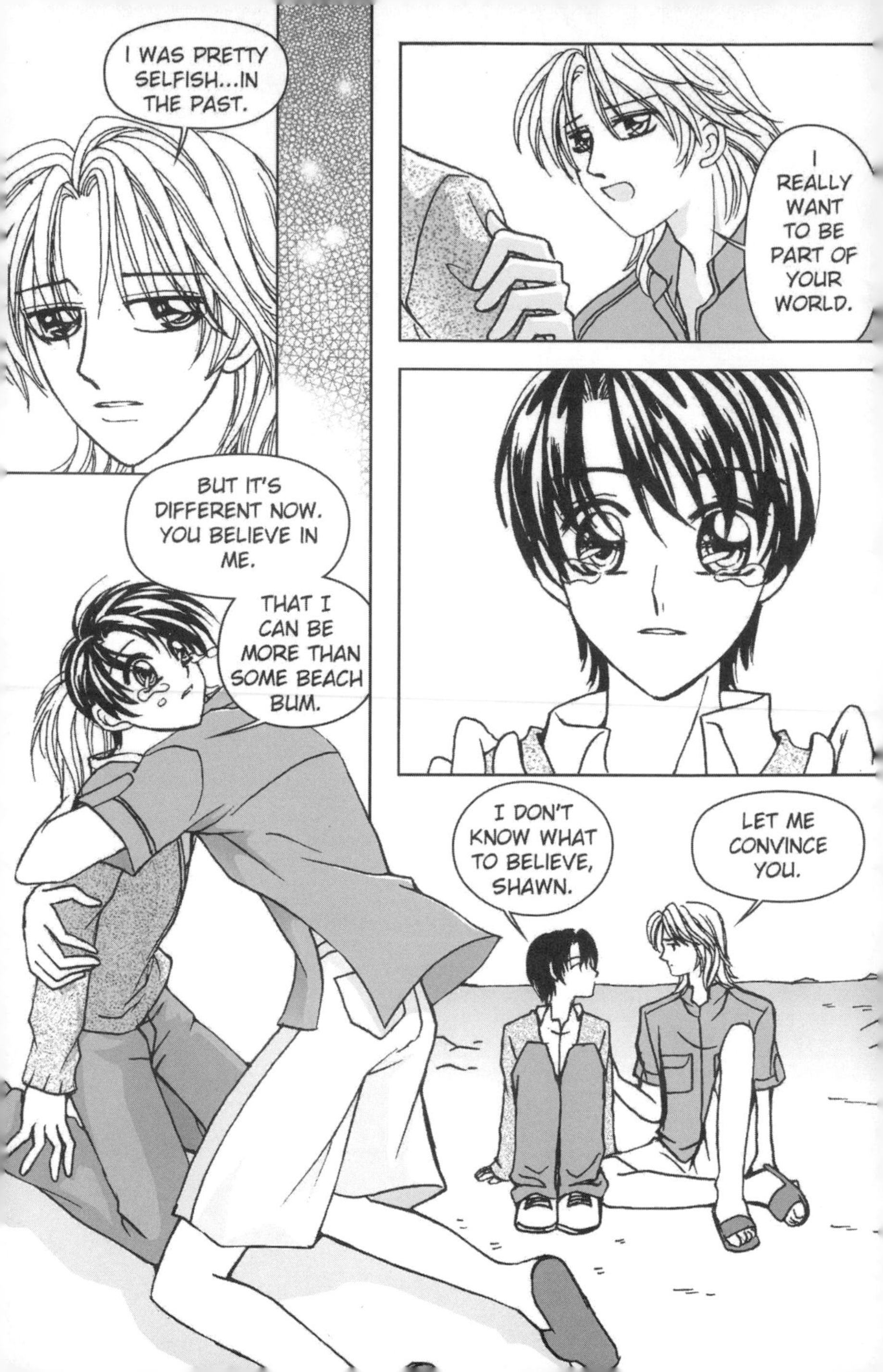
I WAS PRETTY SELFISH...IN THE PAST.
I REALLY WANT TO BE PART OF YOUR WORLD.
BUT IT'S DIFFERENT NOW. YOU BELIEVE IN ME.
THAT I CAN BE MORE THAN SOME BEACH BUM.
I DON'T KNOW WHAT TO BELIEVE, SHAWN.
LET ME CONVINCE YOU.

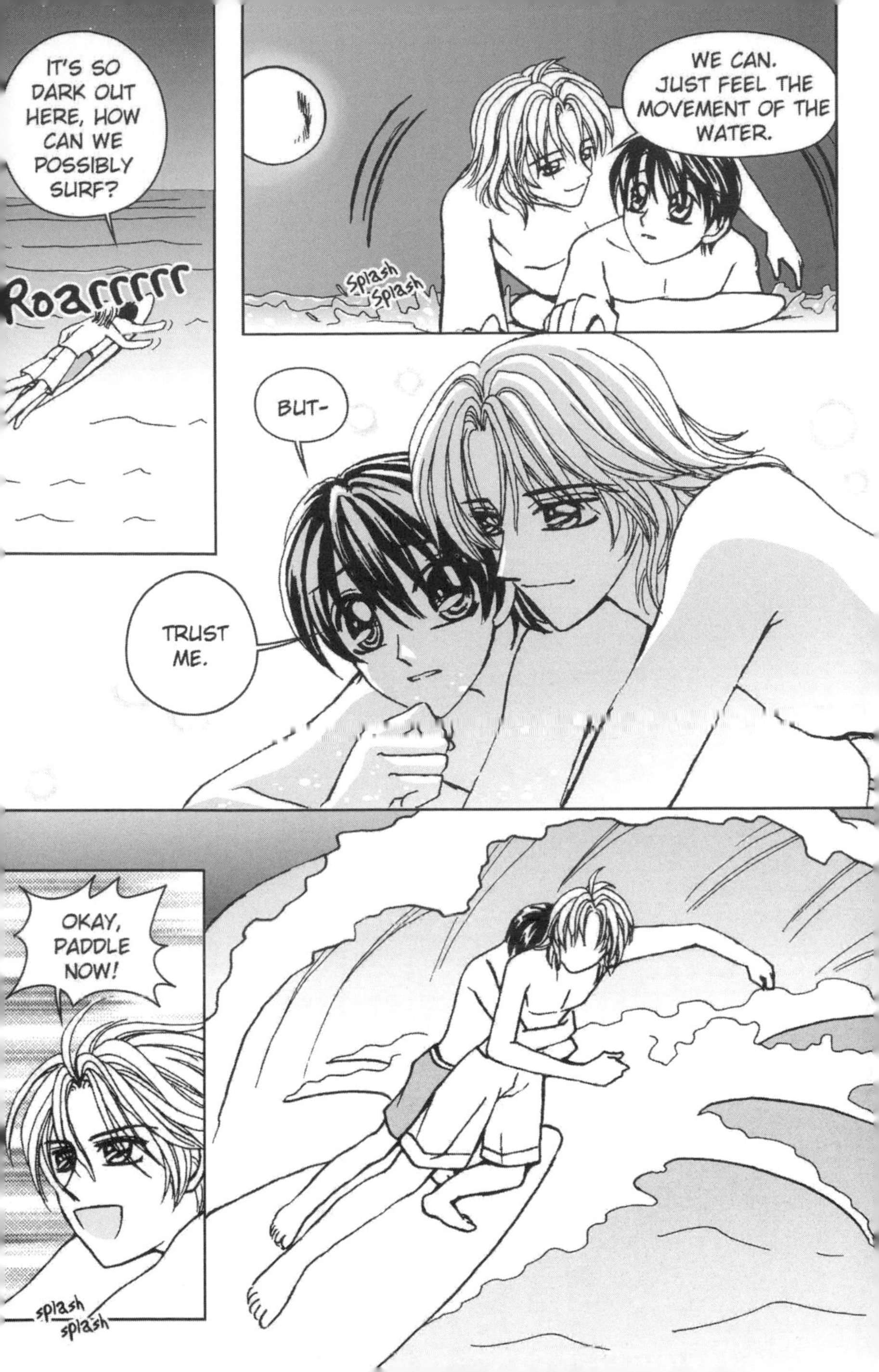
IT'S SO DARK OUT HERE, HOW CAN WE POSSIBLY SURF?
Roarrrrrr
WE CAN. JUST FEEL THE MOVEMENT OF THE WATER.
Splash
Splash
BUT-
TRUST ME.
OKAY, PADDLE NOW!
splash
splash

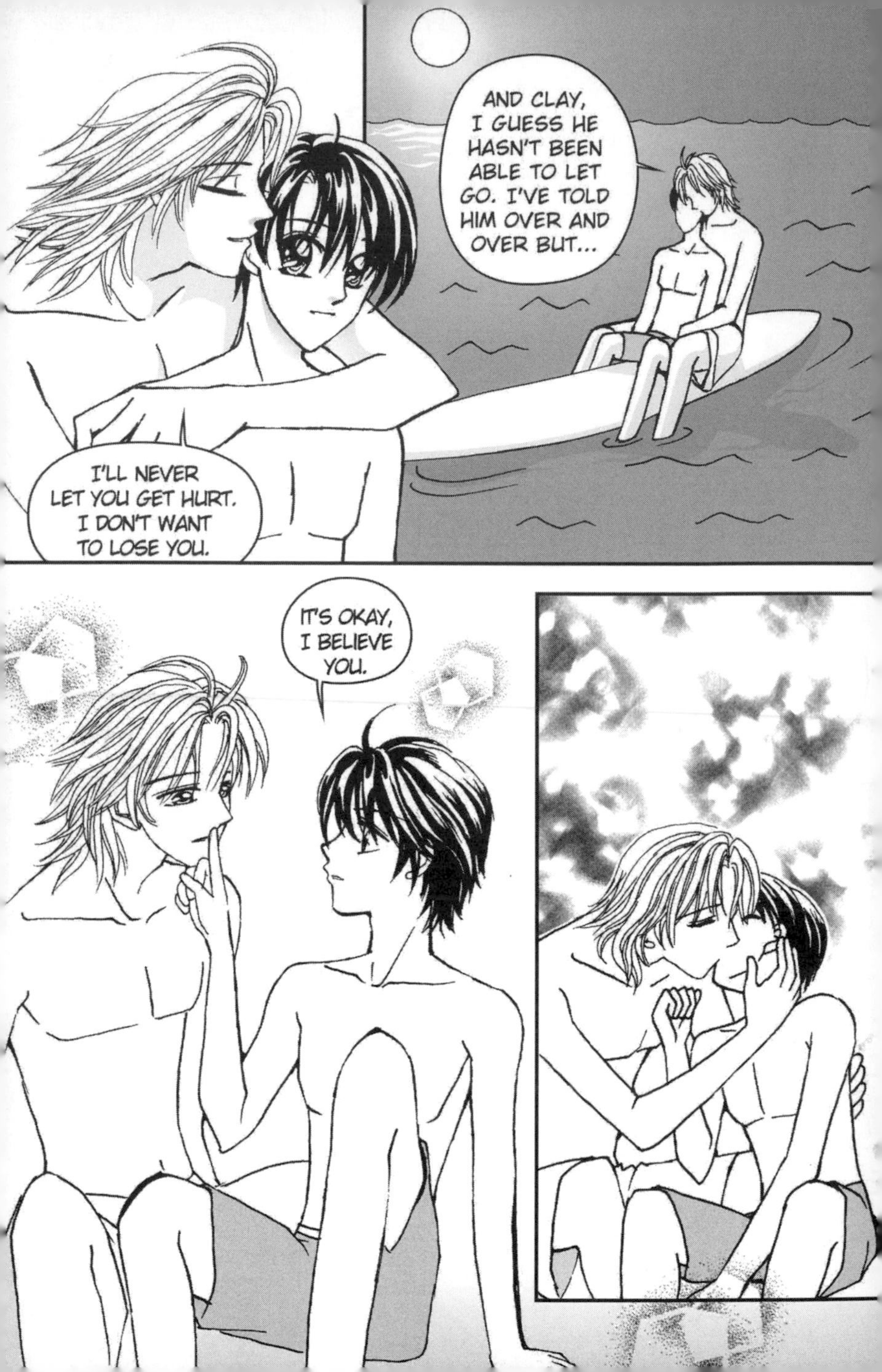
AND CLAY, I GUESS HE HASN'T BEEN ABLE TO LET GO. I'VE TOLD HIM OVER AND OVER BUT...
I'LL NEVER LET YOU GET HURT. I DON'T WANT TO LOSE YOU.
IT'S OKAY, I BELIEVE YOU.

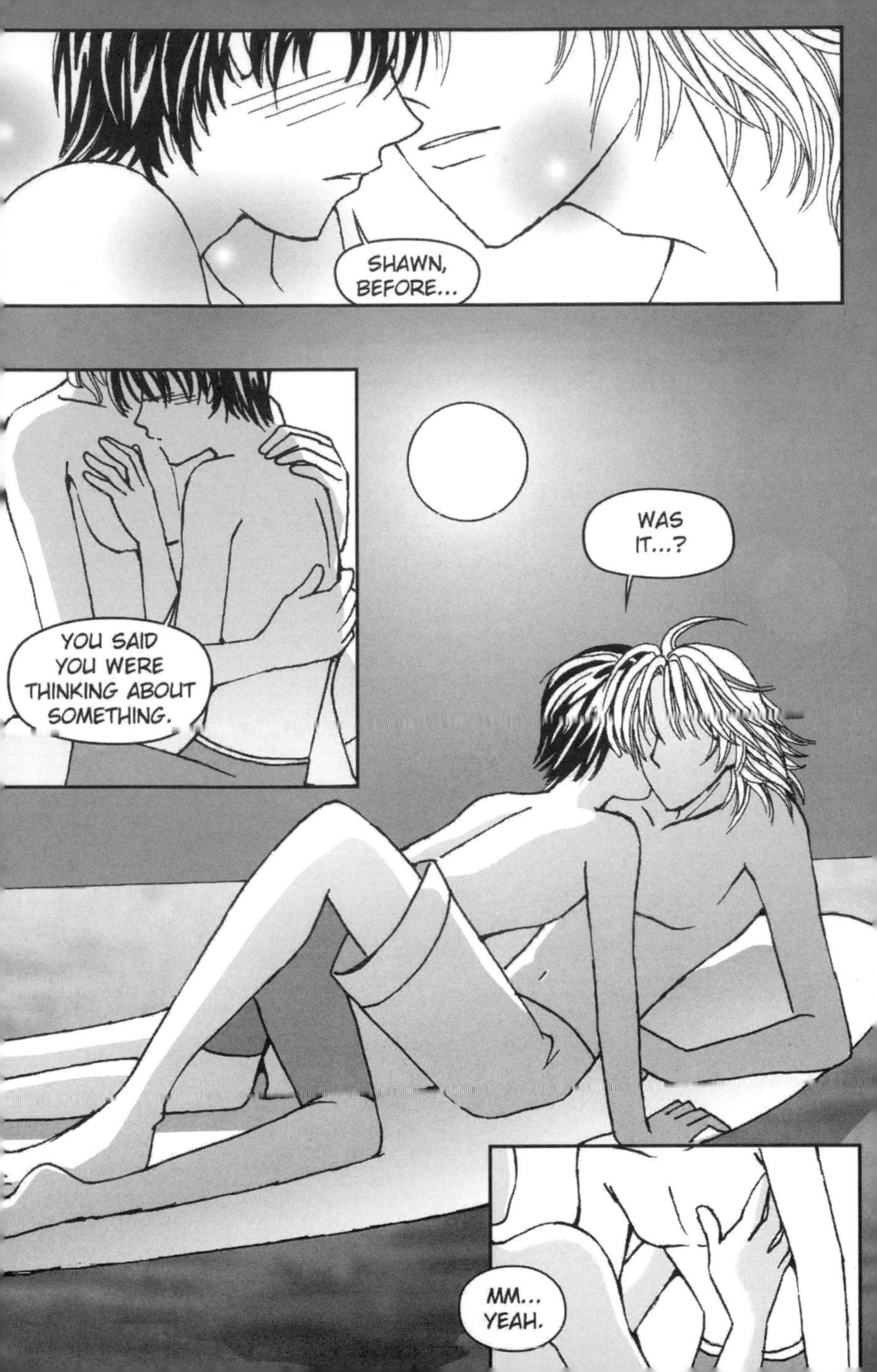
SHAWN, BEFORE...
YOU SAID YOU WERE THINKING ABOUT SOMETHING.
WAS IT...?
MM... YEAH.

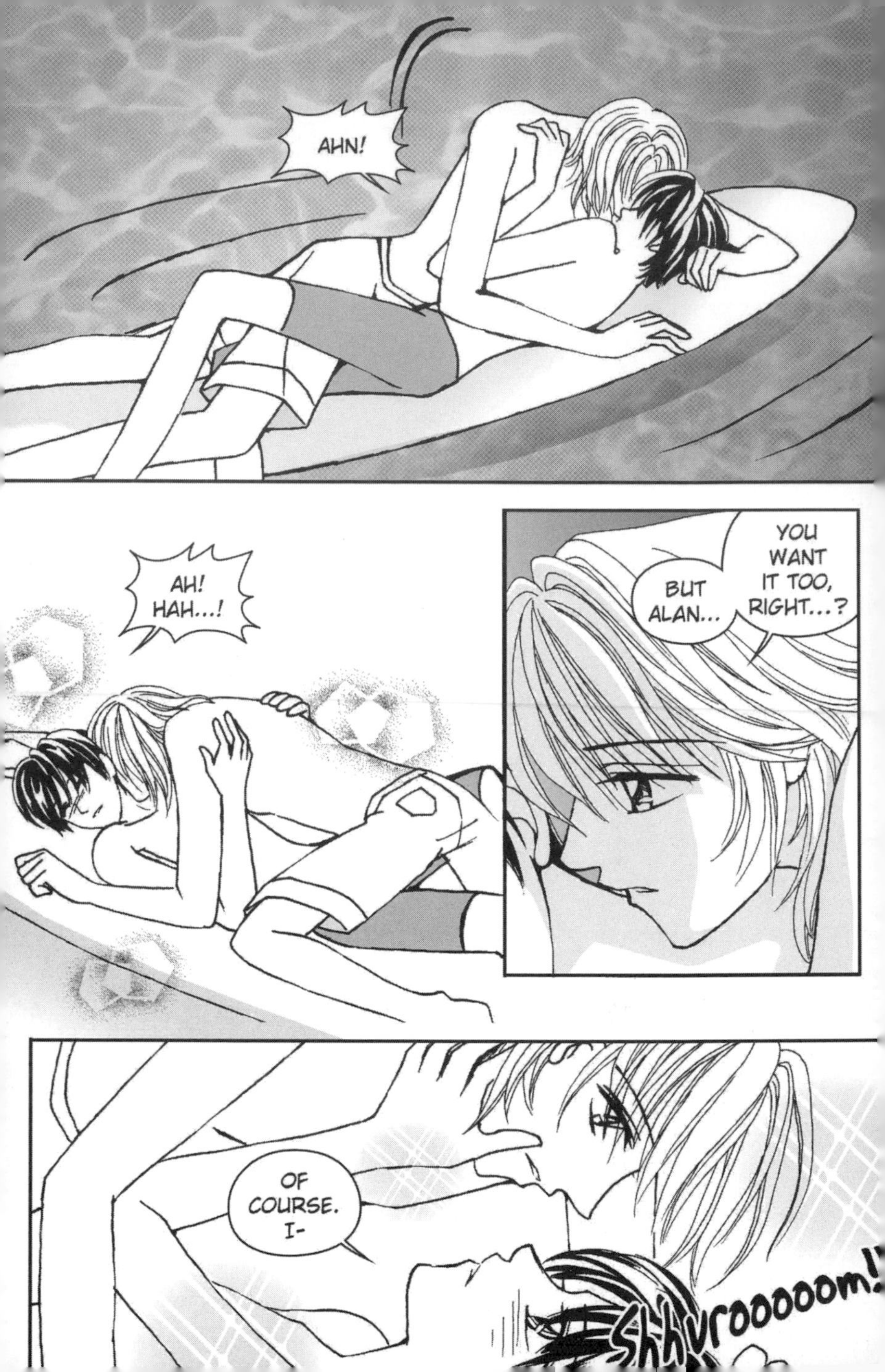
AHN!
AH! HAH...!
YOU WANT IT TOO, RIGHT...?
BUT ALAN...
OF COURSE. I-
SHHUROOOOOM!

Honk! Honk!
WHAT THE-?
THAT'S CLAY'S CAR!
SCREEEEECH!!
WHAT THE HELL ARE YOU DOING?! WERE YOU WATCHING US THE WHOLE TIME?
paddle paddle
DAMN IT, CLAY!
SH-SHUT UP! I LOVED YOU!

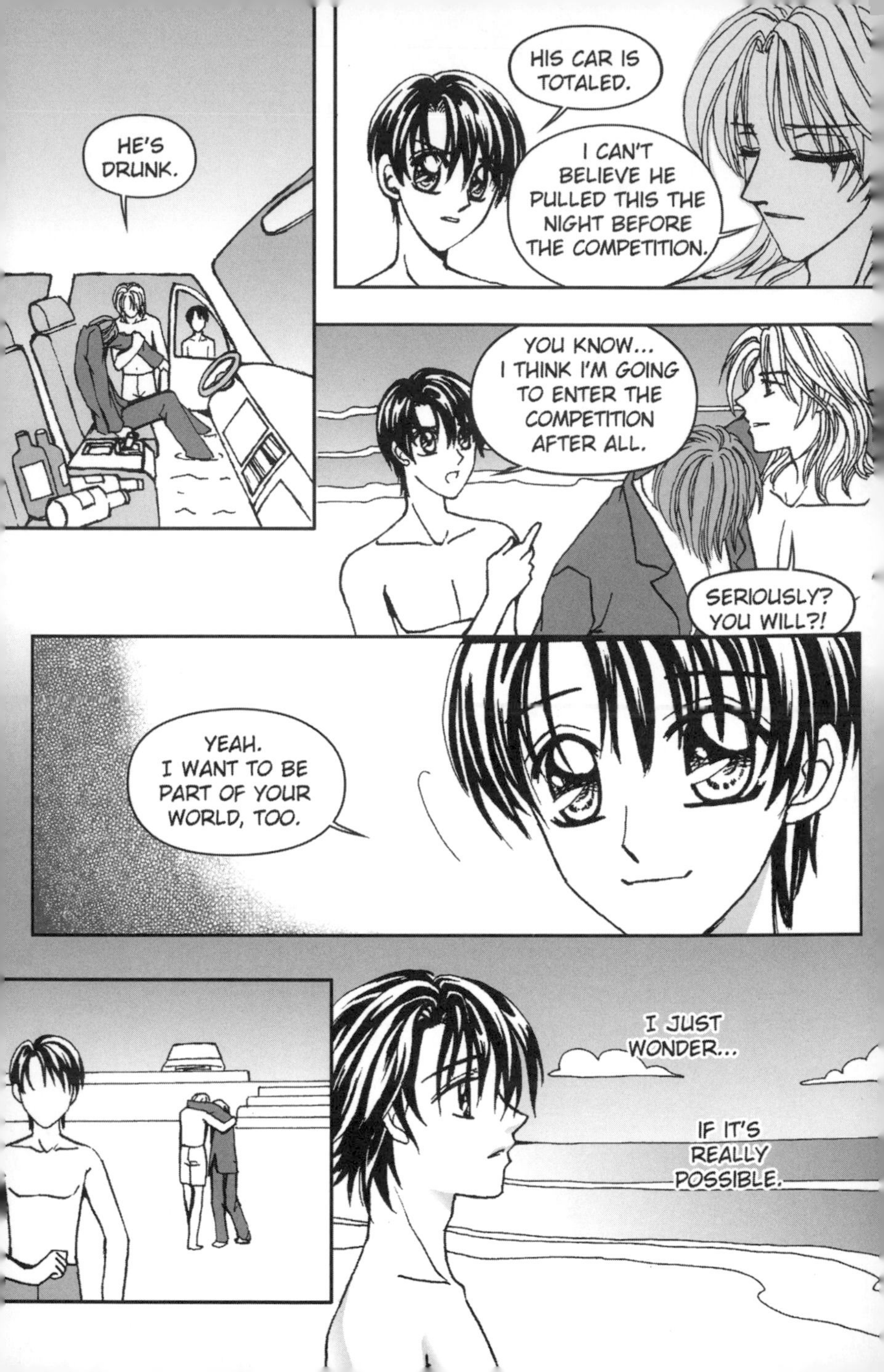
HE'S DRUNK.
HIS CAR IS TOTALED.
I CAN'T BELIEVE HE PULLED THIS THE NIGHT BEFORE THE COMPETITION.
YOU KNOW... I THINK I'M GOING TO ENTER THE COMPETITION AFTER ALL.
SERIOUSLY? YOU WILL?!
YEAH. I WANT TO BE PART OF YOUR WORLD, TOO.
I JUST WONDER...
IF IT'S REALLY POSSIBLE.

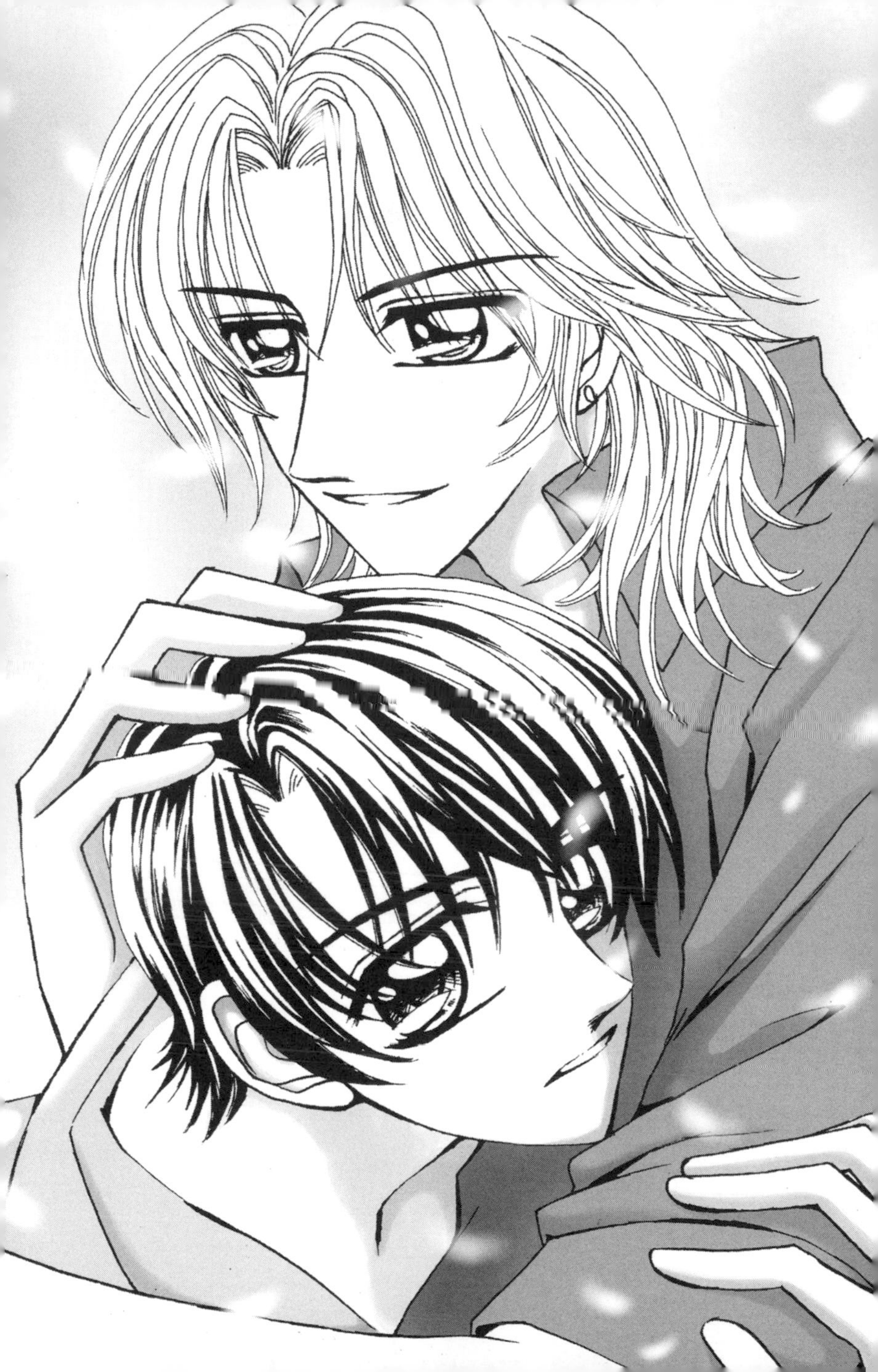

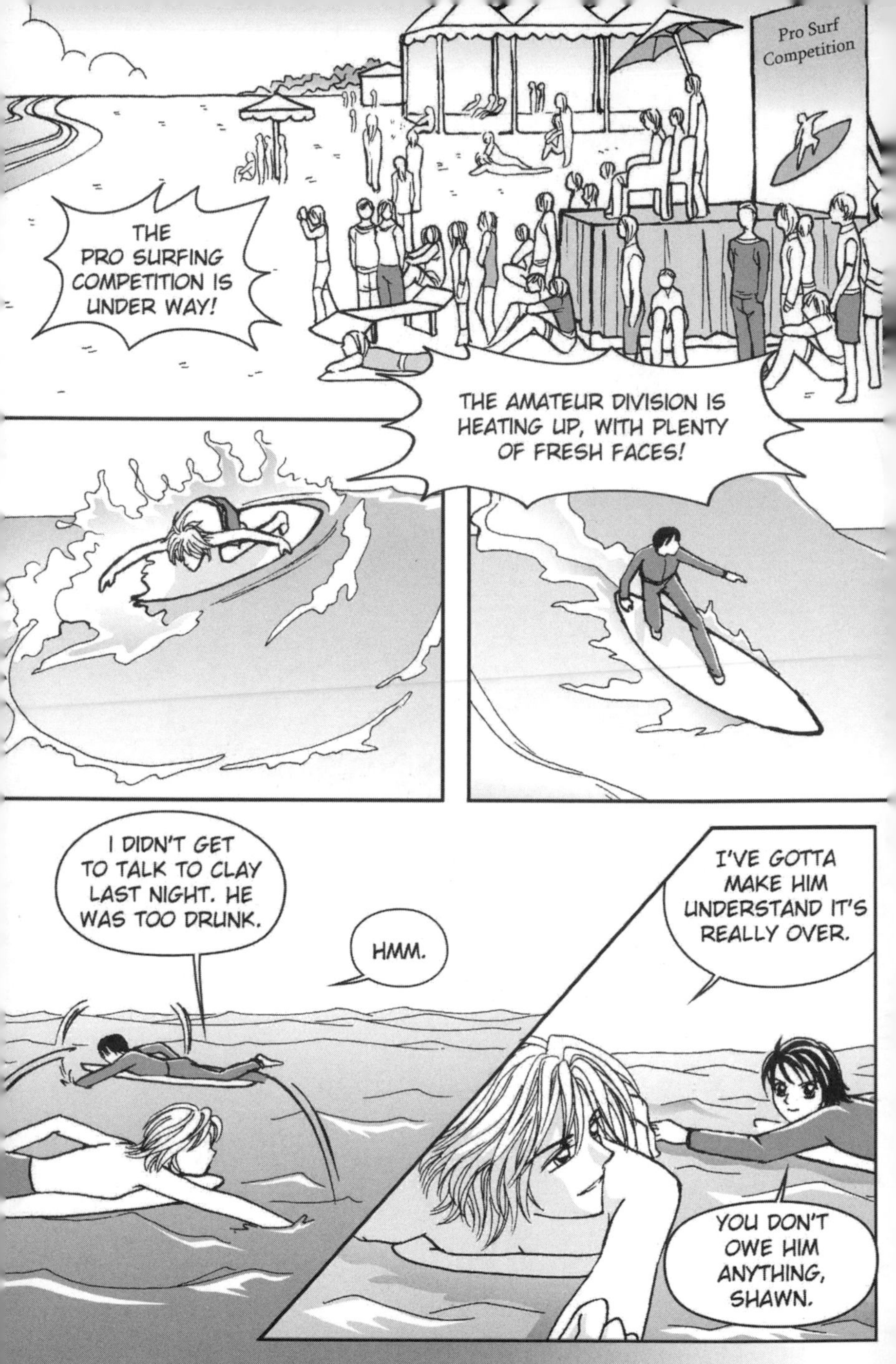
Pro Surf Competition
THE PRO SURFING COMPETITION IS UNDER WAY!
THE AMATEUR DIVISION IS HEATING UP, WITH PLENTY OF FRESH FACES!
I DIDN'T GET TO TALK TO CLAY LAST NIGHT. HE WAS TOO DRUNK.
HMM.
I'VE GOTTA MAKE HIM UNDERSTAND IT'S REALLY OVER.
YOU DON'T OWE HIM ANYTHING, SHAWN.

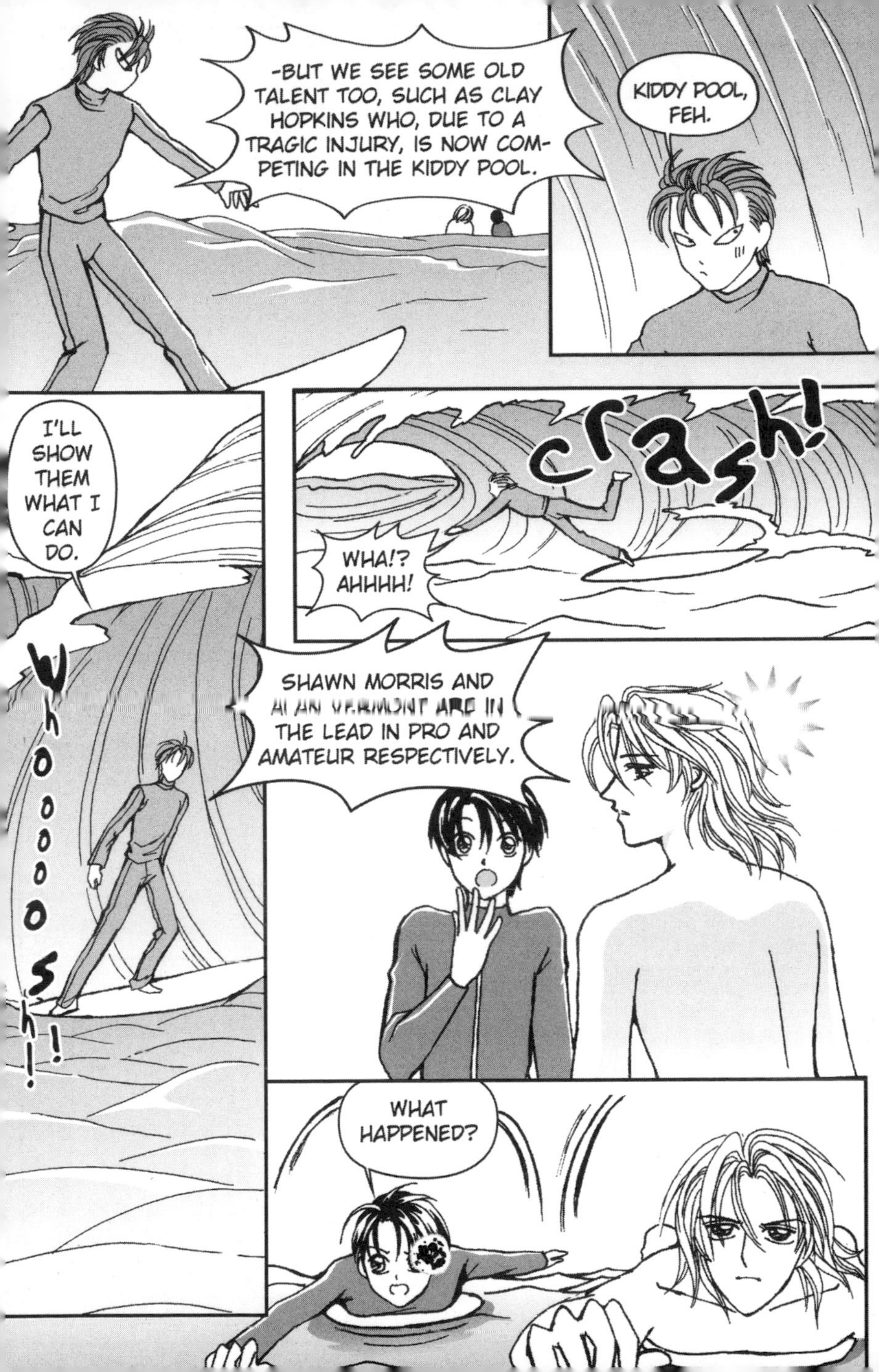
-BUT WE SEE SOME OLD TALENT TOO, SUCH AS CLAY HOPKINS WHO, DUE TO A TRAGIC INJURY, IS NOW COMPETING IN THE KIDDY POOL.
KIDDY POOL, FEH.
I'LL SHOW THEM WHAT I CAN DO.
Whooooosh!!
crash!
WHA!? AHHHH!
SHAWN MORRIS AND ALAN VERMONT ARE IN THE LEAD IN PRO AND AMATEUR RESPECTIVELY.
WHAT HAPPENED?

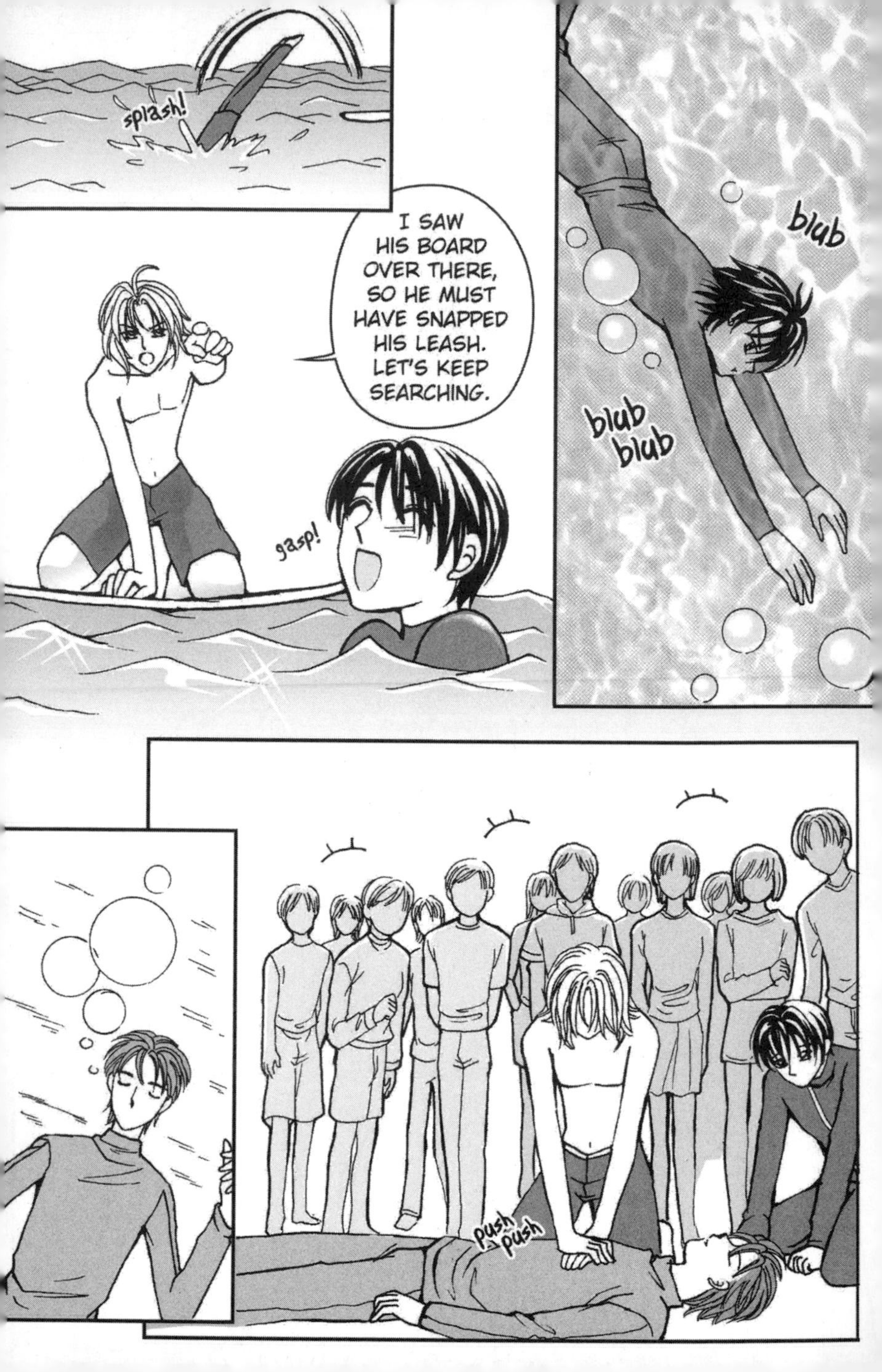
splash!
I SAW HIS BOARD OVER THERE, SO HE MUST HAVE SNAPPED HIS LEASH. LET'S KEEP SEARCHING.
gasp!
blub
blub blub
push push

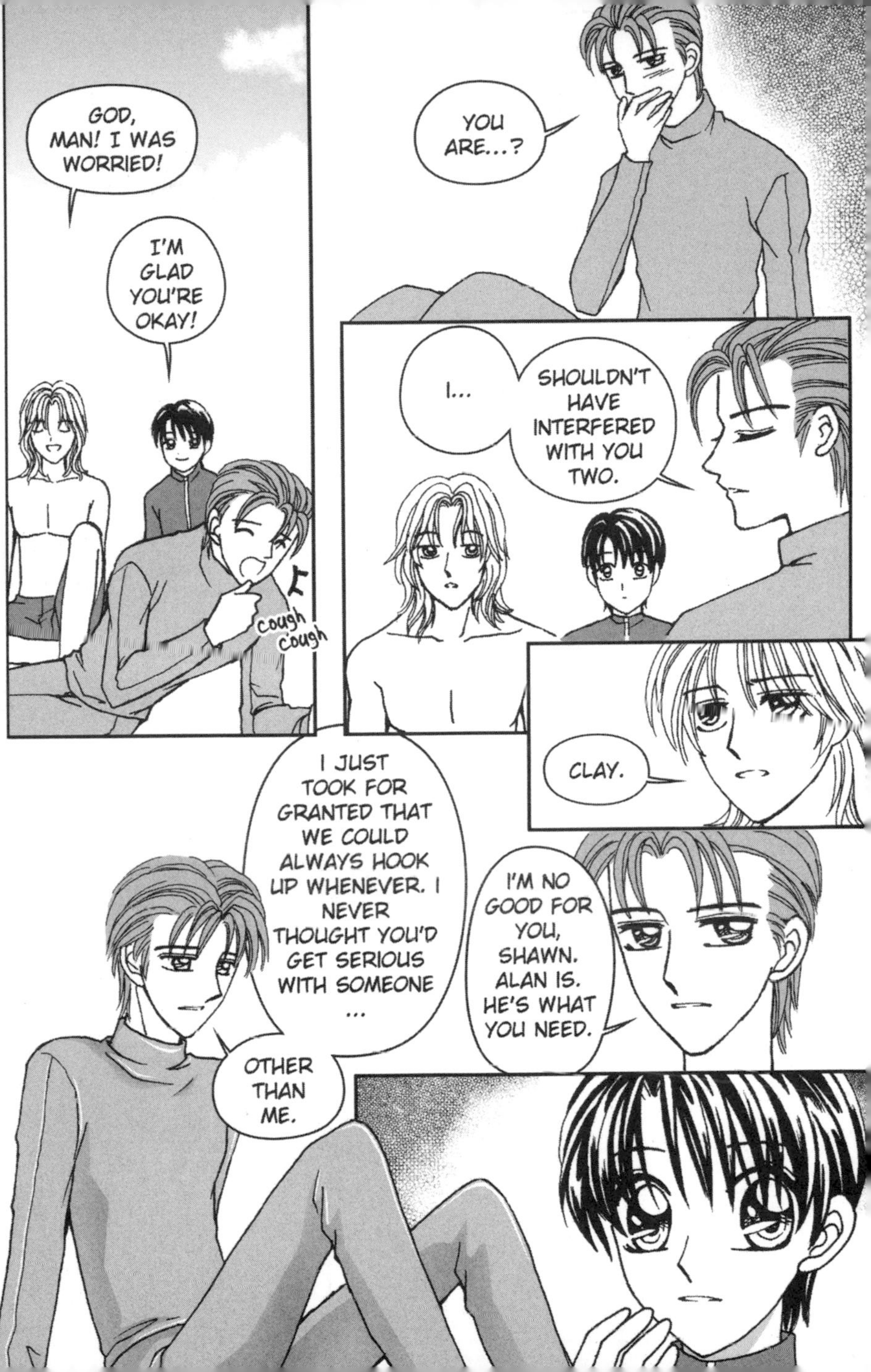
GOD, MAN! I WAS WORRIED!
I'M GLAD YOU'RE OKAY!
cough cough
YOU ARE...?
I...
SHOULDN'T HAVE INTERFERED WITH YOU TWO.
CLAY.
I'M NO GOOD FOR YOU, SHAWN. ALAN IS. HE'S WHAT YOU NEED.
I JUST TOOK FOR GRANTED THAT WE COULD ALWAYS HOOK UP WHENEVER. I NEVER THOUGHT YOU'D GET SERIOUS WITH SOMEONE ...
OTHER THAN ME.

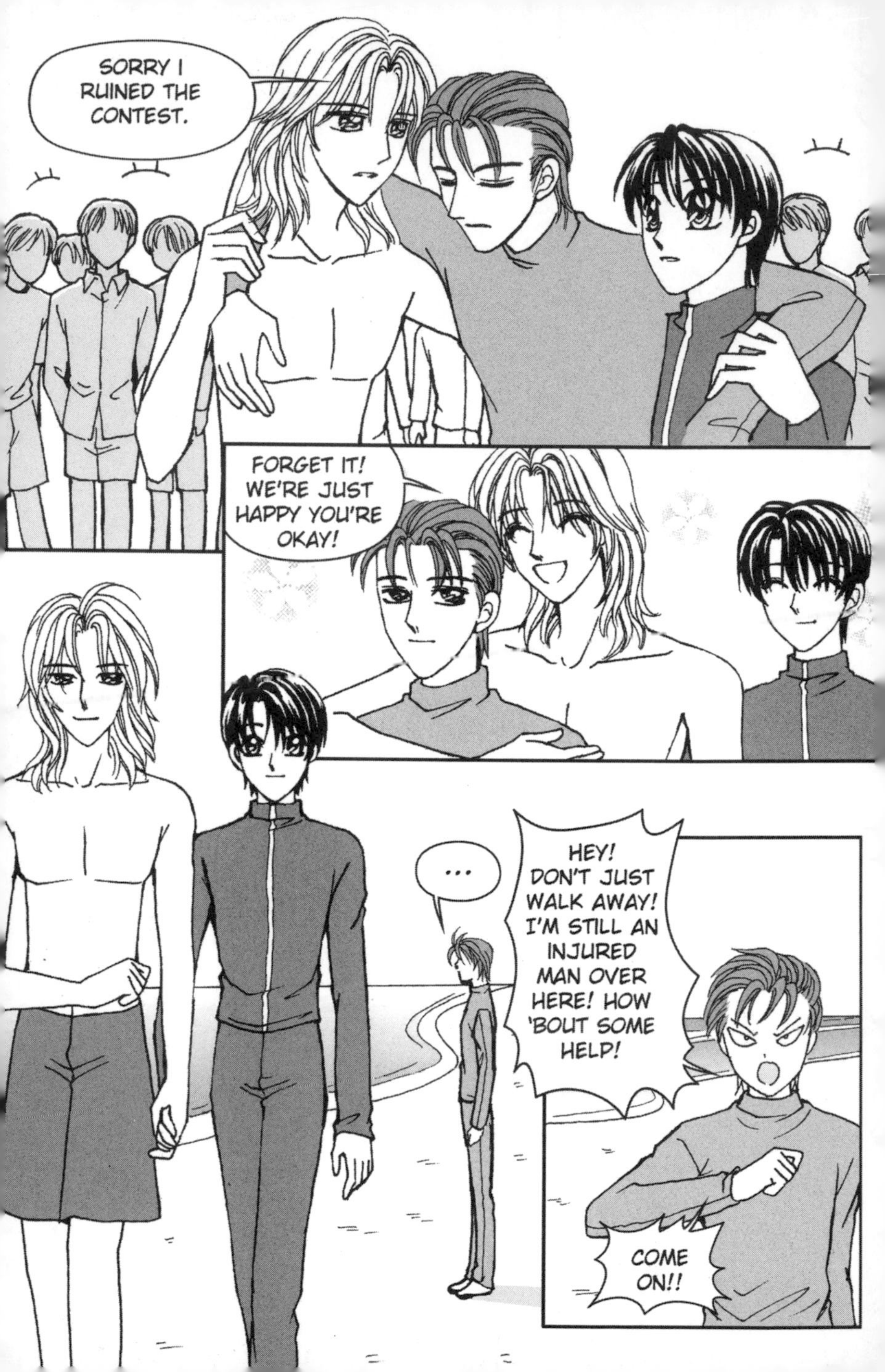
SORRY I RUINED THE CONTEST.
FORGET IT! WE'RE JUST HAPPY YOU'RE OKAY!
...
HEY! DON'T JUST WALK AWAY! I'M STILL AN INJURED MAN OVER HERE! HOW 'BOUT SOME HELP!
COME ON!!

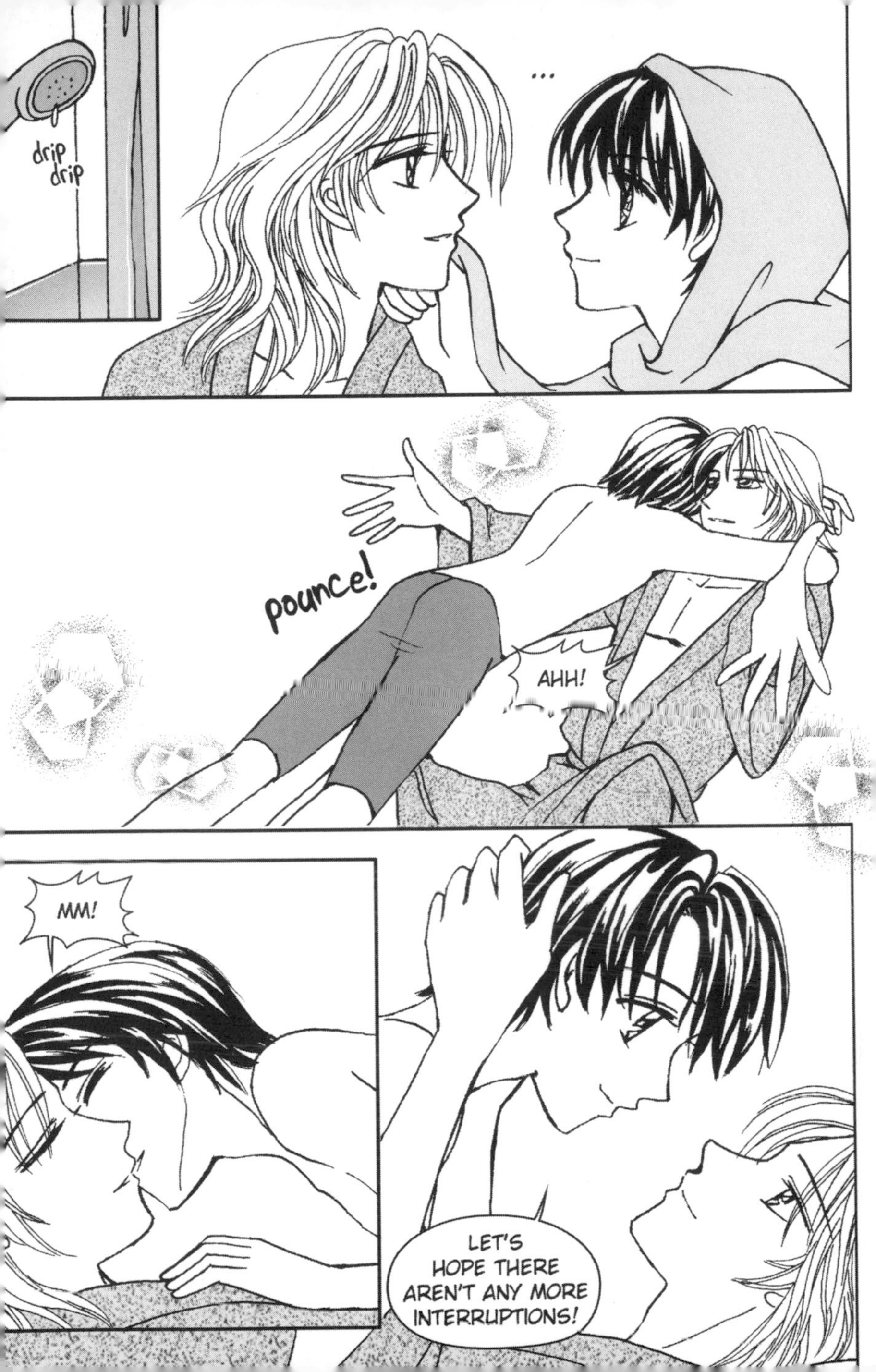
drip
drip
...
pounce!
AHH!
MM!
LET'S HOPE THERE AREN'T ANY MORE INTERRUPTIONS!

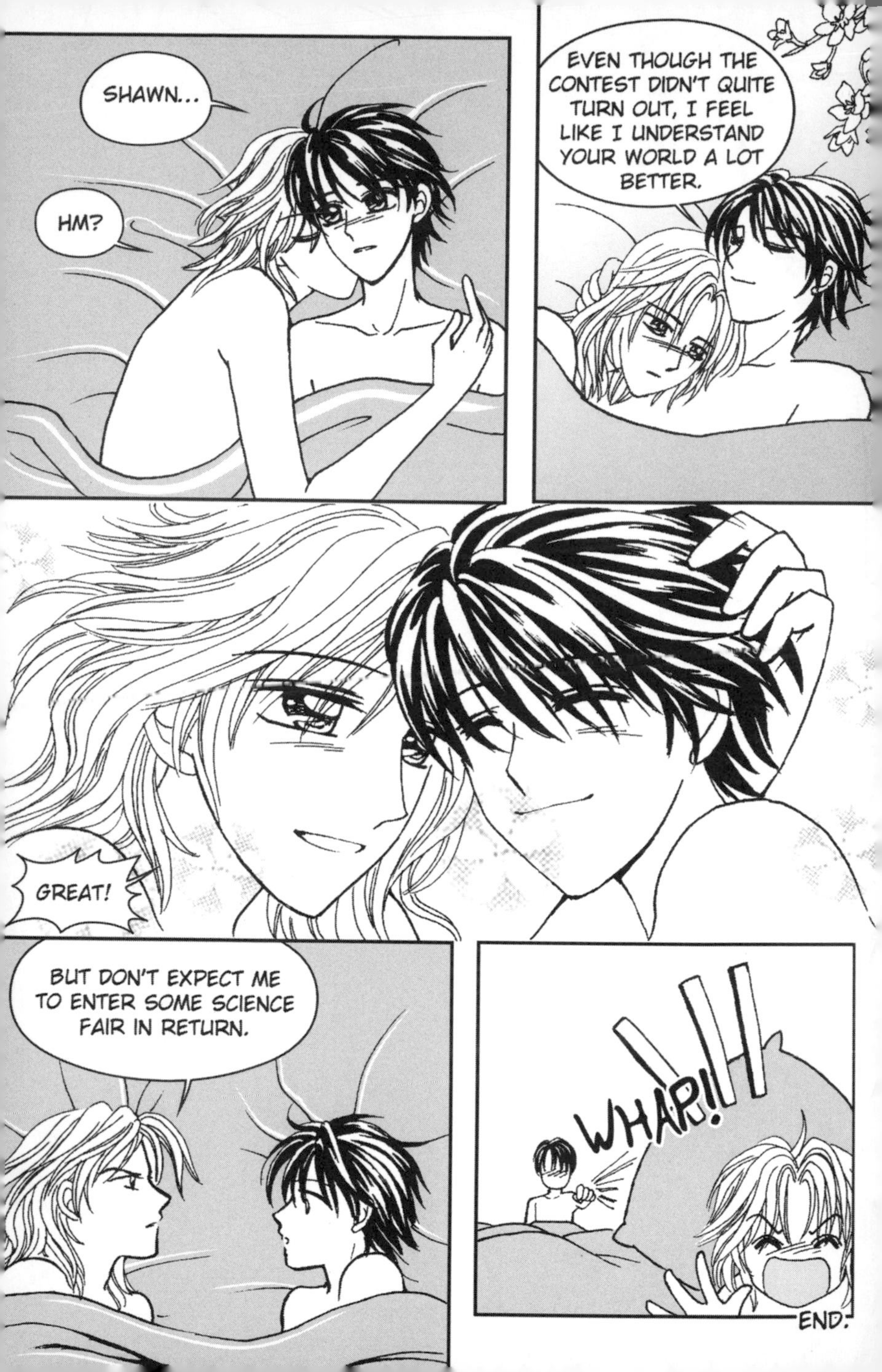
SHAWN...
HM?
EVEN THOUGH THE CONTEST DIDN'T QUITE TURN OUT, I FEEL LIKE I UNDERSTAND YOUR WORLD A LOT BETTER.
GREAT!
BUT DON'T EXPECT ME TO ENTER SOME SCIENCE FAIR IN RETURN.
WHAP!!
END.

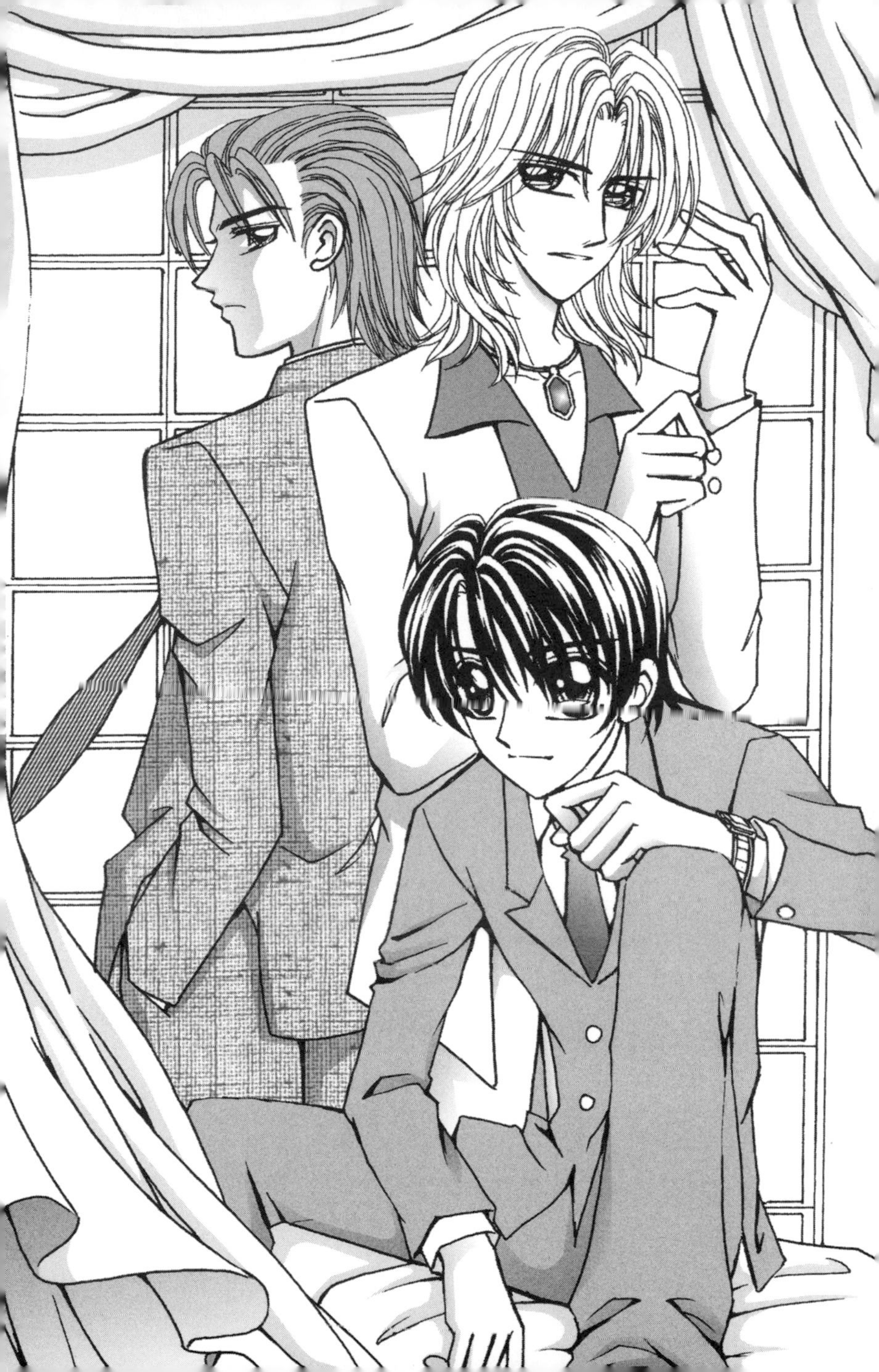

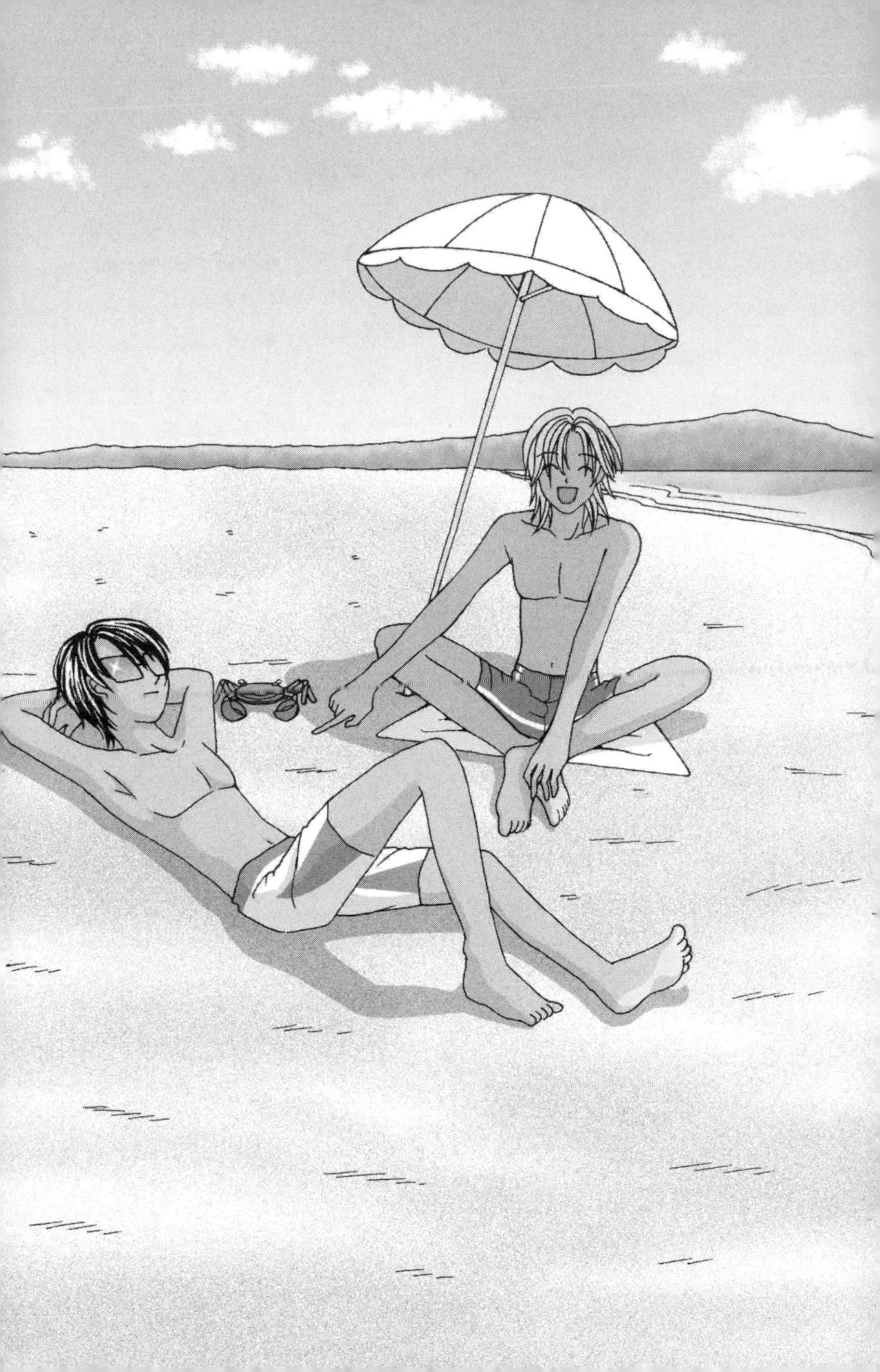

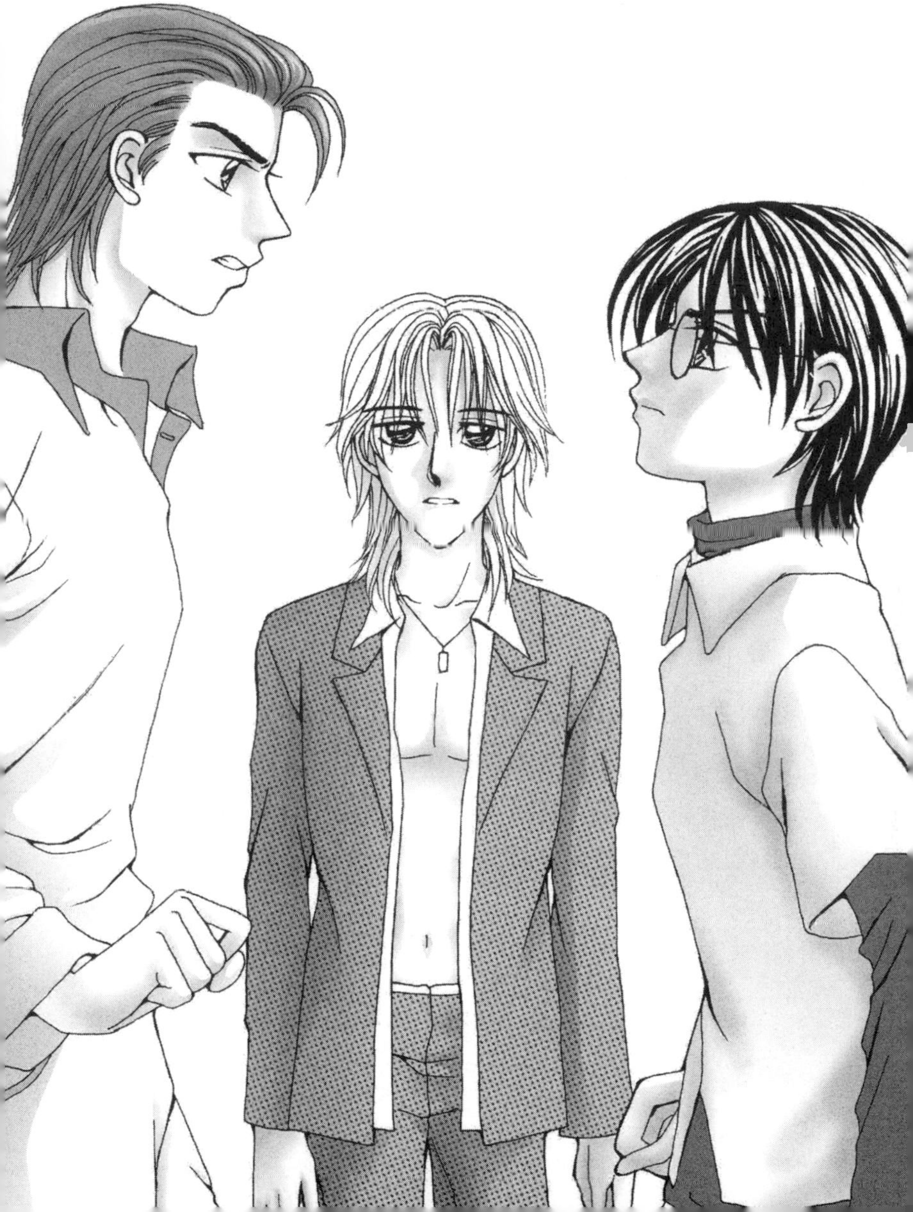

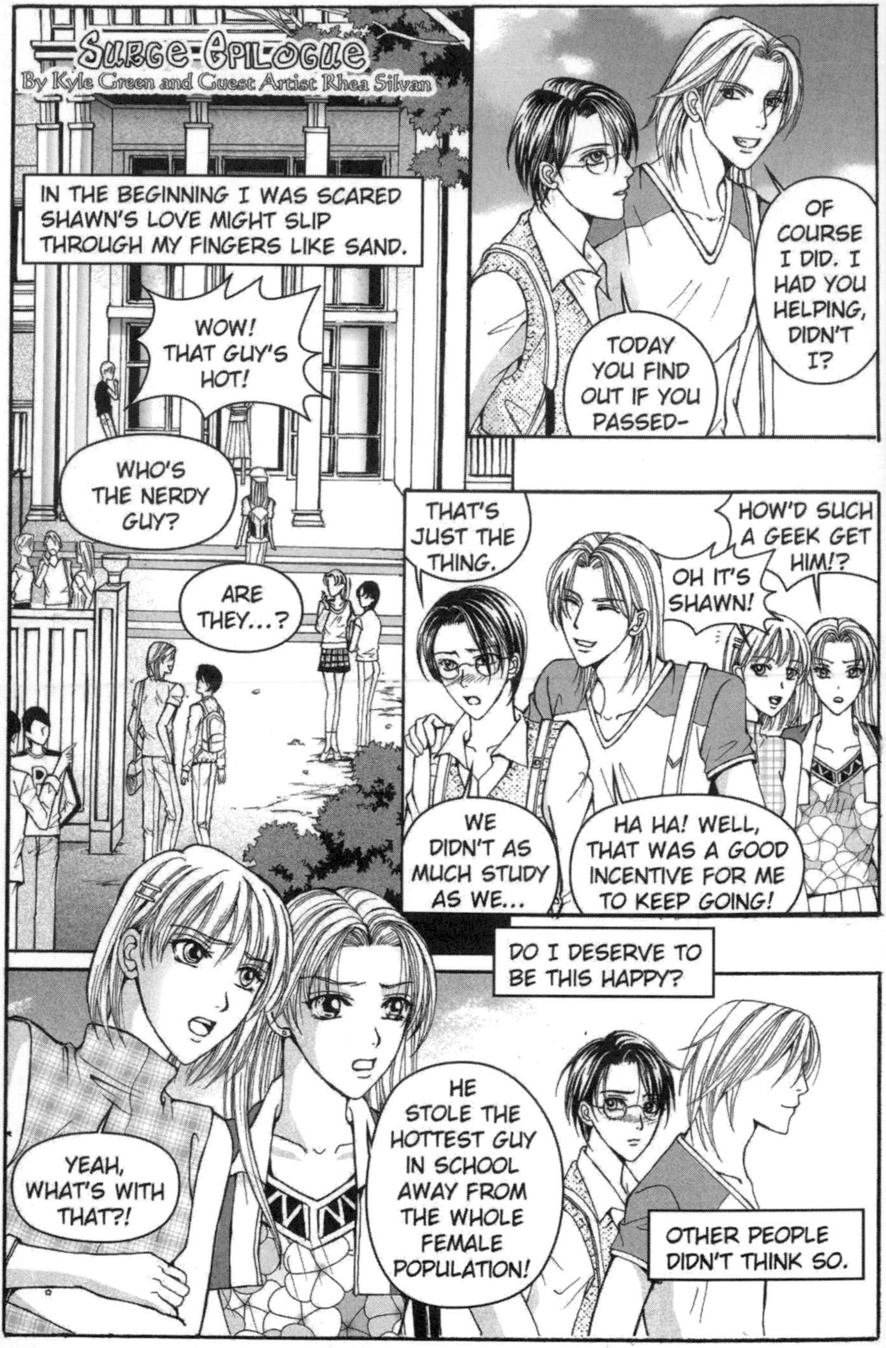
Surge Epilogue
By Kyle Green and Guest Artist Rhea Silvan
IN THE BEGINNING I WAS SCARED SHAWN'S LOVE MIGHT SLIP THROUGH MY FINGERS LIKE SAND.
WOW! THAT GUY'S HOT!
WHO'S THE NERDY GUY?
ARE THEY...?
TODAY YOU FIND OUT IF YOU PASSED-
OF COURSE I DID. I HAD YOU HELPING, DIDN'T I?
THAT'S JUST THE THING.
OH IT'S SHAWN!
HOW'D SUCH A GEEK GET HIM!?
WE DIDN'T AS MUCH STUDY AS WE...
HA HA! WELL, THAT WAS A GOOD INCENTIVE FOR ME TO KEEP GOING!
DO I DESERVE TO BE THIS HAPPY?
YEAH, WHAT'S WITH THAT?!
HE STOLE THE HOTTEST GUY IN SCHOOL AWAY FROM THE WHOLE FEMALE POPULATION!
OTHER PEOPLE DIDN'T THINK SO.

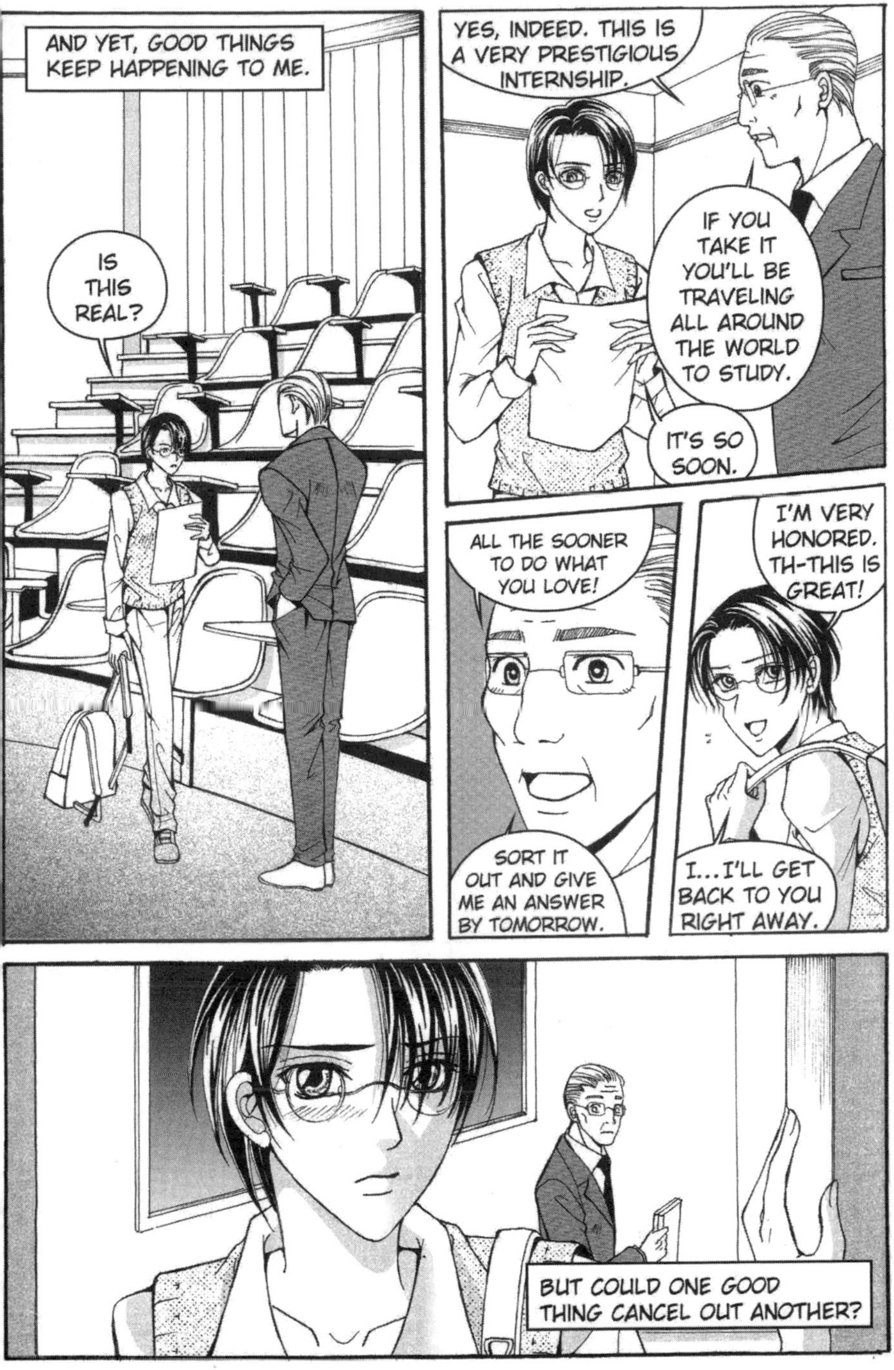
AND YET, GOOD THINGS KEEP HAPPENING TO ME.
IS THIS REAL?
YES, INDEED. THIS IS A VERY PRESTIGIOUS INTERNSHIP.
IF YOU TAKE IT YOU'LL BE TRAVELING ALL AROUND THE WORLD TO STUDY.
IT'S SO SOON.
ALL THE SOONER TO DO WHAT YOU LOVE!
SORT IT OUT AND GIVE ME AN ANSWER BY TOMORROW.
I'M VERY HONORED. TH-THIS IS GREAT!
I...I'LL GET BACK TO YOU RIGHT AWAY.
BUT COULD ONE GOOD THING CANCEL OUT ANOTHER?

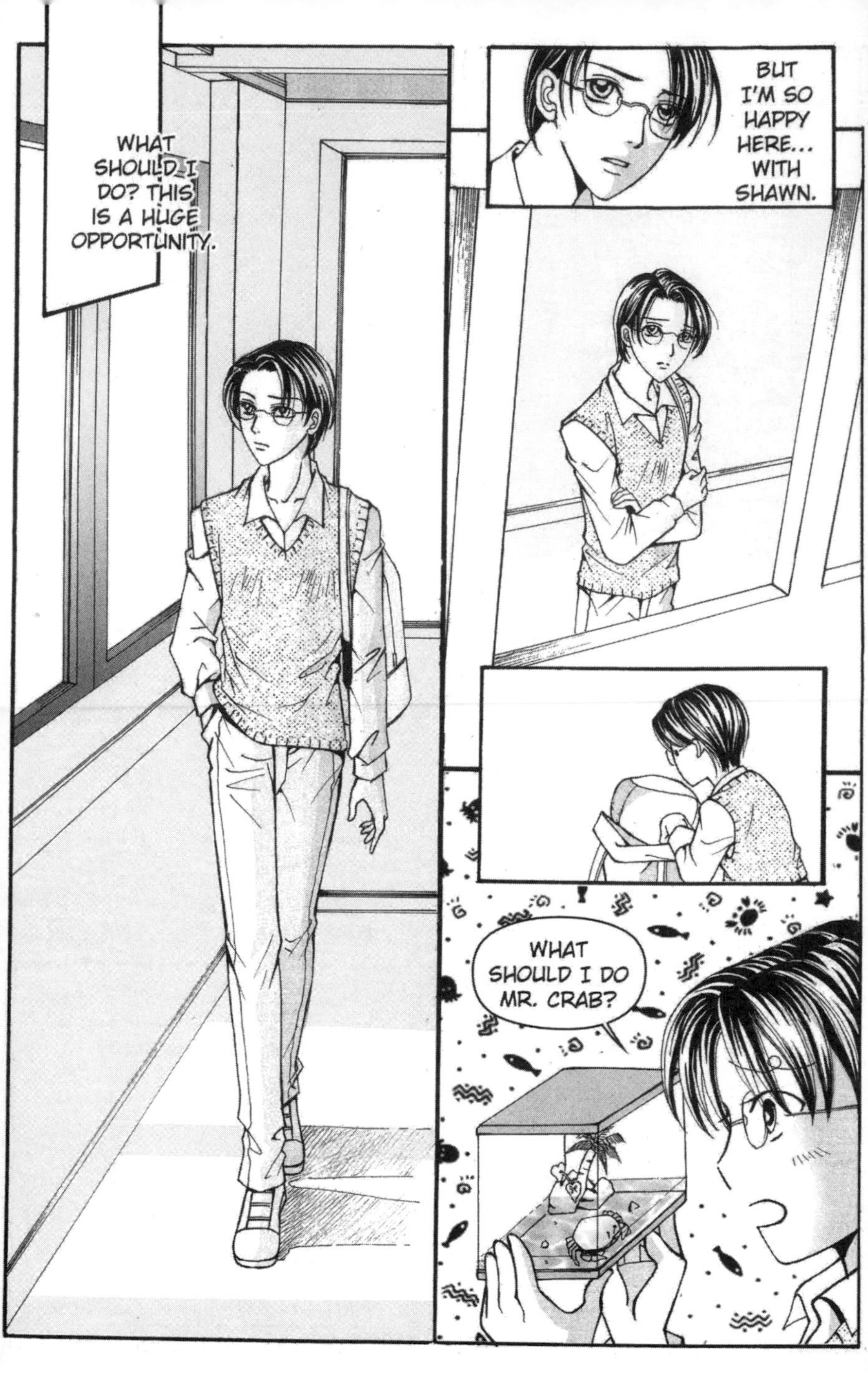
WHAT SHOULD I DO? THIS IS A HUGE OPPORTUNITY.
BUT I'M SO HAPPY HERE... WITH SHAWN.
WHAT SHOULD I DO MR. CRAB?

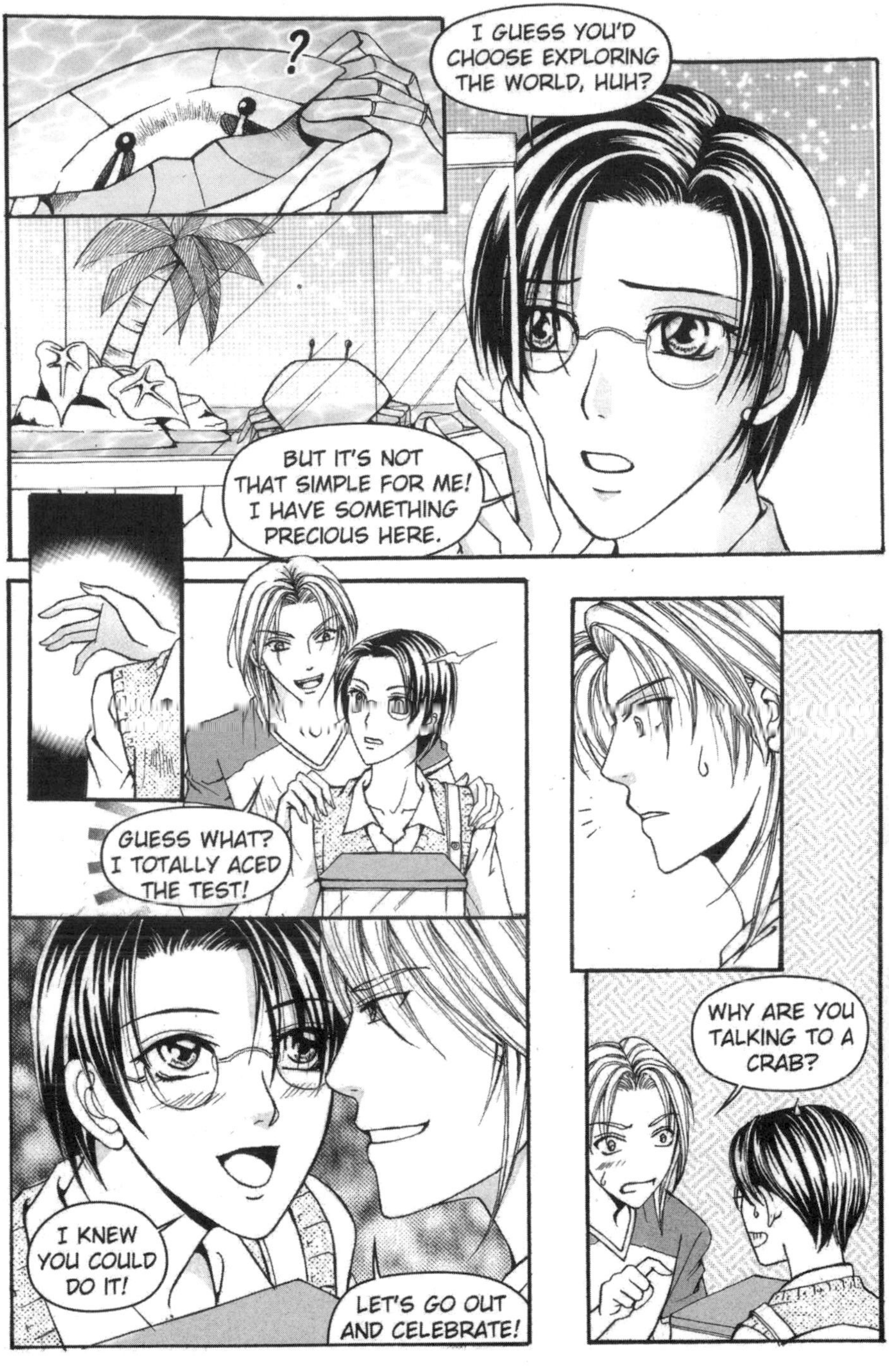
?
I GUESS YOU'D CHOOSE EXPLORING THE WORLD, HUH?
BUT IT'S NOT THAT SIMPLE FOR ME! I HAVE SOMETHING PRECIOUS HERE.
GUESS WHAT? I TOTALLY ACED THE TEST!
I KNEW YOU COULD DO IT!
LET'S GO OUT AND CELEBRATE!
WHY ARE YOU TALKING TO A CRAB?

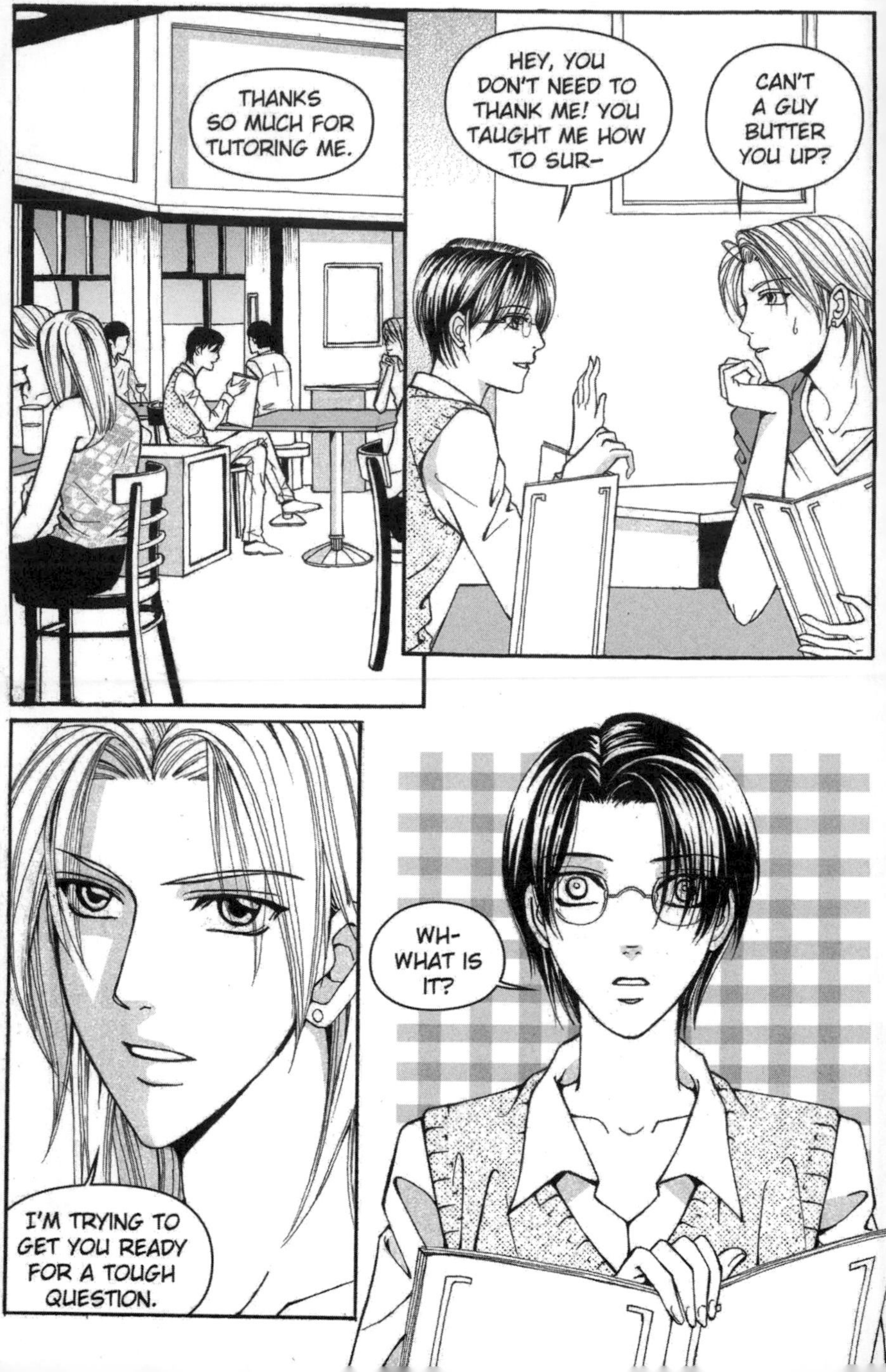
THANKS SO MUCH FOR TUTORING ME.
HEY, YOU DON'T NEED TO THANK ME! YOU TAUGHT ME HOW TO SUR–
CAN'T A GUY BUTTER YOU UP?
WH- WHAT IS IT?
I'M TRYING TO GET YOU READY FOR A TOUGH QUESTION.

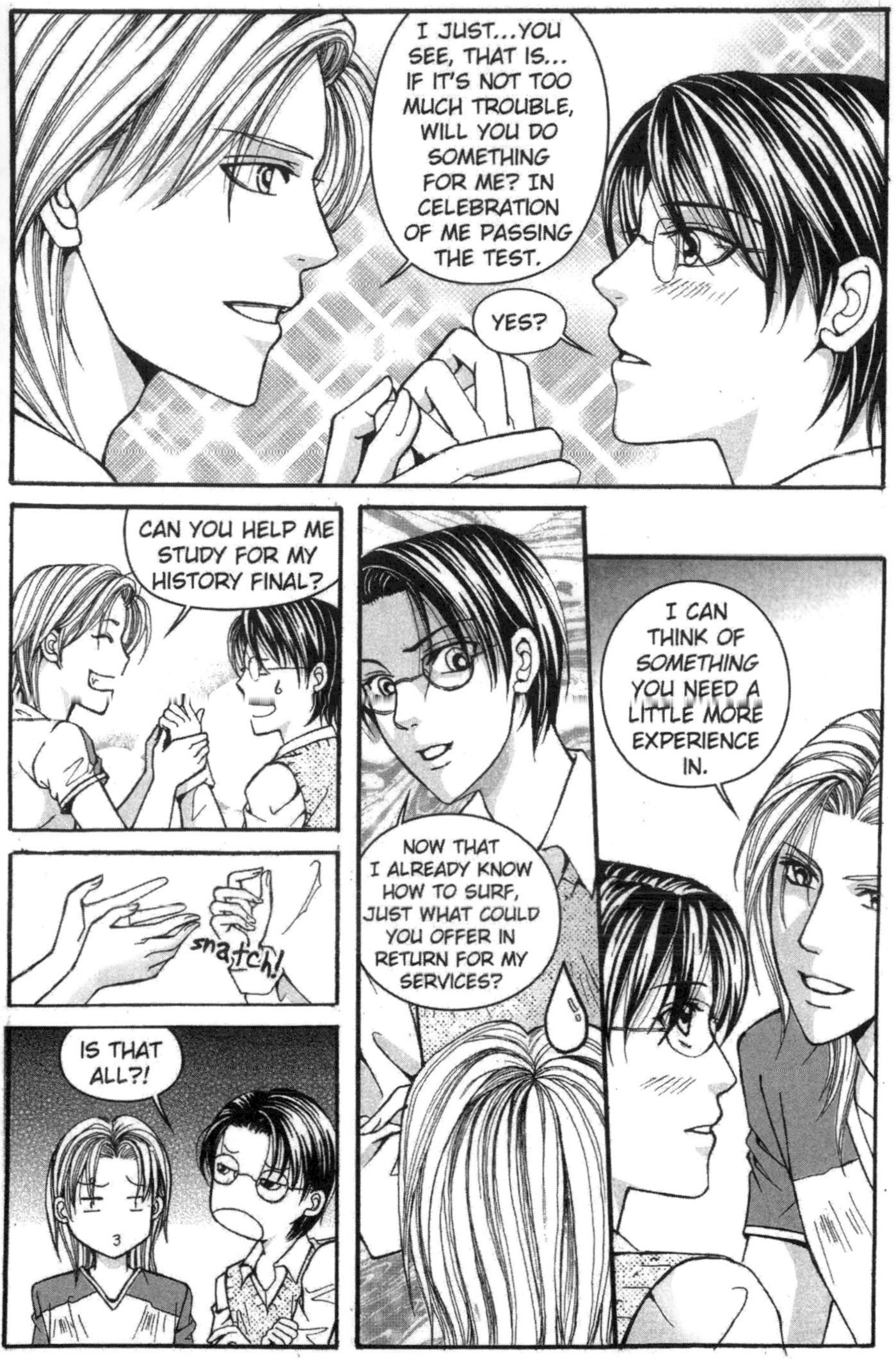
I JUST...YOU SEE, THAT IS... IF IT'S NOT TOO MUCH TROUBLE, WILL YOU DO SOMETHING FOR ME? IN CELEBRATION OF ME PASSING THE TEST.
YES?
CAN YOU HELP ME STUDY FOR MY HISTORY FINAL?
snatch!
IS THAT ALL?!
NOW THAT I ALREADY KNOW HOW TO SURF, JUST WHAT COULD YOU OFFER IN RETURN FOR MY SERVICES?
I CAN THINK OF SOMETHING YOU NEED A LITTLE MORE EXPERIENCE IN.

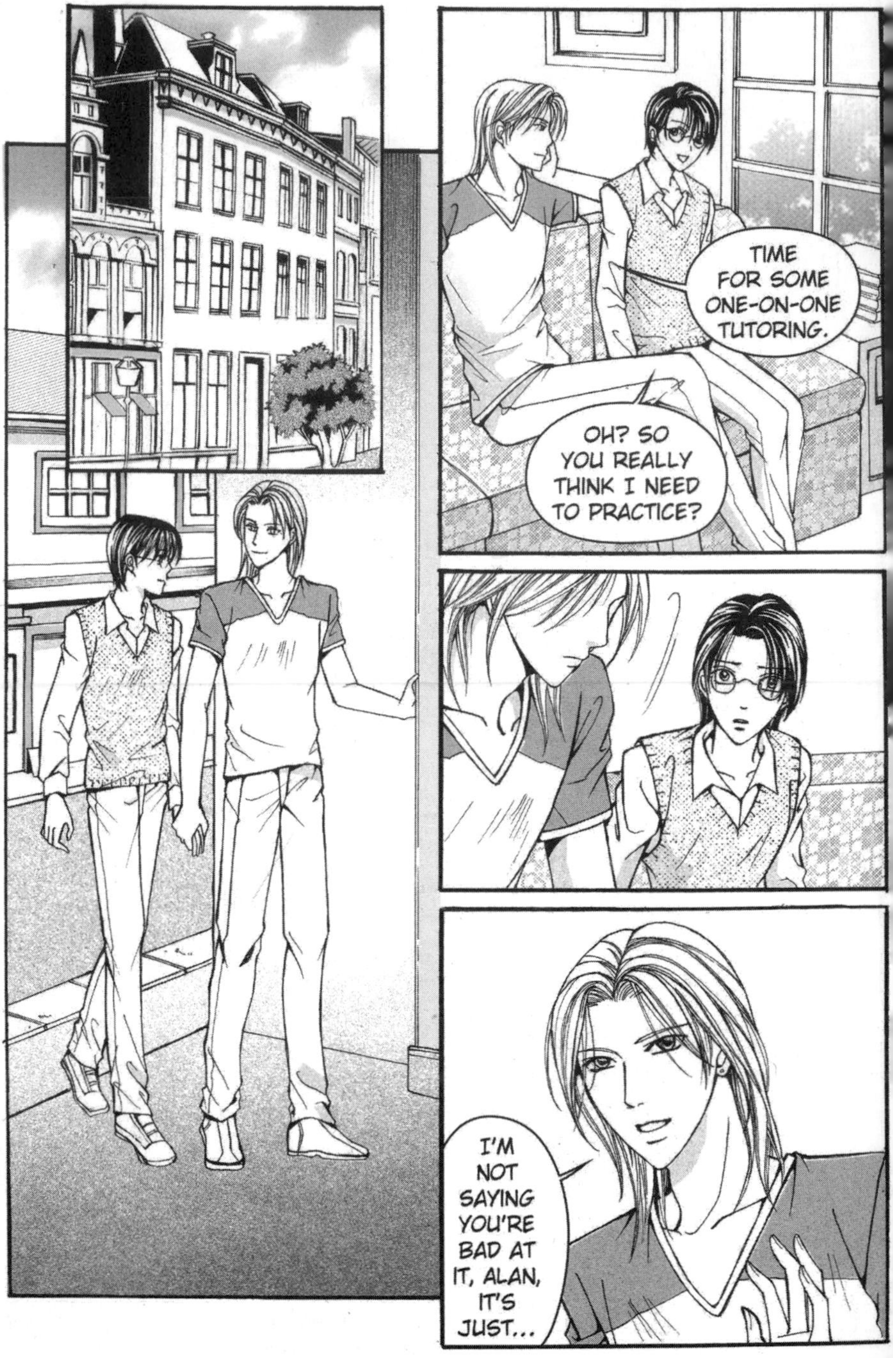
TIME FOR SOME ONE-ON-ONE TUTORING.
OH? SO YOU REALLY THINK I NEED TO PRACTICE?
I'M NOT SAYING YOU'RE BAD AT IT, ALAN, IT'S JUST...

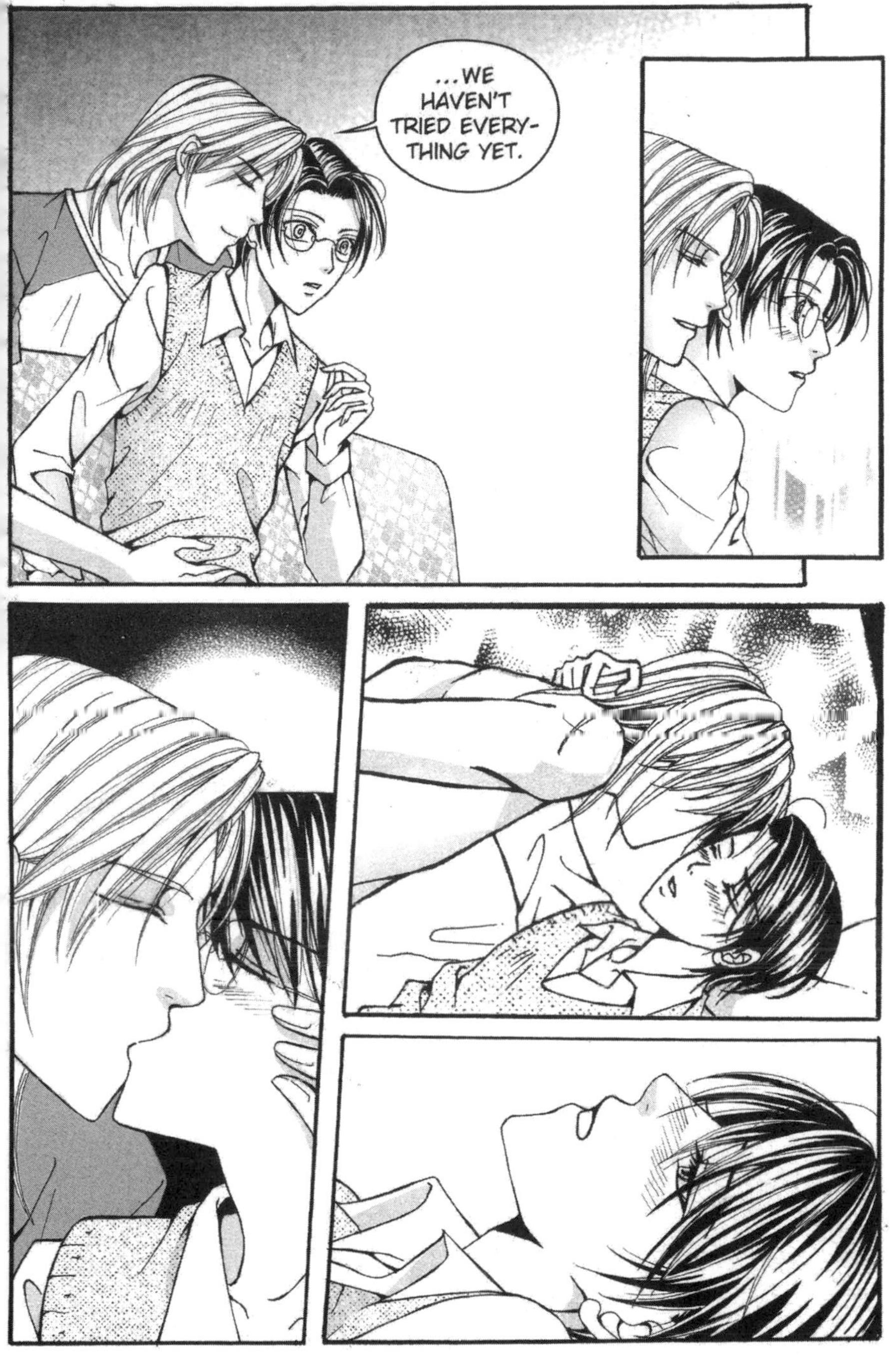
...WE HAVEN'T TRIED EVERY-THING YET.

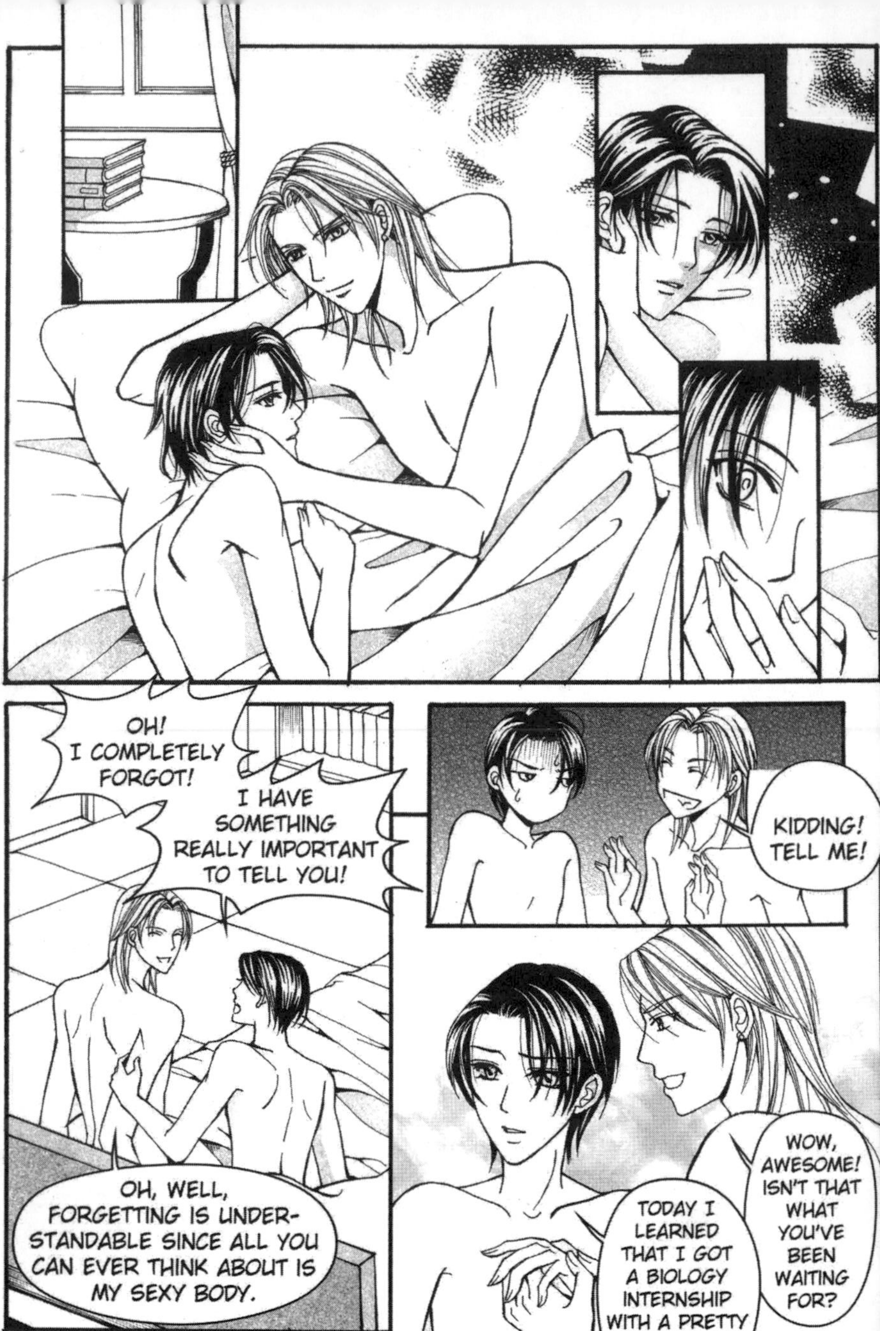
OH!
I COMPLETELY FORGOT!
I HAVE SOMETHING REALLY IMPORTANT TO TELL YOU!
KIDDING! TELL ME!
OH, WELL, FORGETTING IS UNDER-STANDABLE SINCE ALL YOU CAN EVER THINK ABOUT IS MY SEXY BODY.
TODAY I LEARNED THAT I GOT A BIOLOGY INTERNSHIP WITH A PRETTY IMPORTANT COMPANY.
WOW, AWESOME! ISN'T THAT WHAT YOU'VE BEEN WAITING FOR?

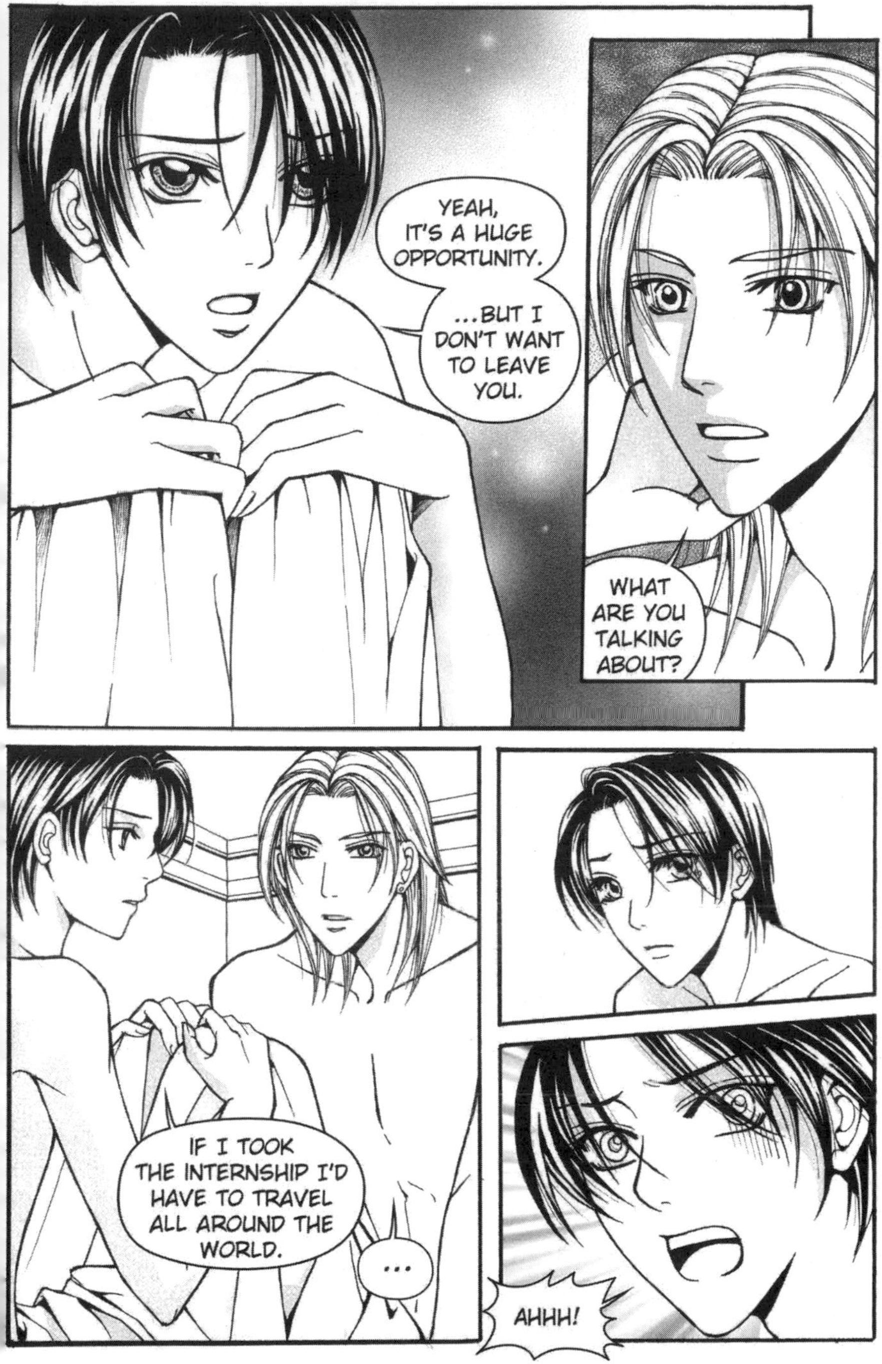
YEAH, IT'S A HUGE OPPORTUNITY.
...BUT I DON'T WANT TO LEAVE YOU.
WHAT ARE YOU TALKING ABOUT?
IF I TOOK THE INTERNSHIP I'D HAVE TO TRAVEL ALL AROUND THE WORLD.
...
AHHH!

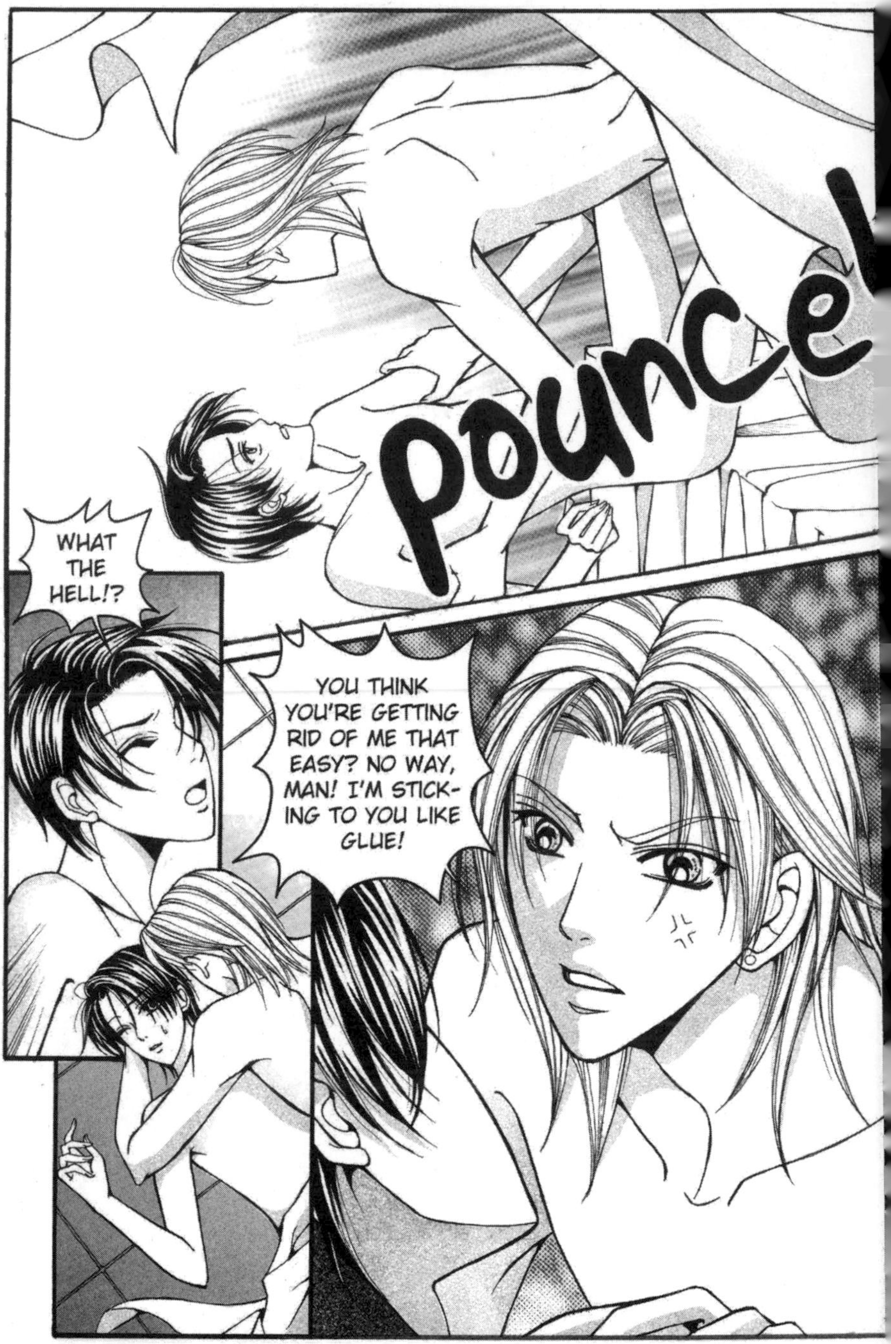
POUNCE!
WHAT THE HELL!?
YOU THINK YOU'RE GETTING RID OF ME THAT EASY? NO WAY, MAN! I'M STICKING TO YOU LIKE GLUE!

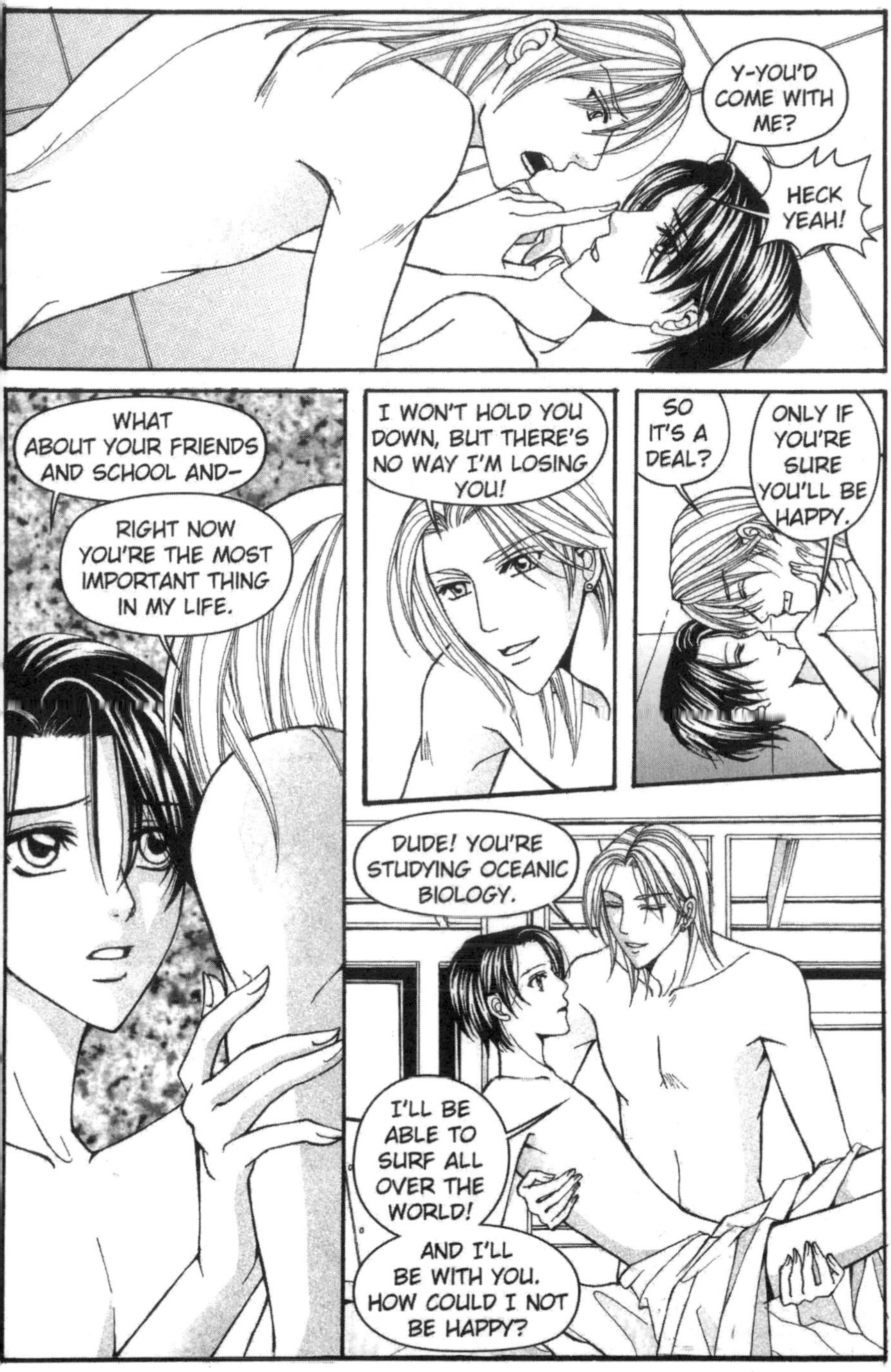
Y-YOU'D COME WITH ME?
HECK YEAH!
WHAT ABOUT YOUR FRIENDS AND SCHOOL AND–
RIGHT NOW YOU'RE THE MOST IMPORTANT THING IN MY LIFE.
I WON'T HOLD YOU DOWN, BUT THERE'S NO WAY I'M LOSING YOU!
SO IT'S A DEAL?
ONLY IF YOU'RE SURE YOU'LL BE HAPPY.
DUDE! YOU'RE STUDYING OCEANIC BIOLOGY.
I'LL BE ABLE TO SURF ALL OVER THE WORLD!
AND I'LL BE WITH YOU. HOW COULD I NOT BE HAPPY?

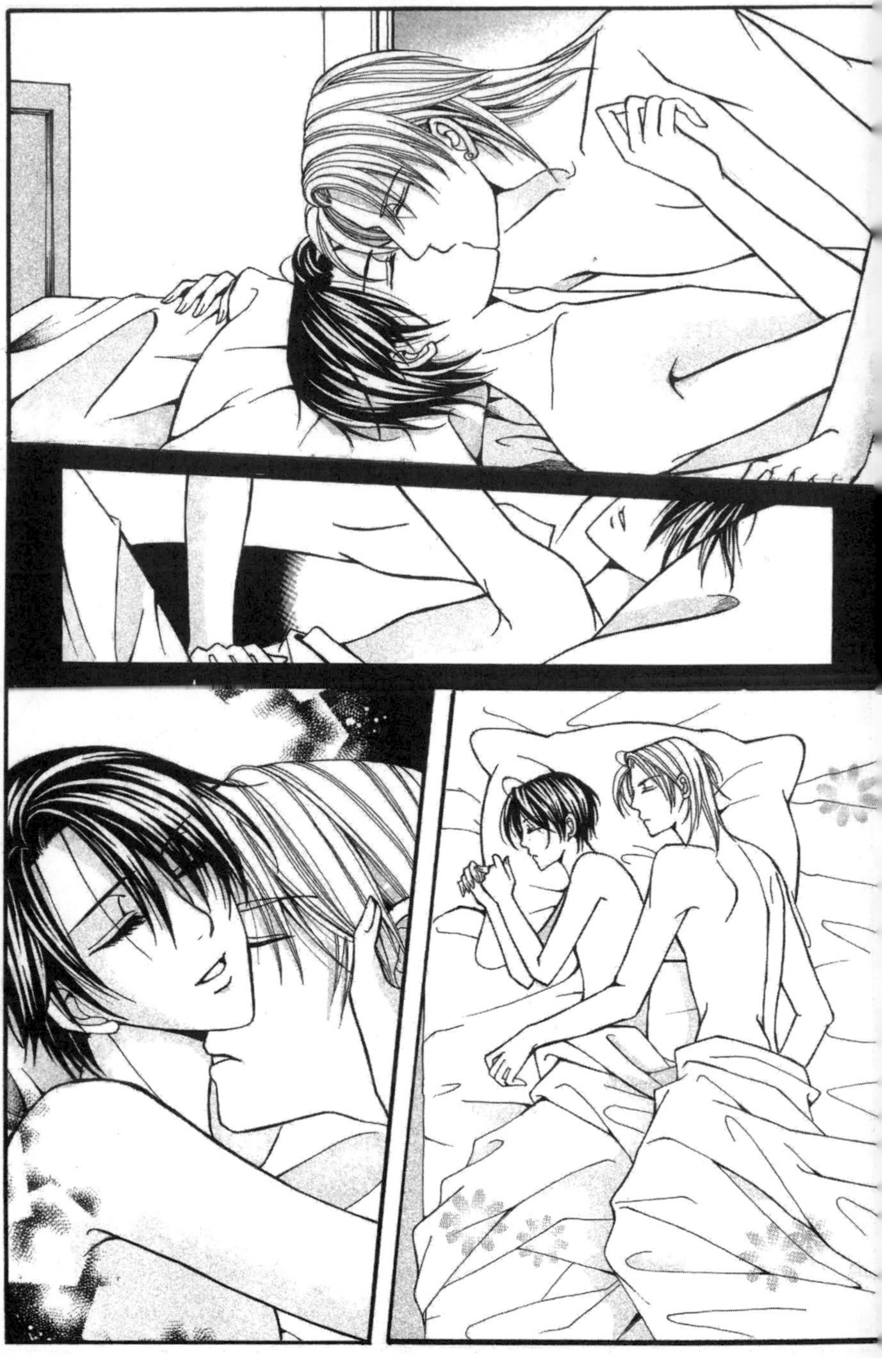

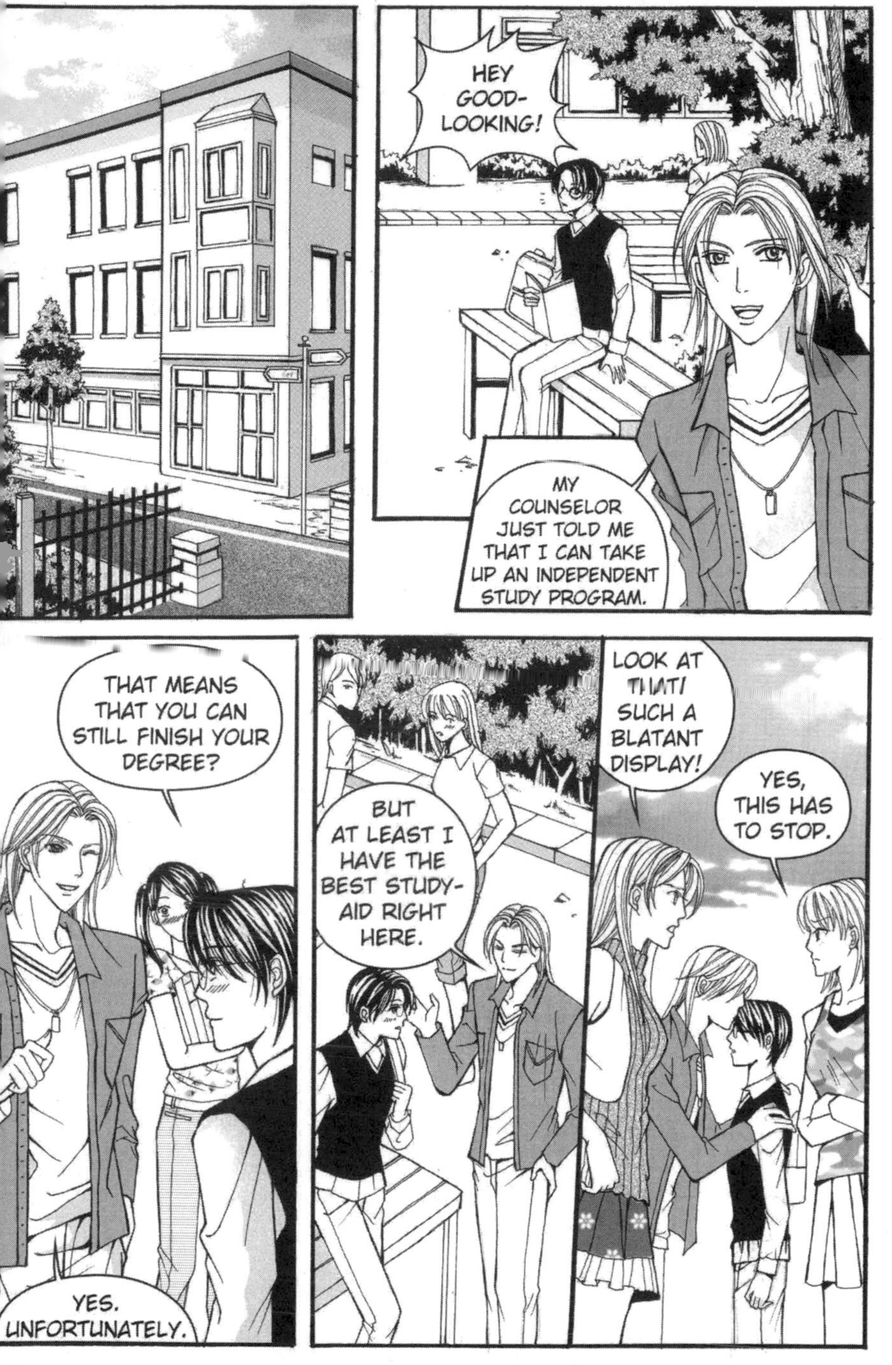
HEY GOOD-LOOKING!
MY COUNSELOR JUST TOLD ME THAT I CAN TAKE UP AN INDEPENDENT STUDY PROGRAM.
THAT MEANS THAT YOU CAN STILL FINISH YOUR DEGREE?
YES. UNFORTUNATELY.
BUT AT LEAST I HAVE THE BEST STUDY-AID RIGHT HERE.
LOOK AT THAT! SUCH A BLATANT DISPLAY!
YES, THIS HAS TO STOP.

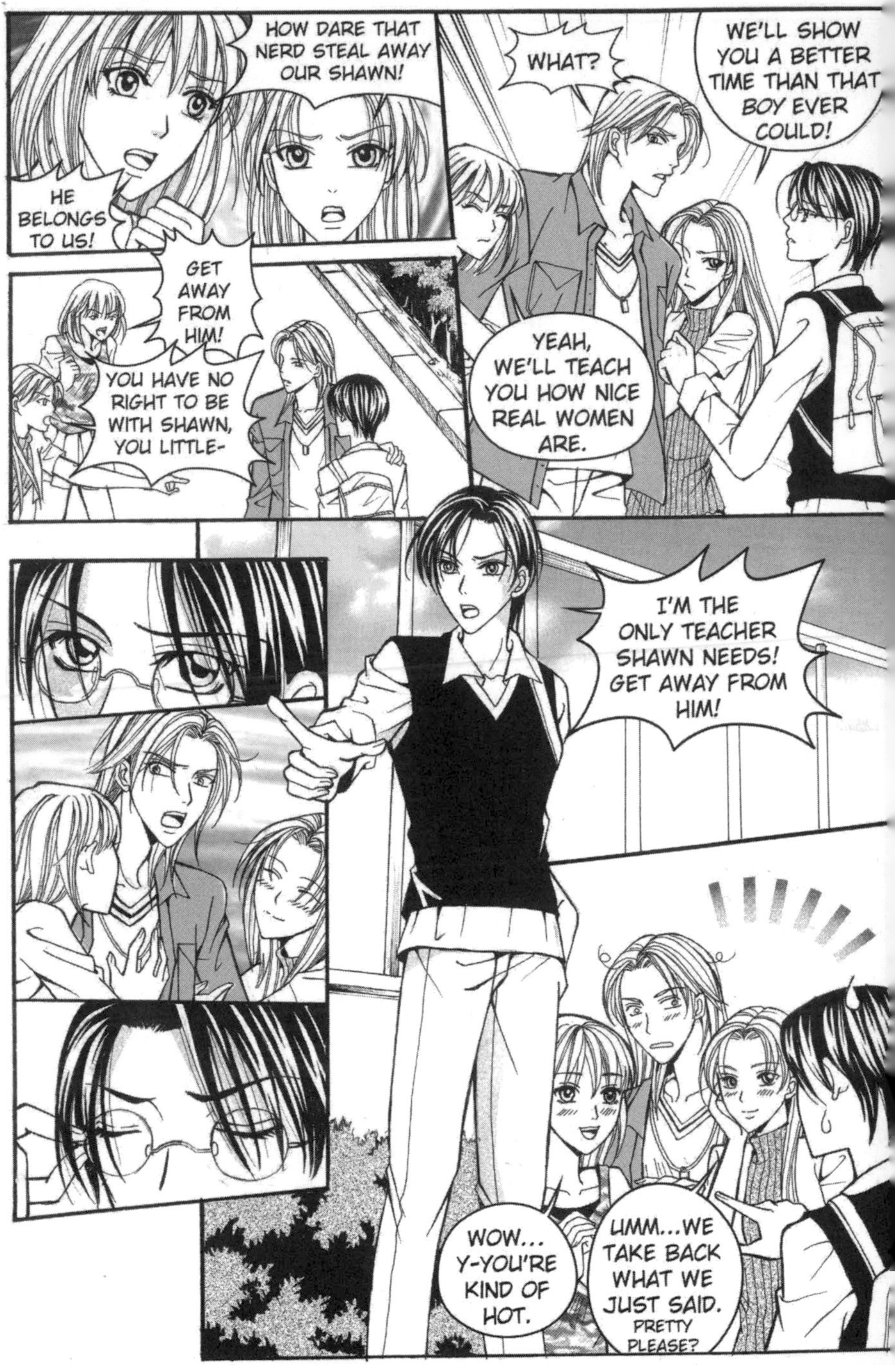
HOW DARE THAT NERD STEAL AWAY OUR SHAWN!
HE BELONGS TO US!
WHAT?
WE'LL SHOW YOU A BETTER TIME THAN THAT BOY EVER COULD!
GET AWAY FROM HIM!
YOU HAVE NO RIGHT TO BE WITH SHAWN, YOU LITTLE-
YEAH, WE'LL TEACH YOU HOW NICE REAL WOMEN ARE.
I'M THE ONLY TEACHER SHAWN NEEDS! GET AWAY FROM HIM!
WOW... Y-YOU'RE KIND OF HOT.
UMM...WE TAKE BACK WHAT WE JUST SAID.
PRETTY PLEASE?

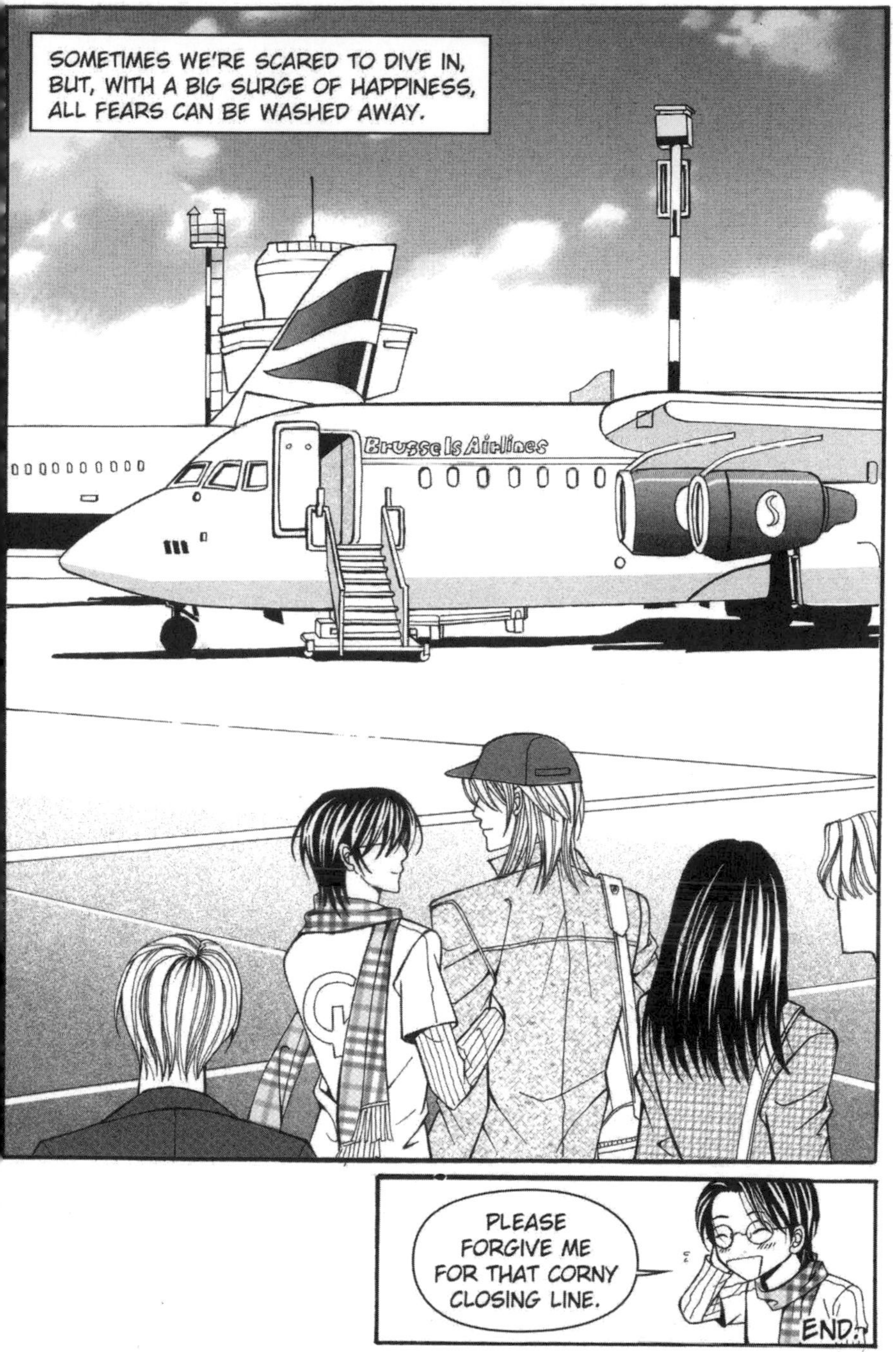
SOMETIMES WE'RE SCARED TO DIVE IN, BUT, WITH A BIG SURGE OF HAPPINESS, ALL FEARS CAN BE WASHED AWAY.
Brussels Airlines
PLEASE FORGIVE ME FOR THAT CORNY CLOSING LINE.
END.

Alan

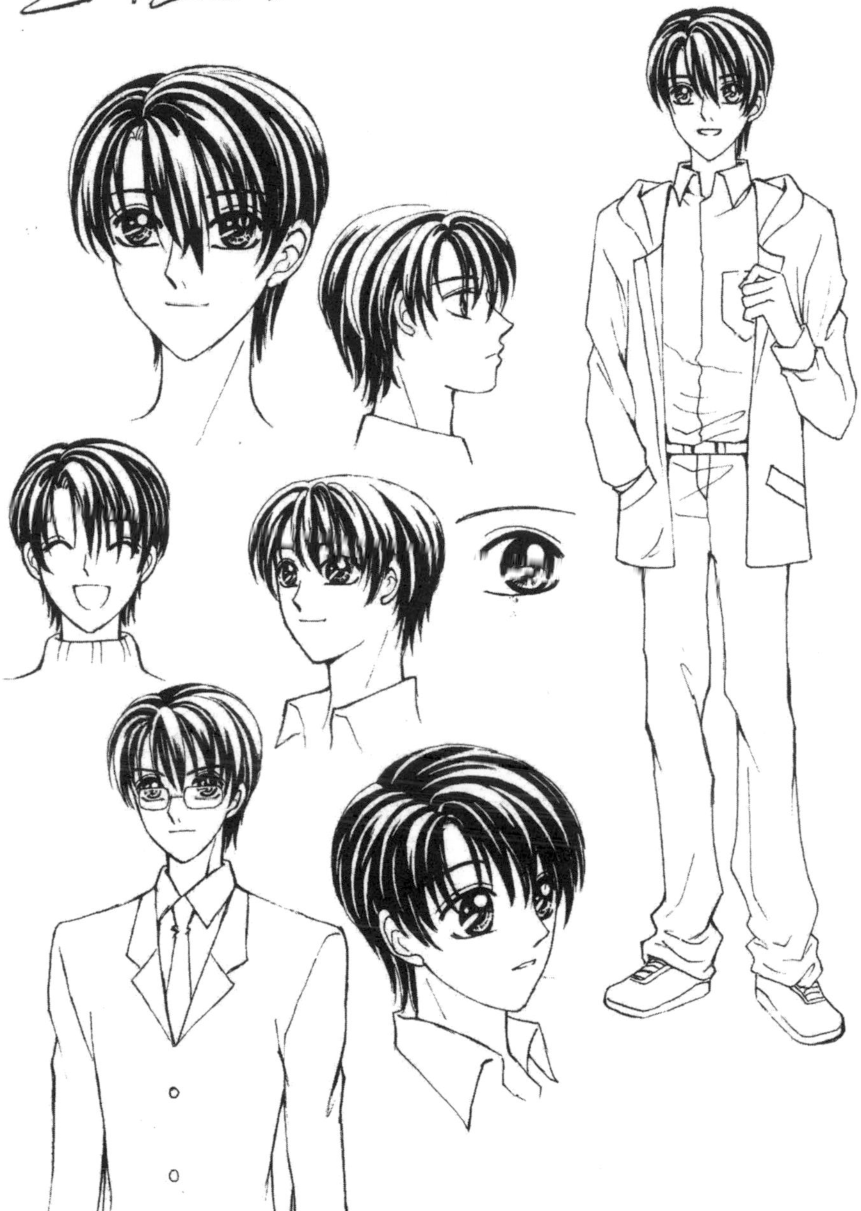

Shawn

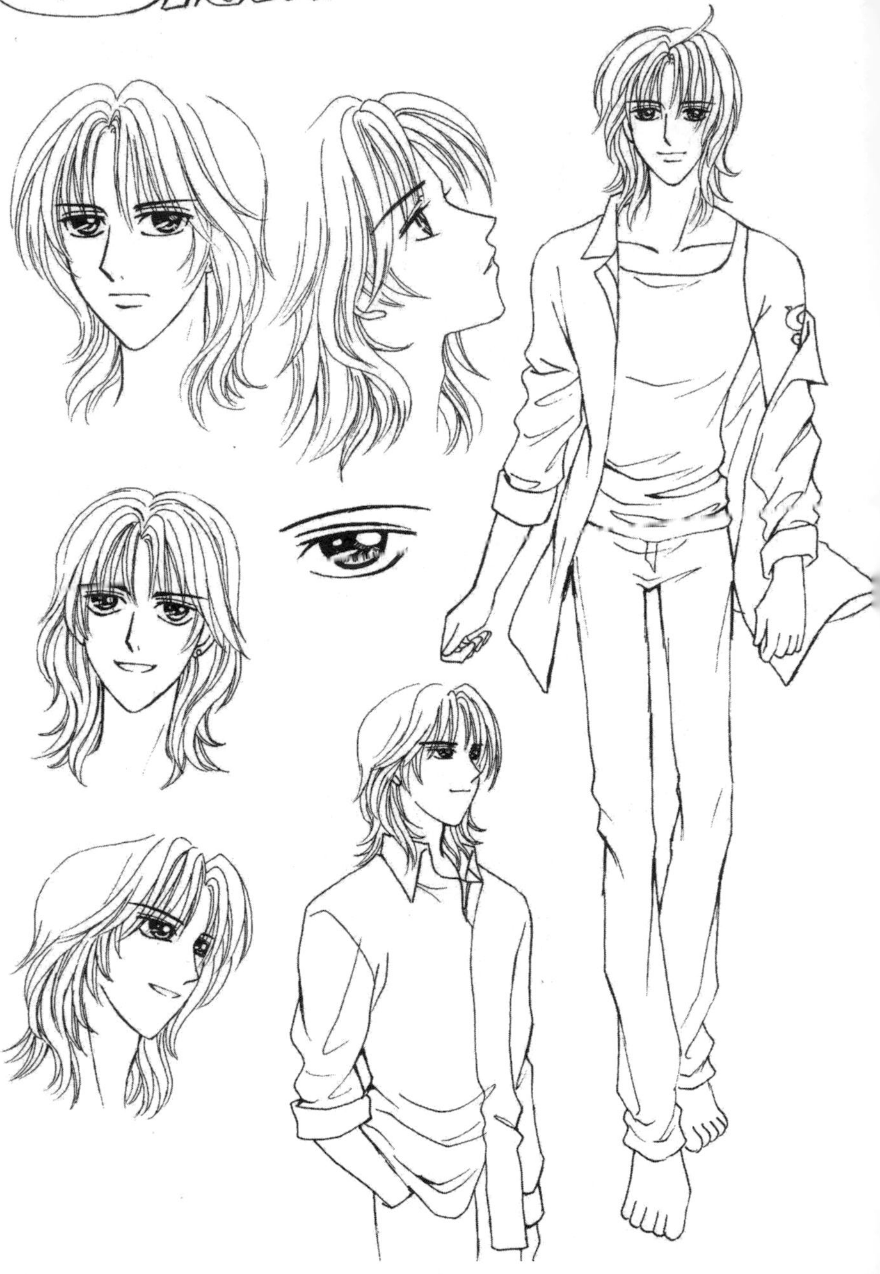

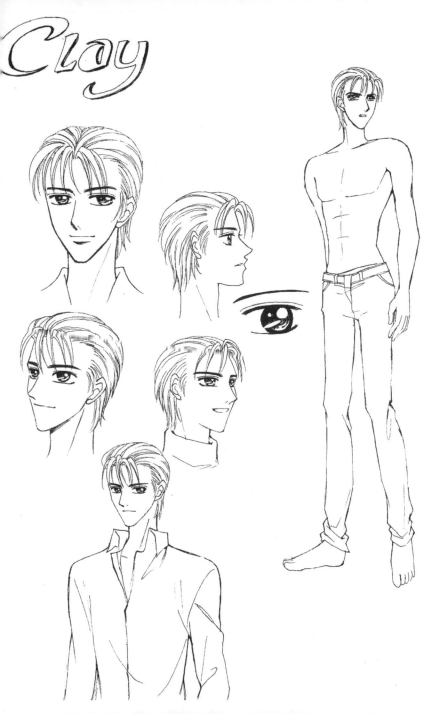

Clay

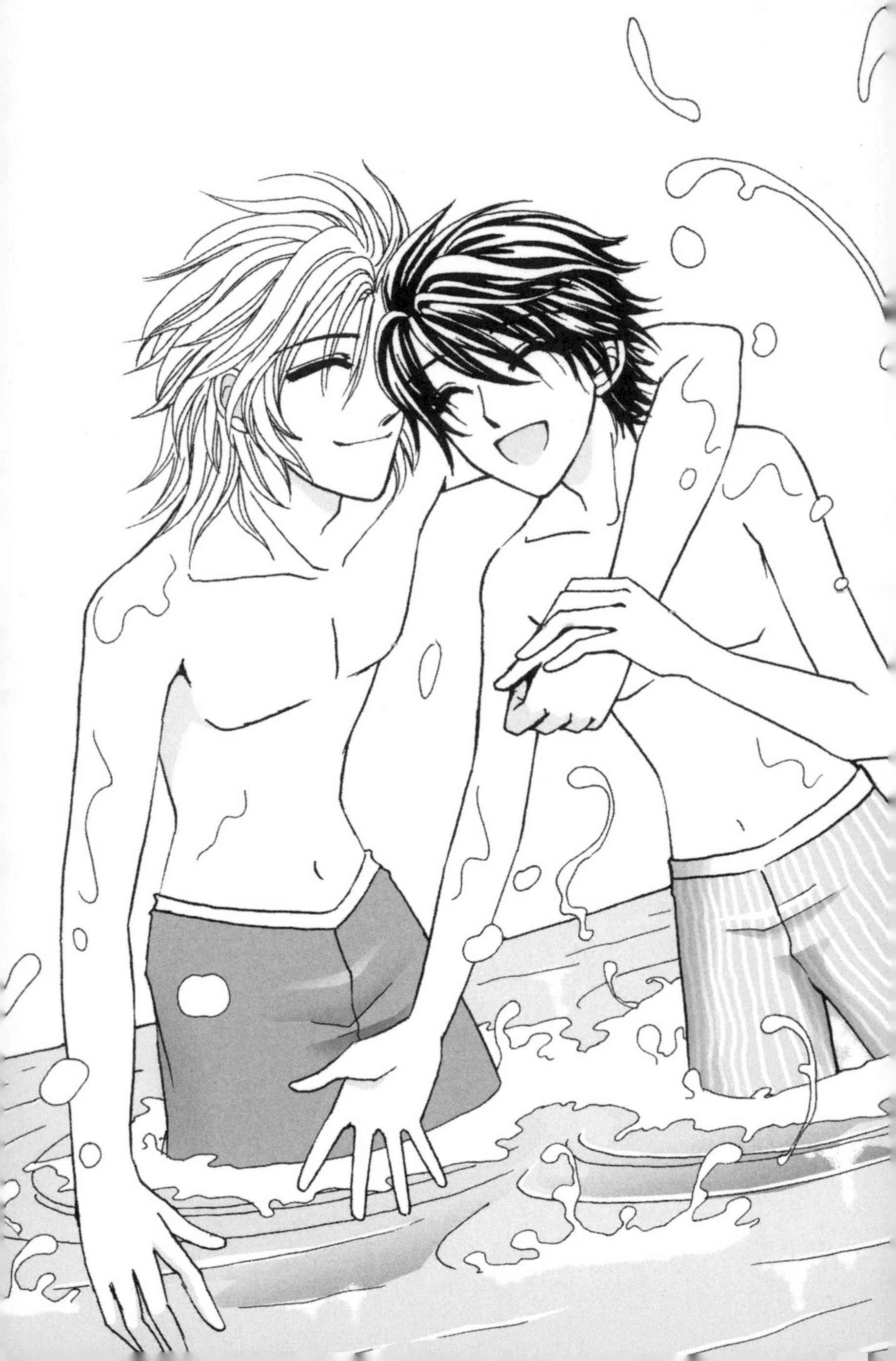

Available Now!

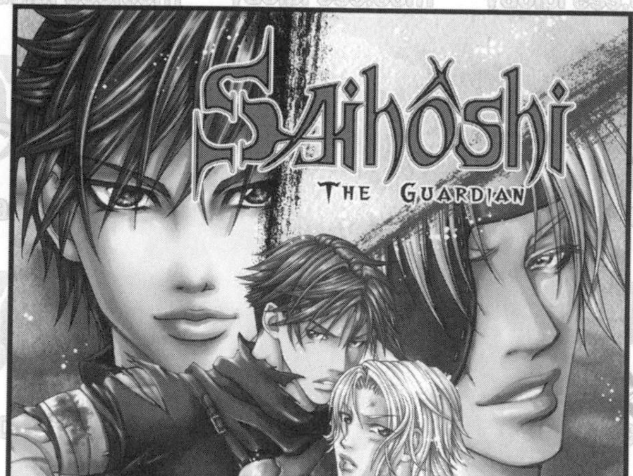

Saihôshi
THE GUARDIAN
By KÔSEN

Saihôshi the Guardian
by KÔSEN

The Guardian Sastre must escort the spoiled Prince Anel to a neighboring kingdom where tensions run high. Anel is enchanted by his noble bodyguard, but Sastre becomes more interested in Kaleth, the spirited lover of Prince Anel.

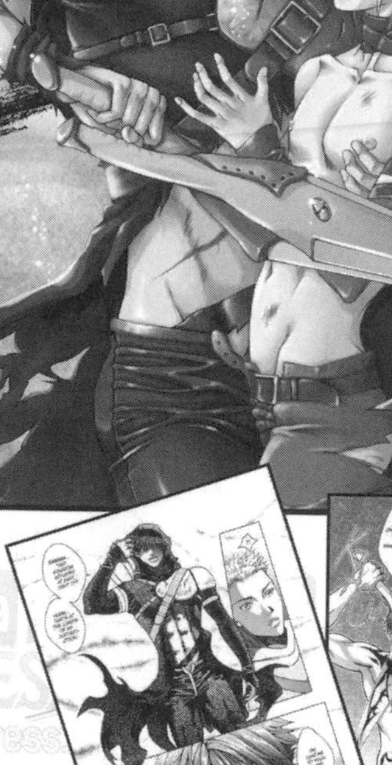

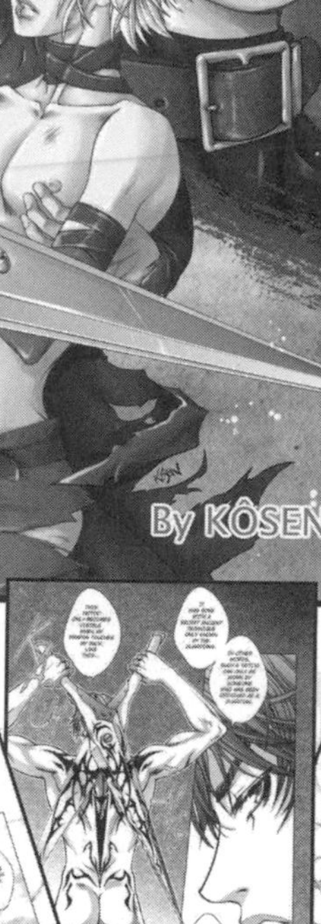

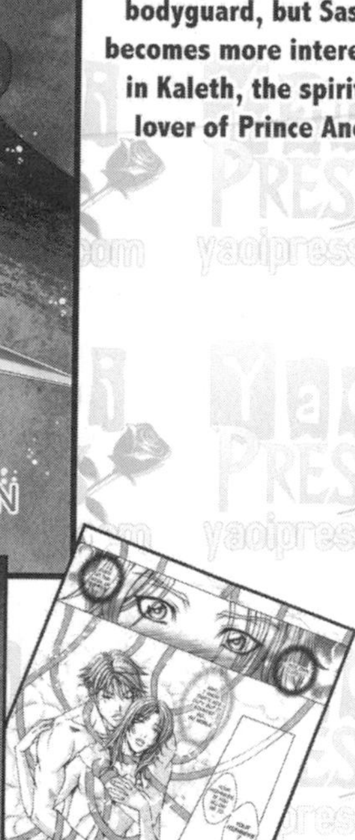

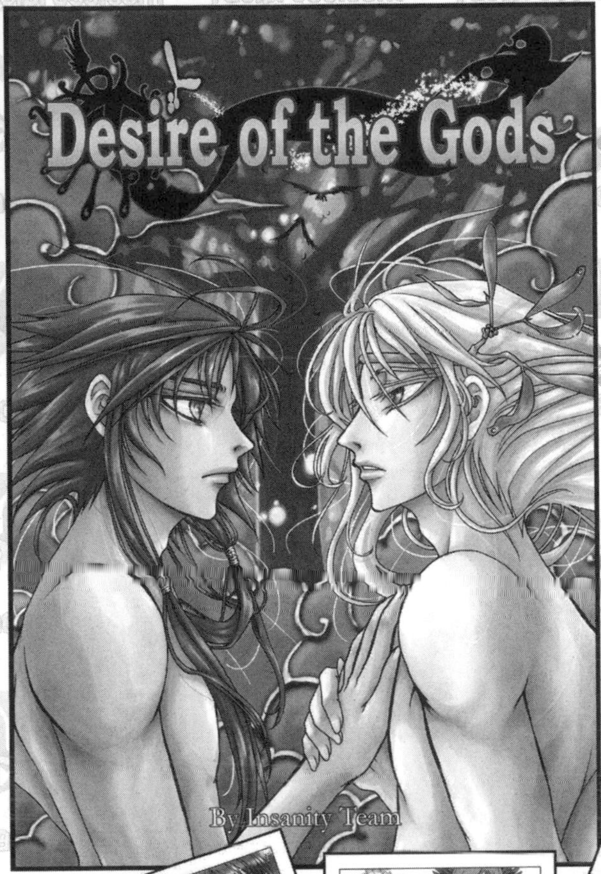
Desire of the Gods
By Insanity Team

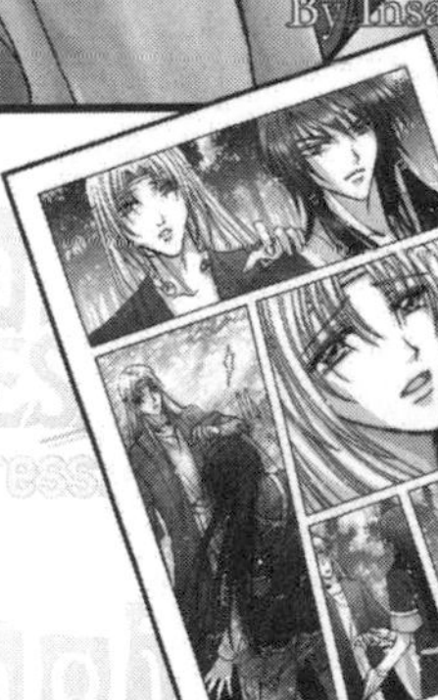

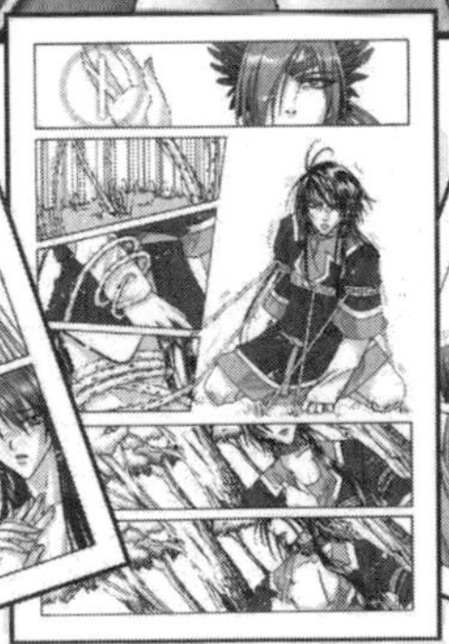

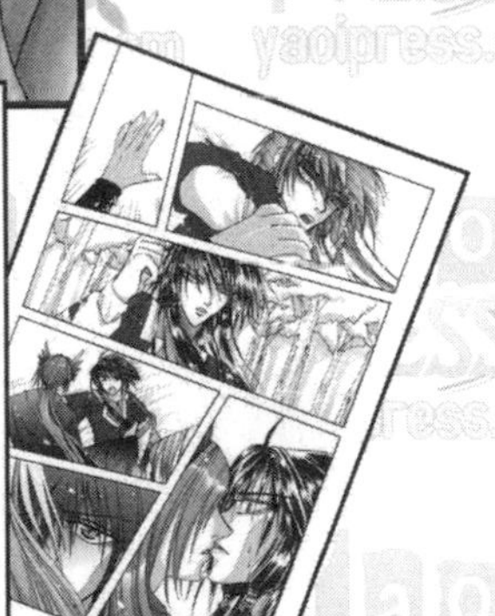

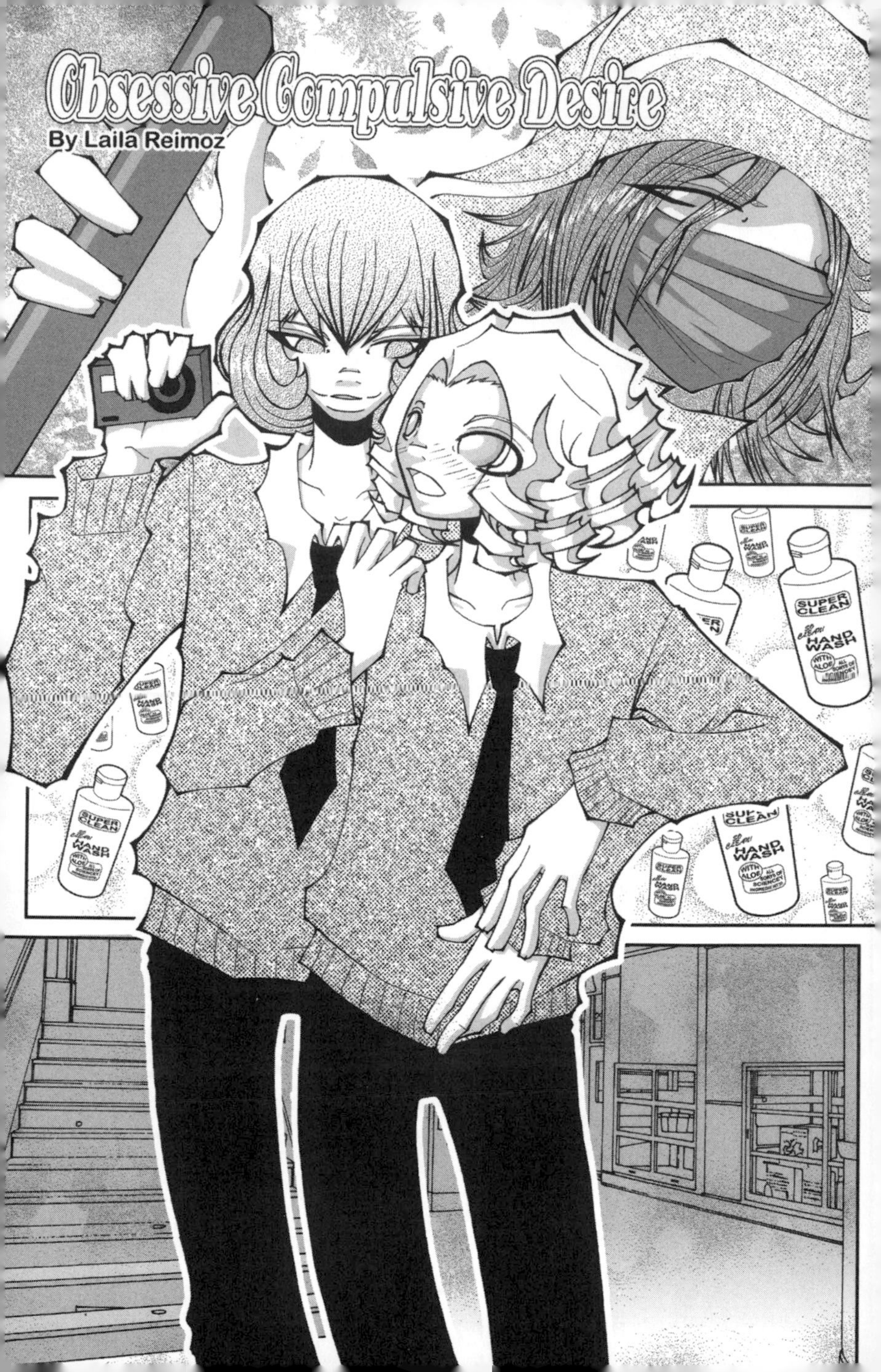
Obsessive Compulsive Desire
By Laila Reimoz
SUPER CLEAN
HAND WASH
WITH ALOE

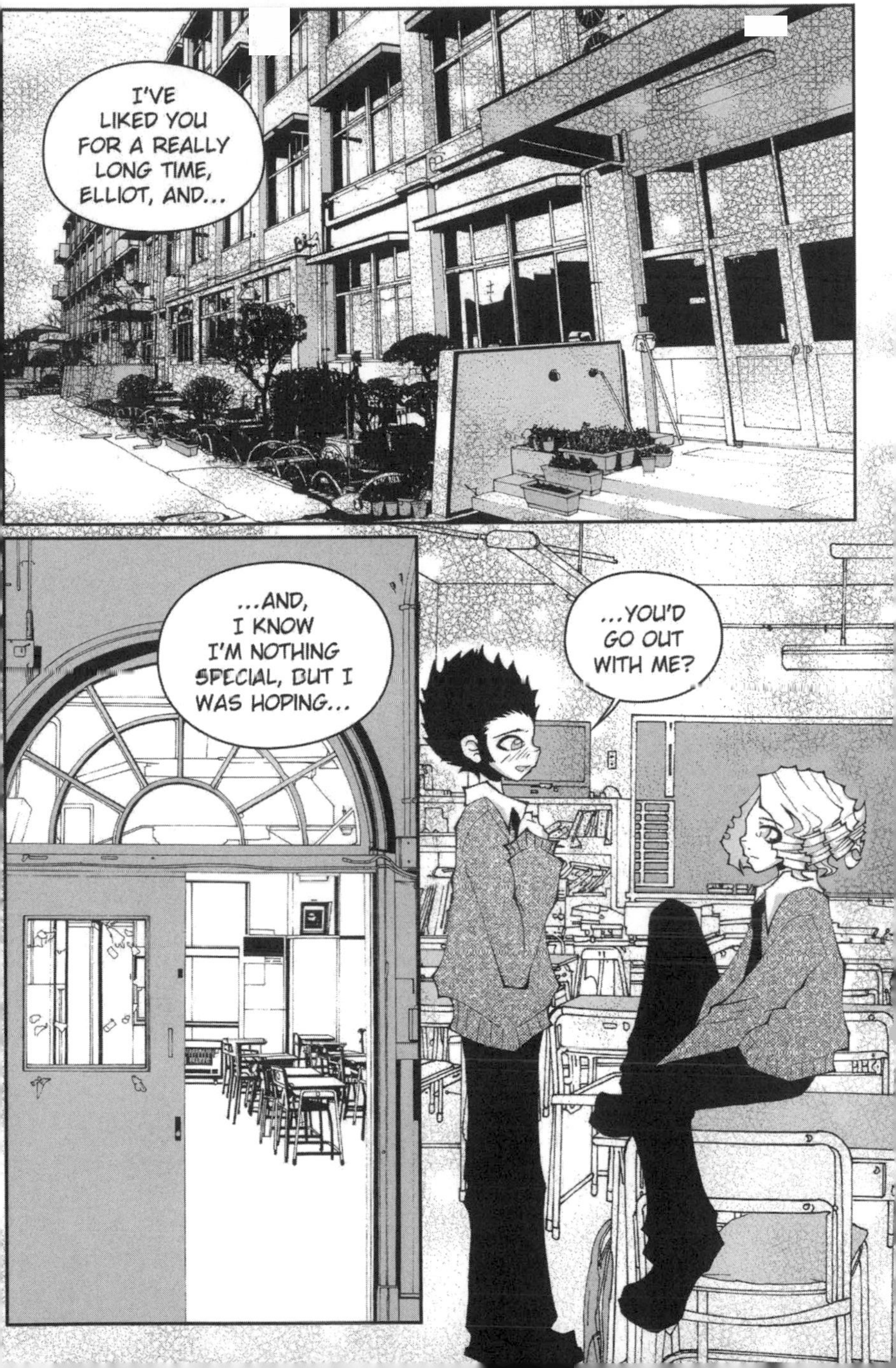
I'VE LIKED YOU FOR A REALLY LONG TIME, ELLIOT, AND...
...AND, I KNOW I'M NOTHING SPECIAL, BUT I WAS HOPING...
...YOU'D GO OUT WITH ME?

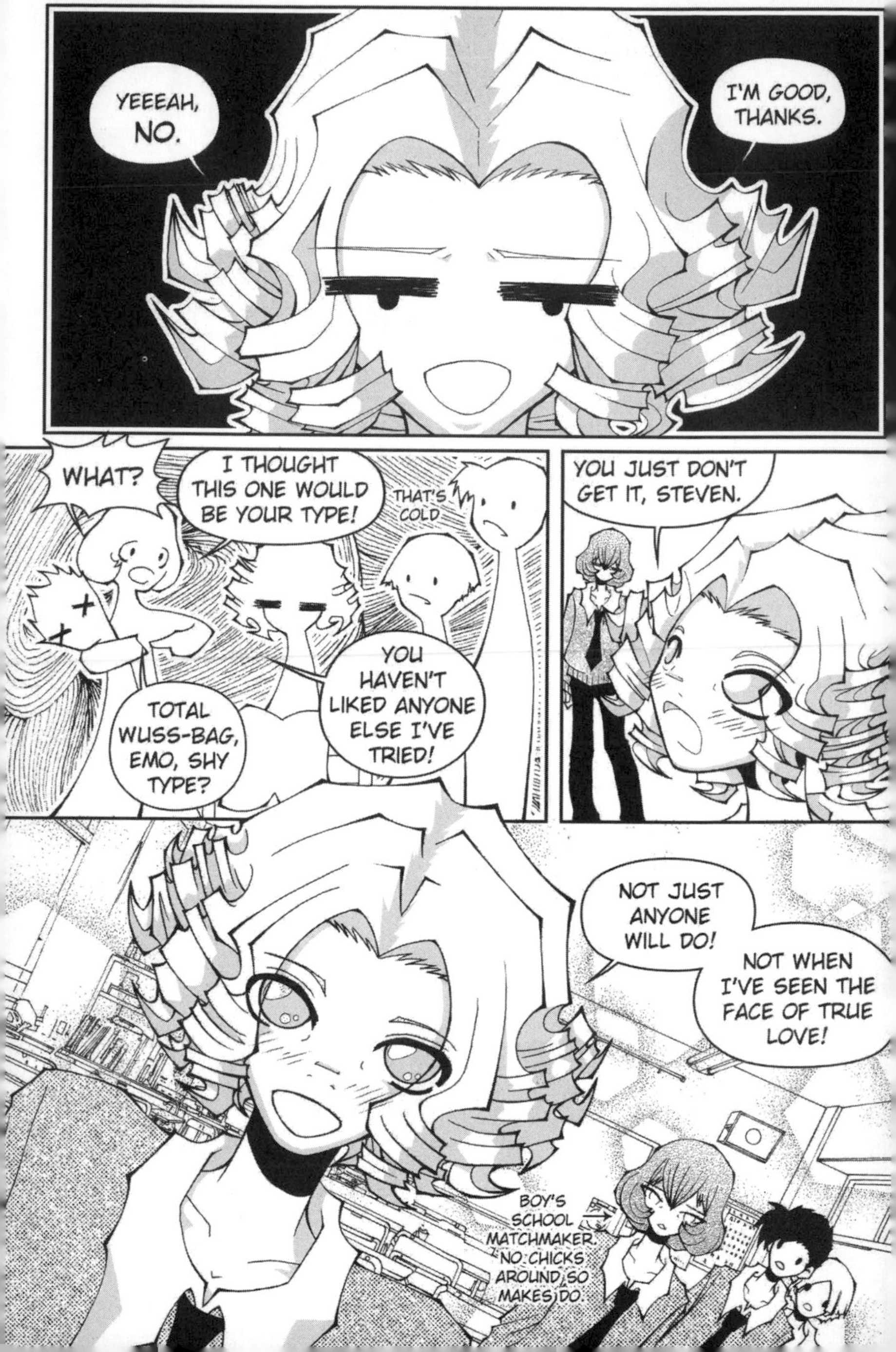
YEEEAH, NO.
I'M GOOD, THANKS.
WHAT?
I THOUGHT THIS ONE WOULD BE YOUR TYPE!
THAT'S COLD
TOTAL WUSS-BAG, EMO, SHY TYPE?
YOU HAVEN'T LIKED ANYONE ELSE I'VE TRIED!
YOU JUST DON'T GET IT, STEVEN.
NOT JUST ANYONE WILL DO!
NOT WHEN I'VE SEEN THE FACE OF TRUE LOVE!
BOY'S SCHOOL MATCHMAKER. NO CHICKS AROUND SO MAKES DO.

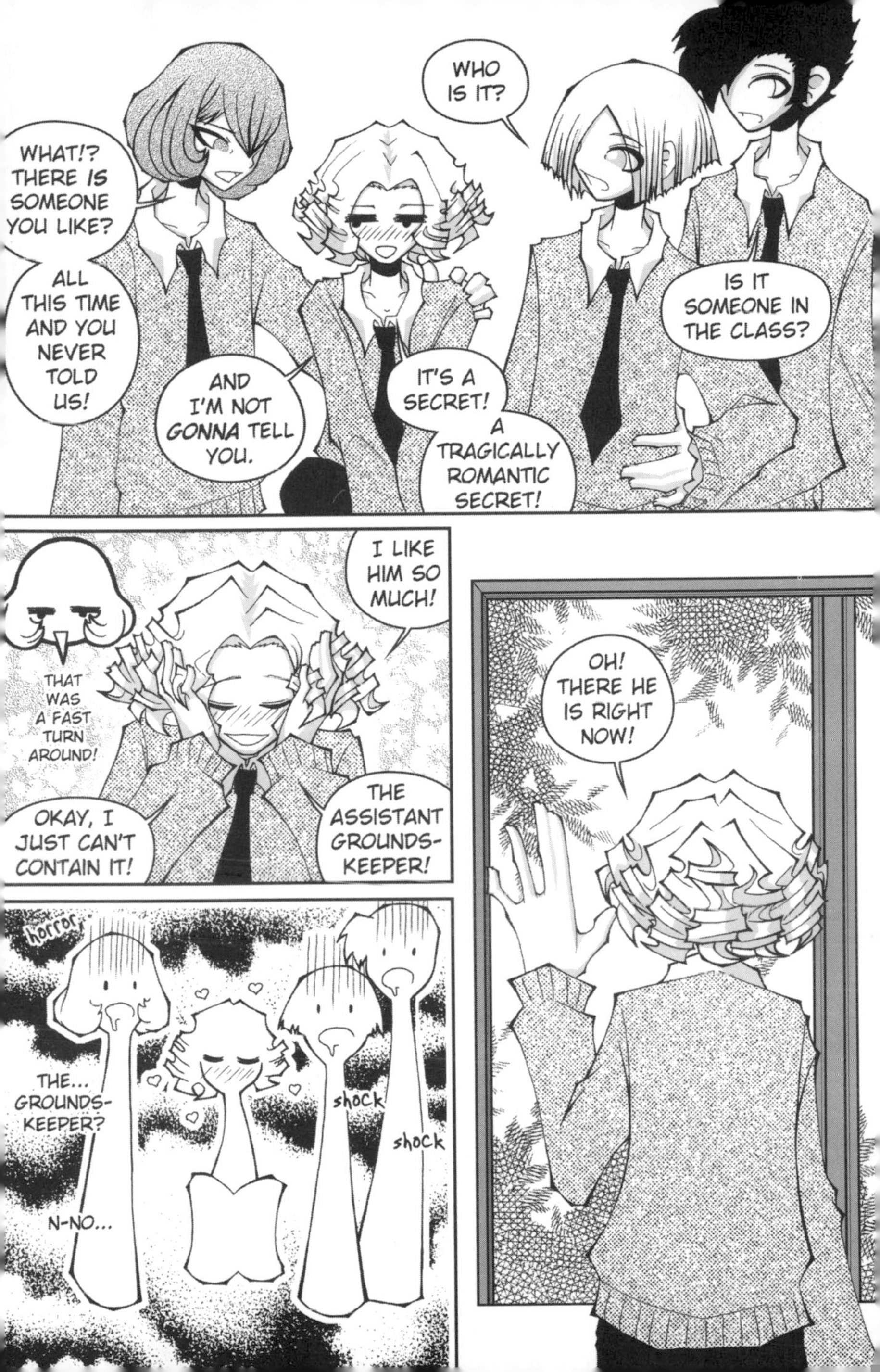
WHO IS IT?
WHAT!? THERE IS SOMEONE YOU LIKE?
ALL THIS TIME AND YOU NEVER TOLD US!
IS IT SOMEONE IN THE CLASS?
AND I'M NOT GONNA TELL YOU.
IT'S A SECRET!
A TRAGICALLY ROMANTIC SECRET!
I LIKE HIM SO MUCH!
THAT WAS A FAST TURN AROUND!
OKAY, I JUST CAN'T CONTAIN IT!
THE ASSISTANT GROUNDS-KEEPER!
OH! THERE HE IS RIGHT NOW!
horror
THE... GROUNDS-KEEPER?
shock
shock
N-NO...

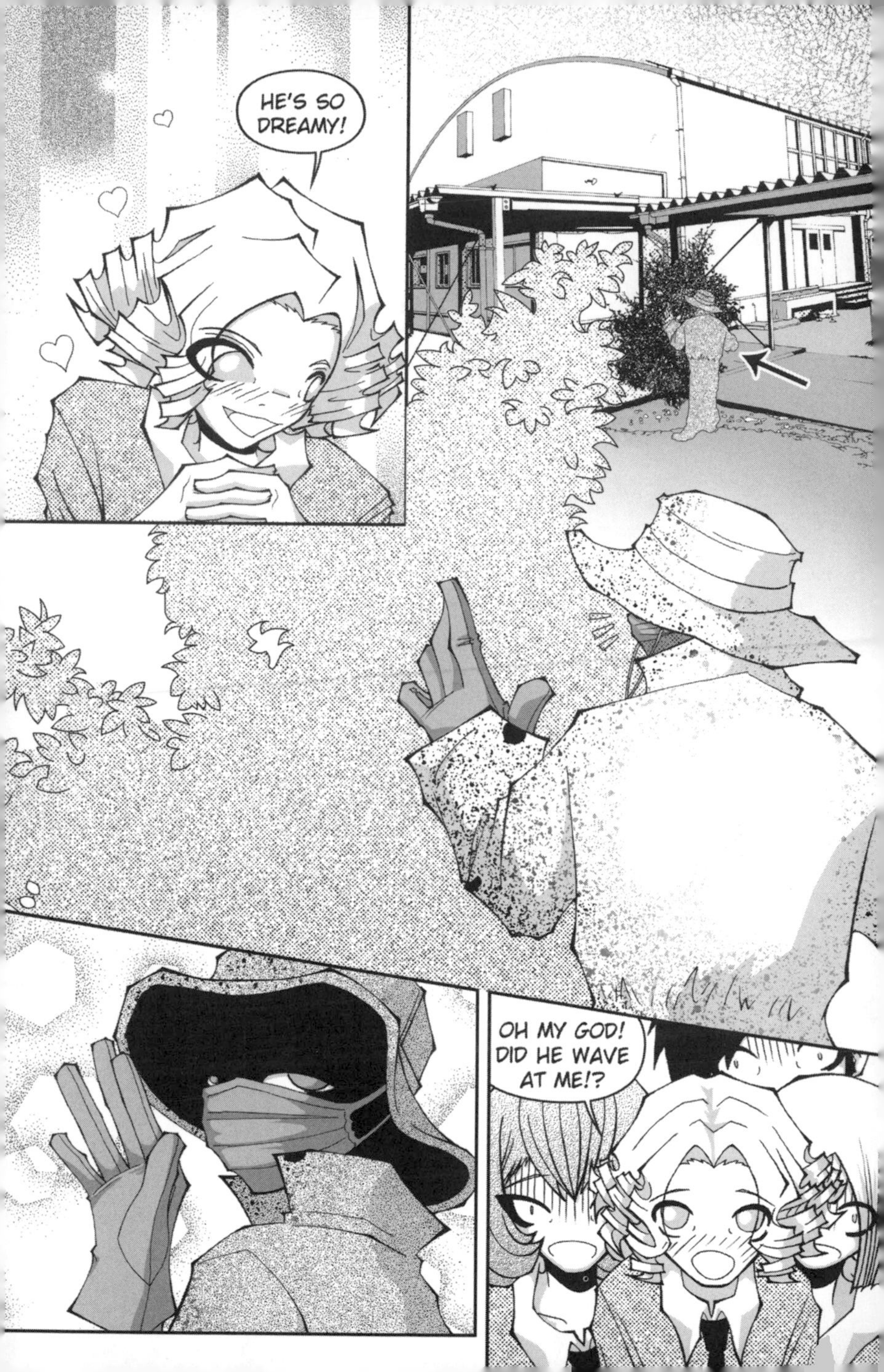
HE'S SO DREAMY!
OH MY GOD! DID HE WAVE AT ME!?

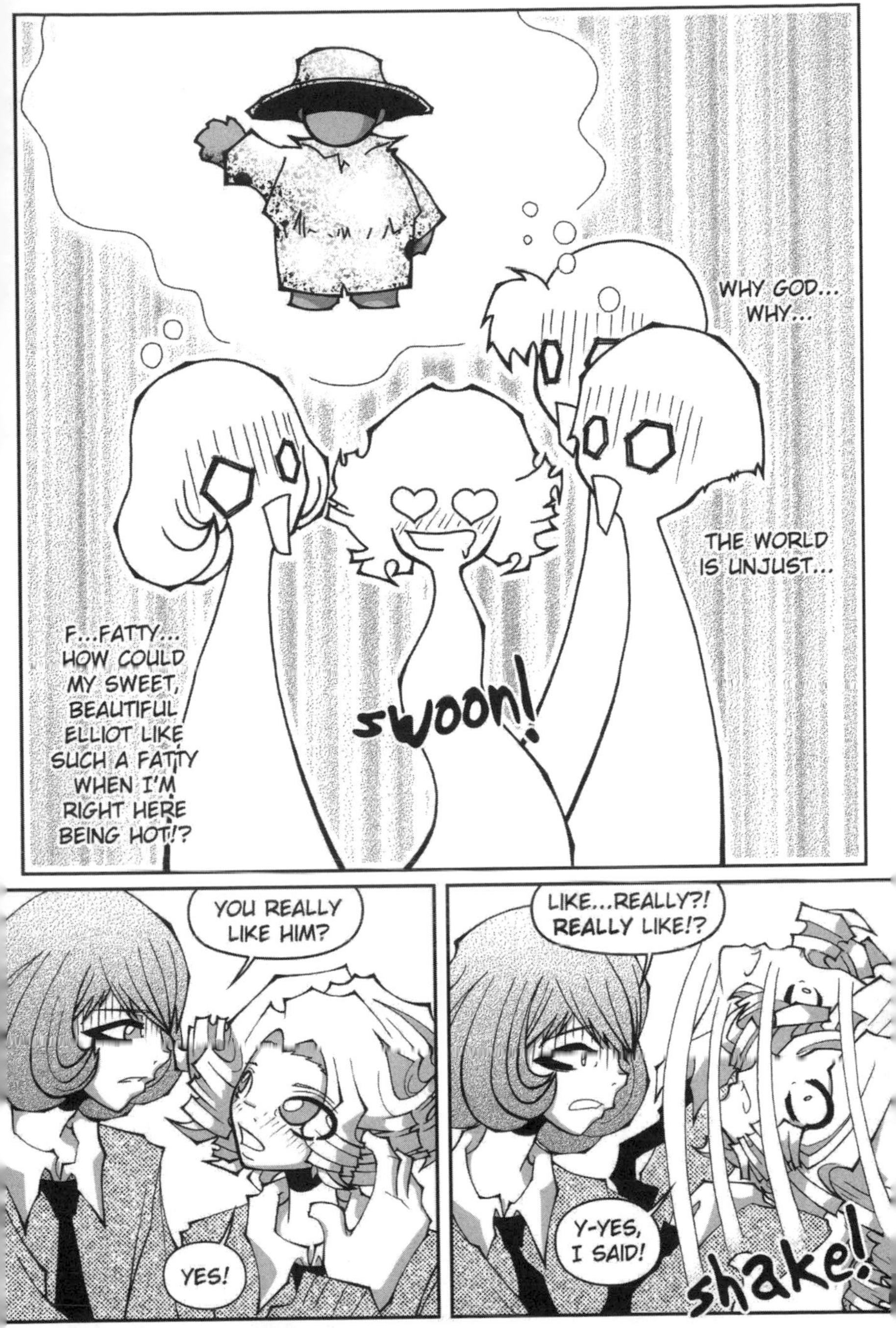
WHY GOD... WHY...
THE WORLD IS UNJUST...
F...FATTY... HOW COULD MY SWEET, BEAUTIFUL ELLIOT LIKE SUCH A FATTY WHEN I'M RIGHT HERE BEING HOT!?
SWOON!
YOU REALLY LIKE HIM?
YES!
LIKE...REALLY?! REALLY LIKE!?
Y-YES, I SAID!
SHAKE!

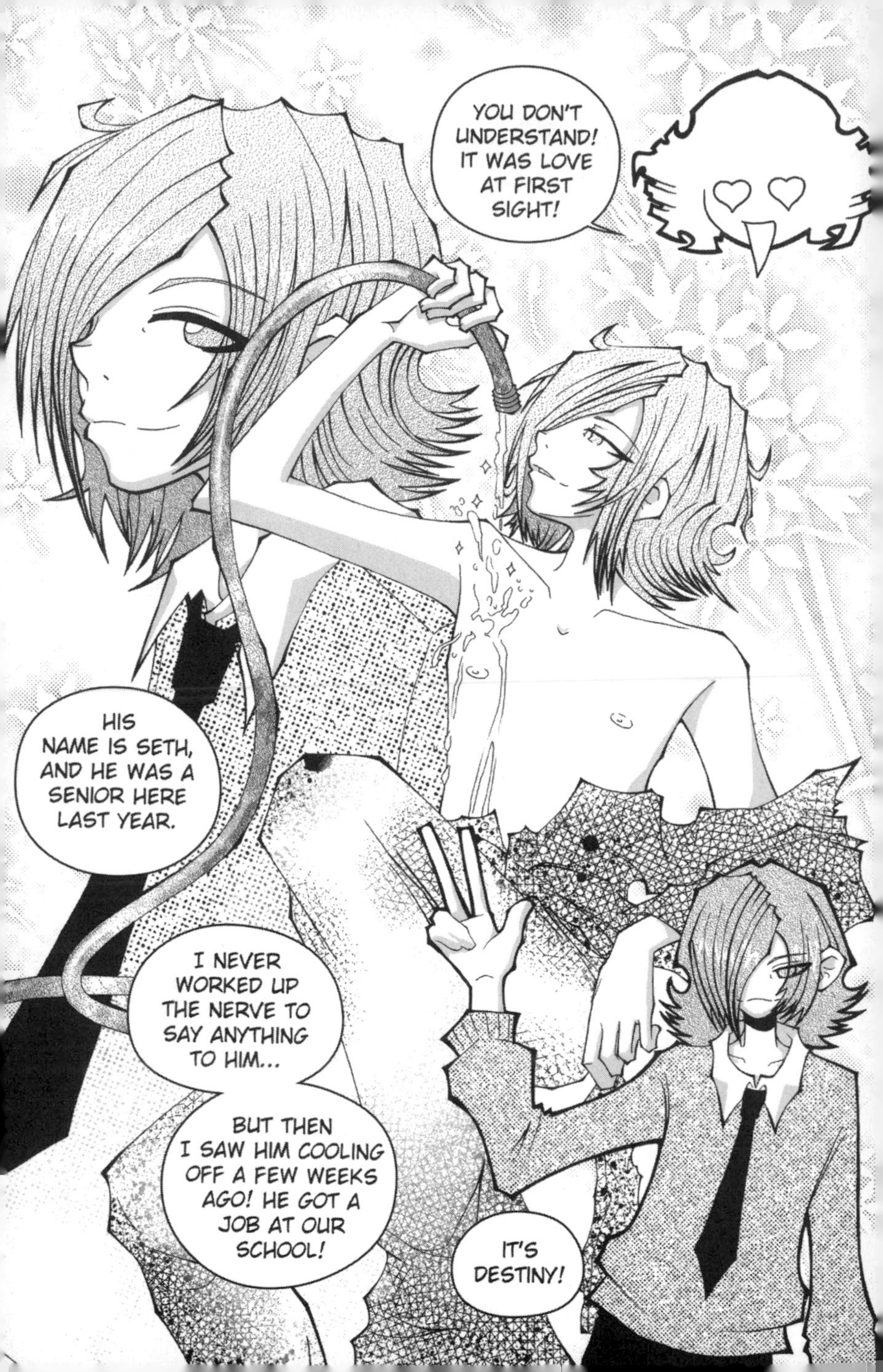
YOU DON'T UNDERSTAND! IT WAS LOVE AT FIRST SIGHT!
HIS NAME IS SETH, AND HE WAS A SENIOR HERE LAST YEAR.
I NEVER WORKED UP THE NERVE TO SAY ANYTHING TO HIM...
BUT THEN I SAW HIM COOLING OFF A FEW WEEKS AGO! HE GOT A JOB AT OUR SCHOOL!
IT'S DESTINY!

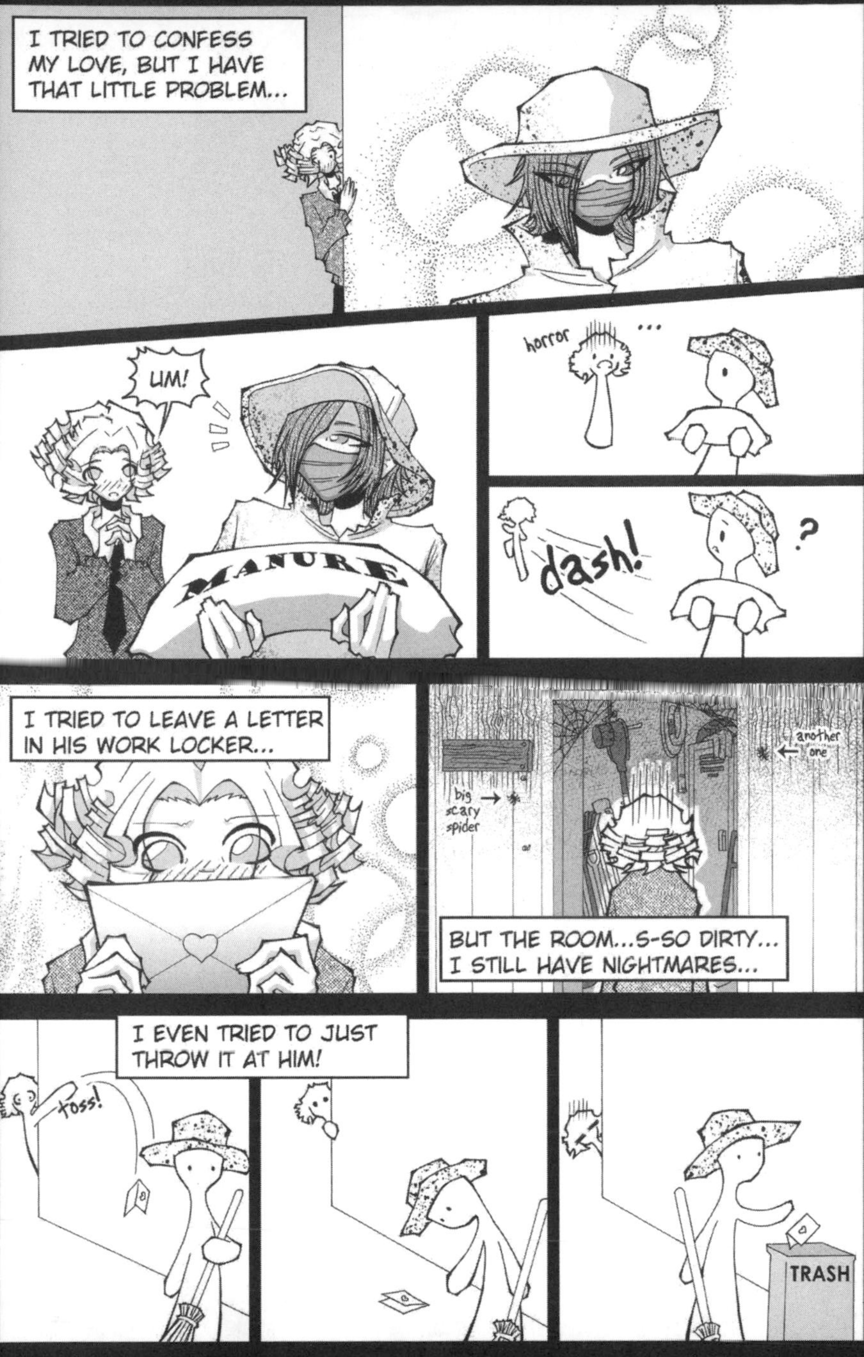
I TRIED TO CONFESS MY LOVE, BUT I HAVE THAT LITTLE PROBLEM...
UM!
MANURE
horror
...
dash!
?
I TRIED TO LEAVE A LETTER IN HIS WORK LOCKER...
another one
big scary spider
BUT THE ROOM...S-SO DIRTY... I STILL HAVE NIGHTMARES...
I EVEN TRIED TO JUST THROW IT AT HIM!
toss!
TRASH

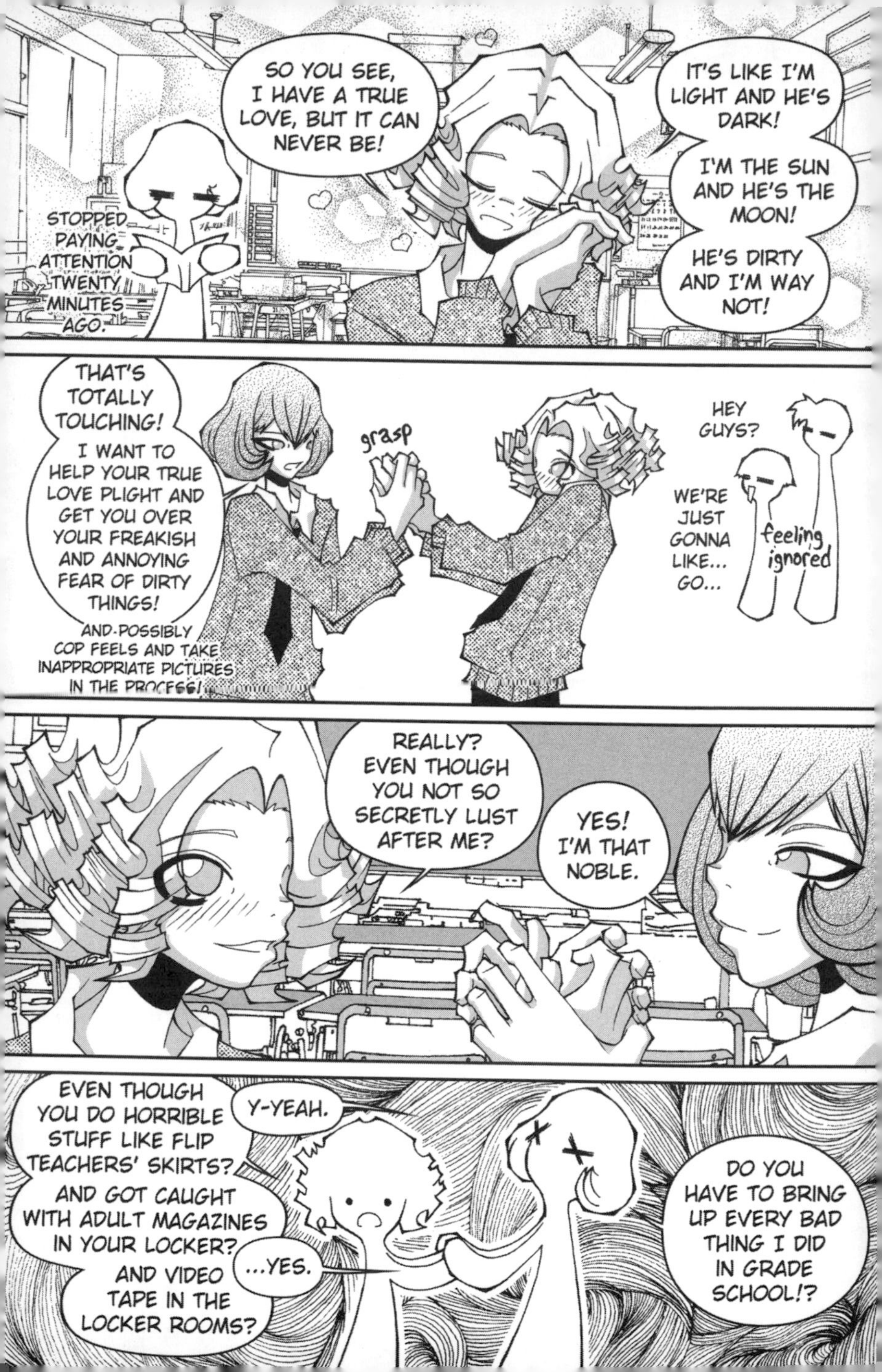

SO YOU SEE, I HAVE A TRUE LOVE, BUT IT CAN NEVER BE!
IT'S LIKE I'M LIGHT AND HE'S DARK!
I'M THE SUN AND HE'S THE MOON!
HE'S DIRTY AND I'M WAY NOT!
STOPPED PAYING ATTENTION TWENTY MINUTES AGO.
THAT'S TOTALLY TOUCHING!
I WANT TO HELP YOUR TRUE LOVE PLIGHT AND GET YOU OVER YOUR FREAKISH AND ANNOYING FEAR OF DIRTY THINGS!
AND POSSIBLY COP FEELS AND TAKE INAPPROPRIATE PICTURES IN THE PROCESS!
grasp
HEY GUYS?
WE'RE JUST GONNA LIKE... GO...
feeling ignored
REALLY? EVEN THOUGH YOU NOT SO SECRETLY LUST AFTER ME?
YES! I'M THAT NOBLE.
EVEN THOUGH YOU DO HORRIBLE STUFF LIKE FLIP TEACHERS' SKIRTS?
Y-YEAH.
AND GOT CAUGHT WITH ADULT MAGAZINES IN YOUR LOCKER?
AND VIDEO TAPE IN THE LOCKER ROOMS?
...YES.
DO YOU HAVE TO BRING UP EVERY BAD THING I DID IN GRADE SCHOOL!?

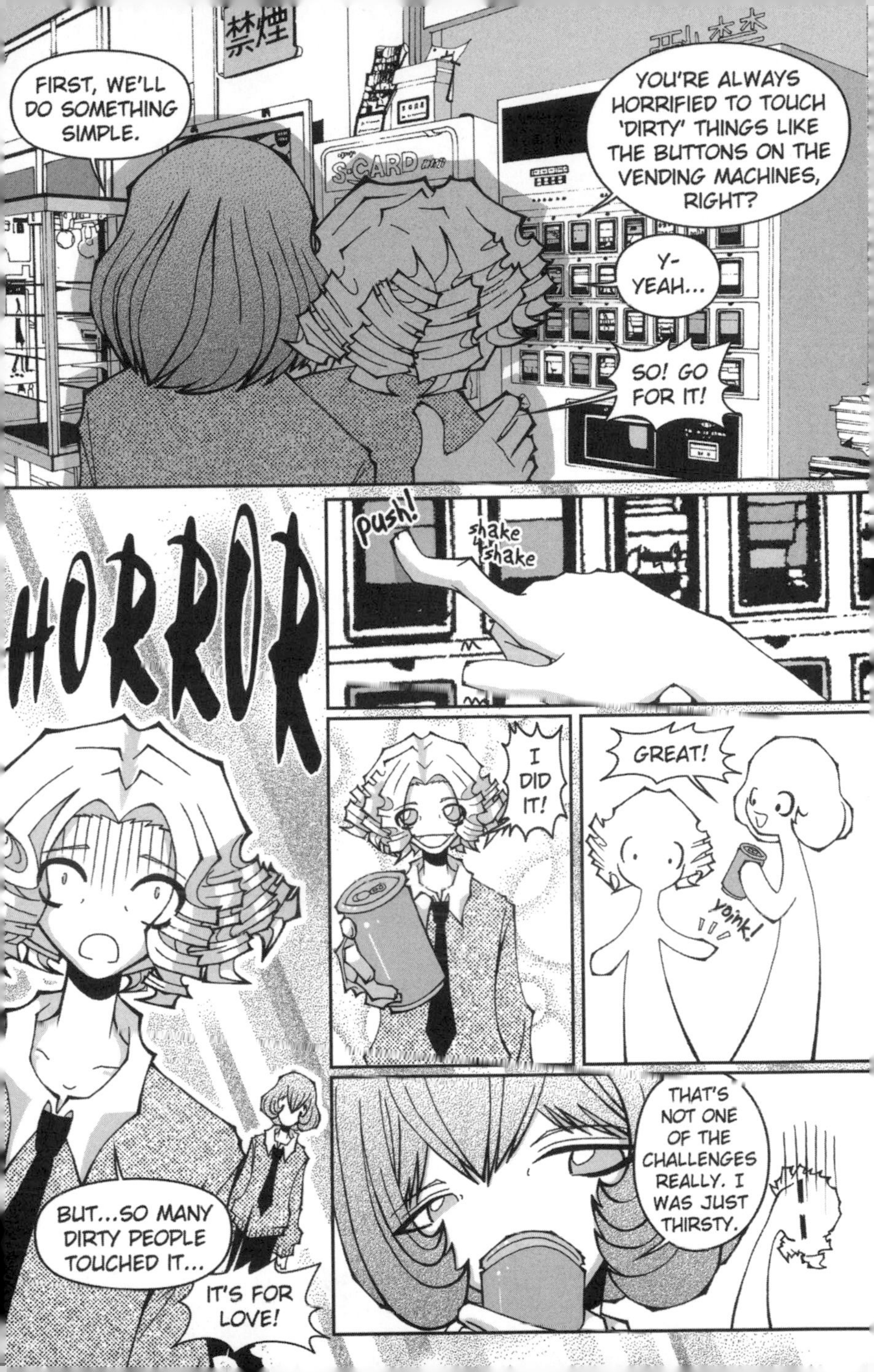
FIRST, WE'LL DO SOMETHING SIMPLE.
YOU'RE ALWAYS HORRIFIED TO TOUCH 'DIRTY' THINGS LIKE THE BUTTONS ON THE VENDING MACHINES, RIGHT?
Y-YEAH...
SO! GO FOR IT!
S-CARD
HORROR
push!
shake shake
I DID IT!
GREAT!
yoink!
BUT...SO MANY DIRTY PEOPLE TOUCHED IT...
IT'S FOR LOVE!
THAT'S NOT ONE OF THE CHALLENGES REALLY. I WAS JUST THIRSTY.

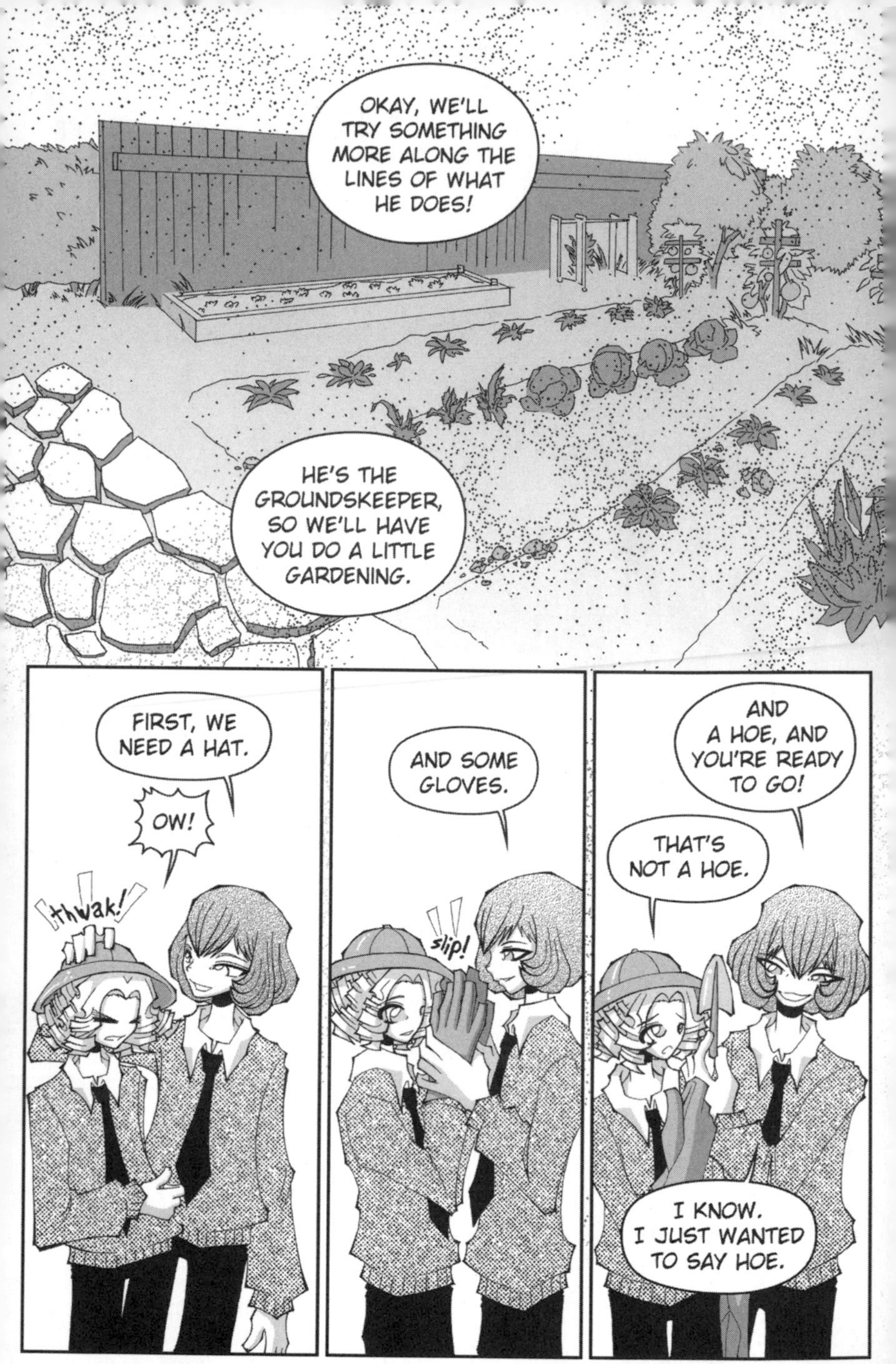
OKAY, WE'LL TRY SOMETHING MORE ALONG THE LINES OF WHAT HE DOES!
HE'S THE GROUNDSKEEPER, SO WE'LL HAVE YOU DO A LITTLE GARDENING.
FIRST, WE NEED A HAT.
OW!
thwak!
AND SOME GLOVES.
slip!
AND A HOE, AND YOU'RE READY TO GO!
THAT'S NOT A HOE.
I KNOW. I JUST WANTED TO SAY HOE.

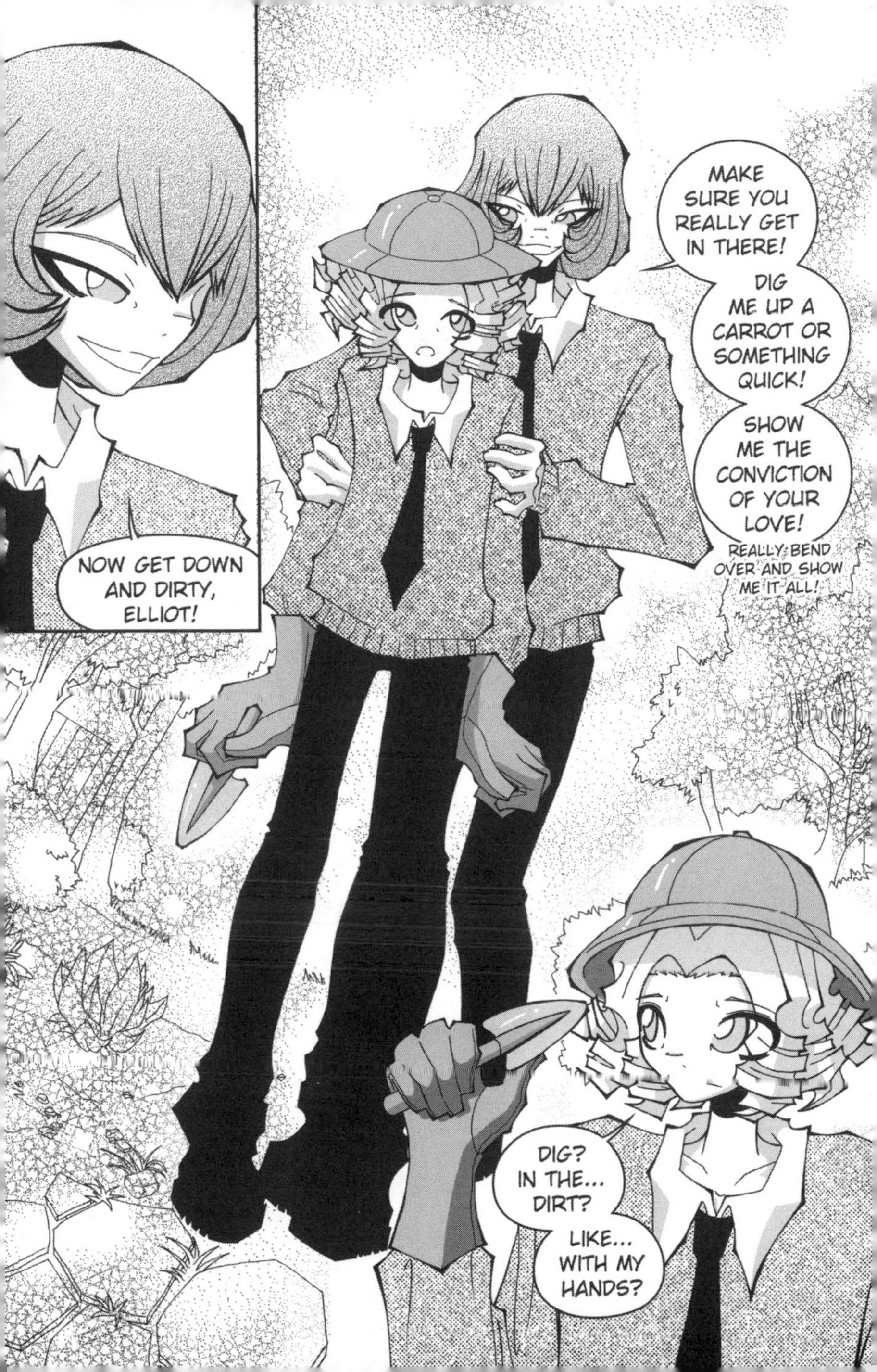
MAKE SURE YOU REALLY GET IN THERE!
DIG ME UP A CARROT OR SOMETHING QUICK!
SHOW ME THE CONVICTION OF YOUR LOVE!
REALLY BEND OVER AND SHOW ME IT ALL!
NOW GET DOWN AND DIRTY, ELLIOT!
DIG? IN THE... DIRT?
LIKE... WITH MY HANDS?

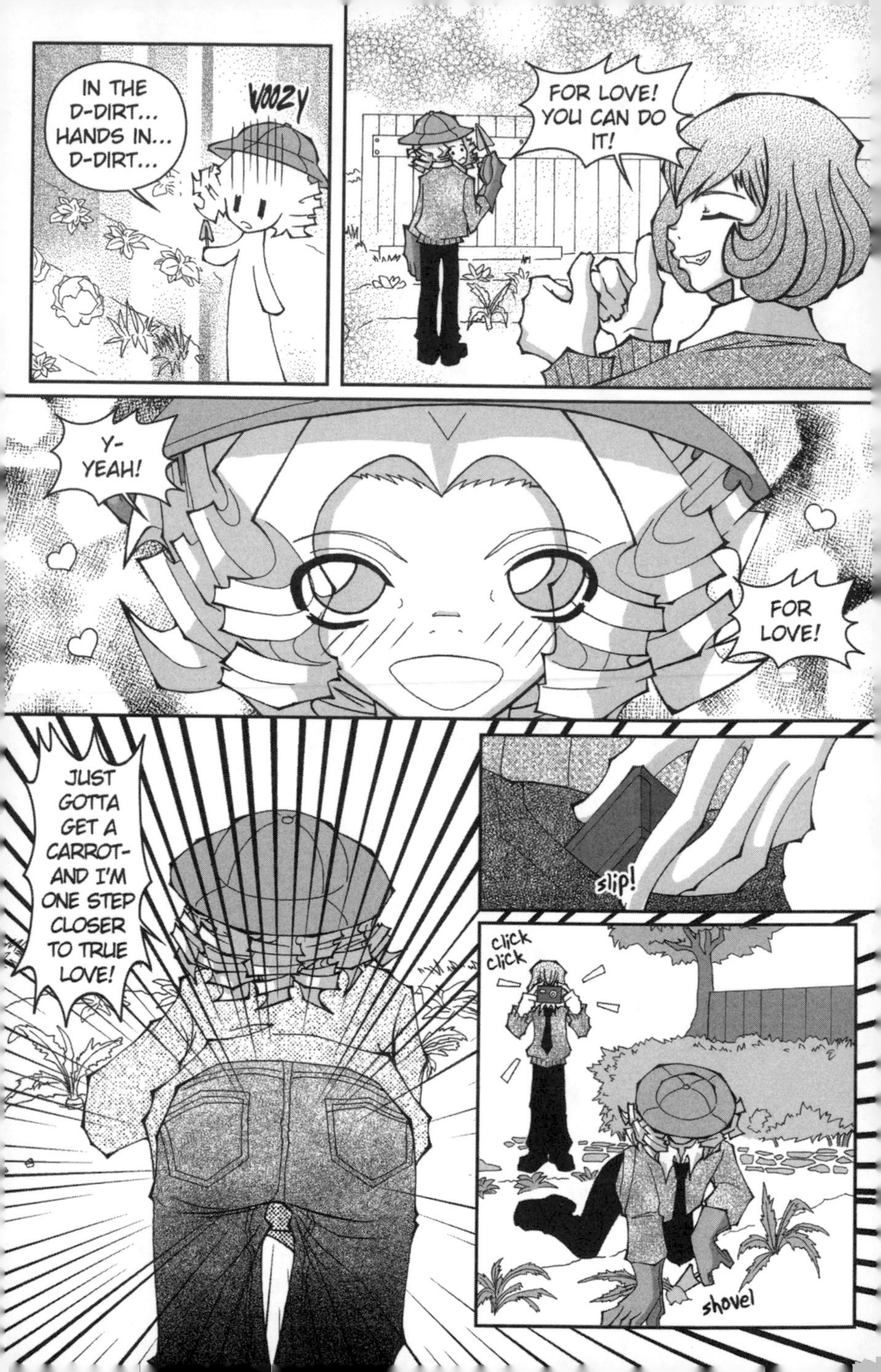
IN THE D-DIRT... HANDS IN... D-DIRT...
WOOZY
FOR LOVE! YOU CAN DO IT!
Y-YEAH!
FOR LOVE!
JUST GOTTA GET A CARROT- AND I'M ONE STEP CLOSER TO TRUE LOVE!
slip!
click click
shovel

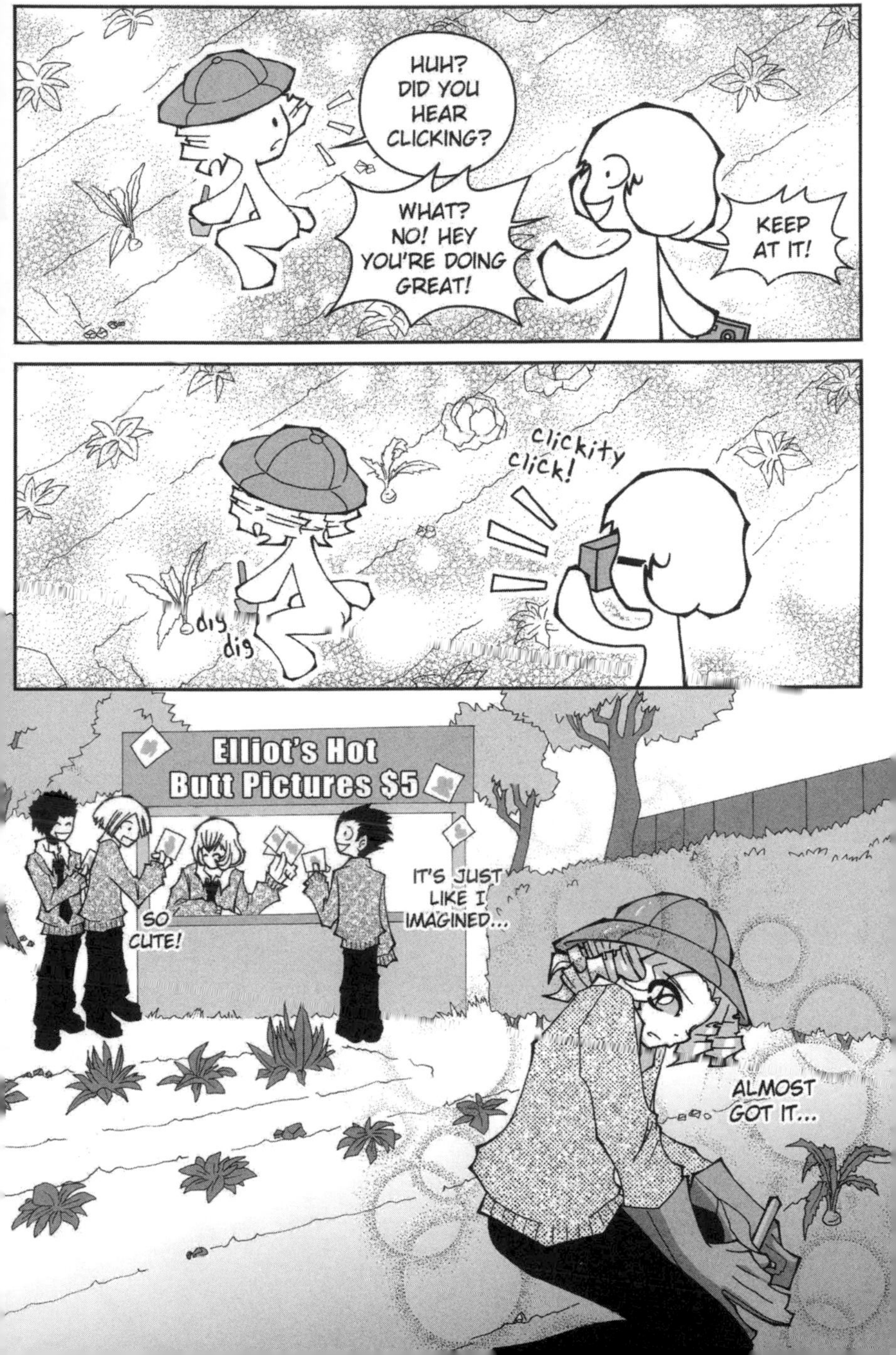
HUH? DID YOU HEAR CLICKING?
WHAT? NO! HEY YOU'RE DOING GREAT!
KEEP AT IT!
clickity click!
dig dig
Elliot's Hot Butt Pictures $5
SO CUTE!
IT'S JUST LIKE I IMAGINED...
ALMOST GOT IT...

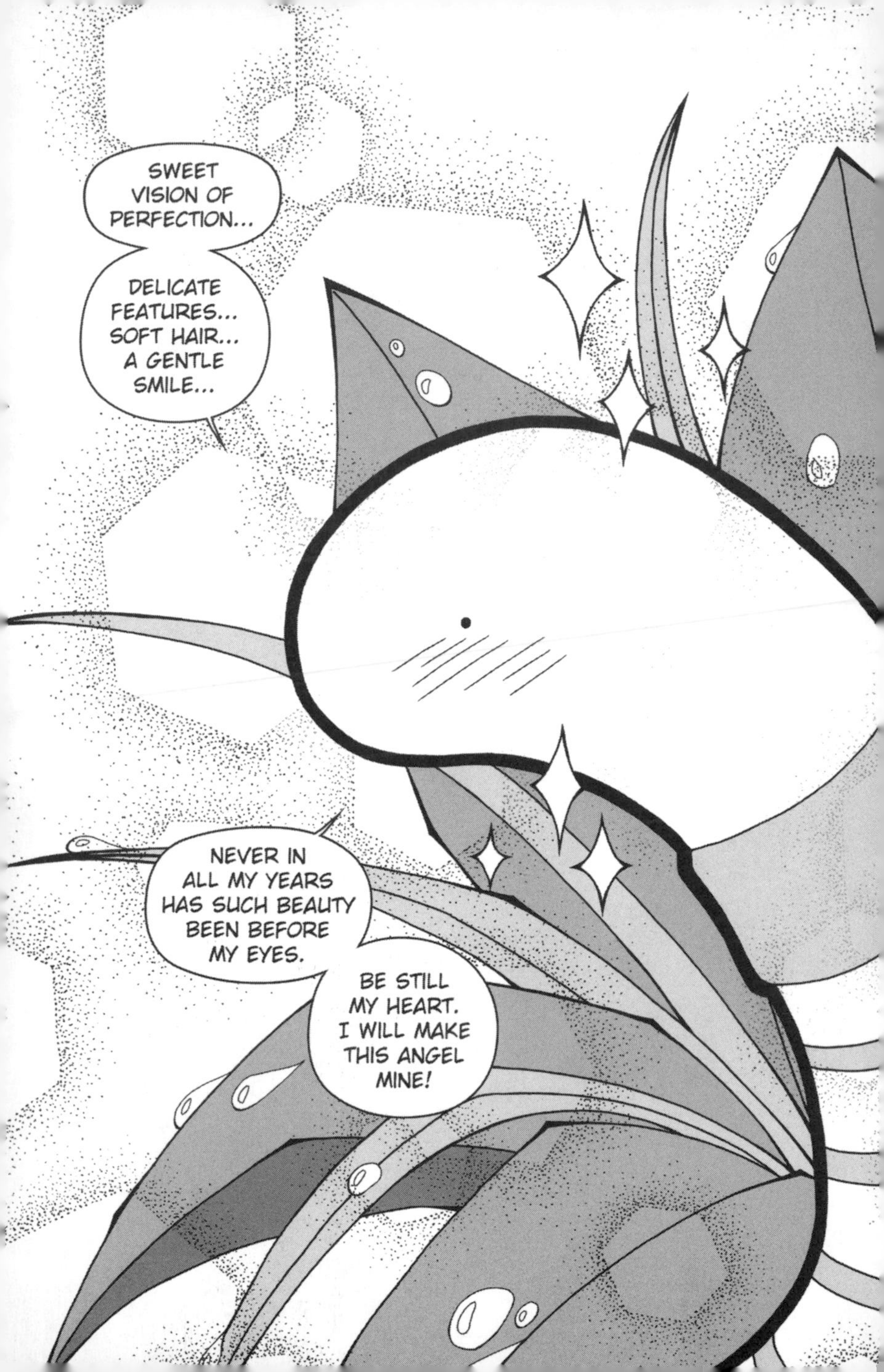
SWEET VISION OF PERFECTION...
DELICATE FEATURES... SOFT HAIR... A GENTLE SMILE...
NEVER IN ALL MY YEARS HAS SUCH BEAUTY BEEN BEFORE MY EYES.
BE STILL MY HEART. I WILL MAKE THIS ANGEL MINE!

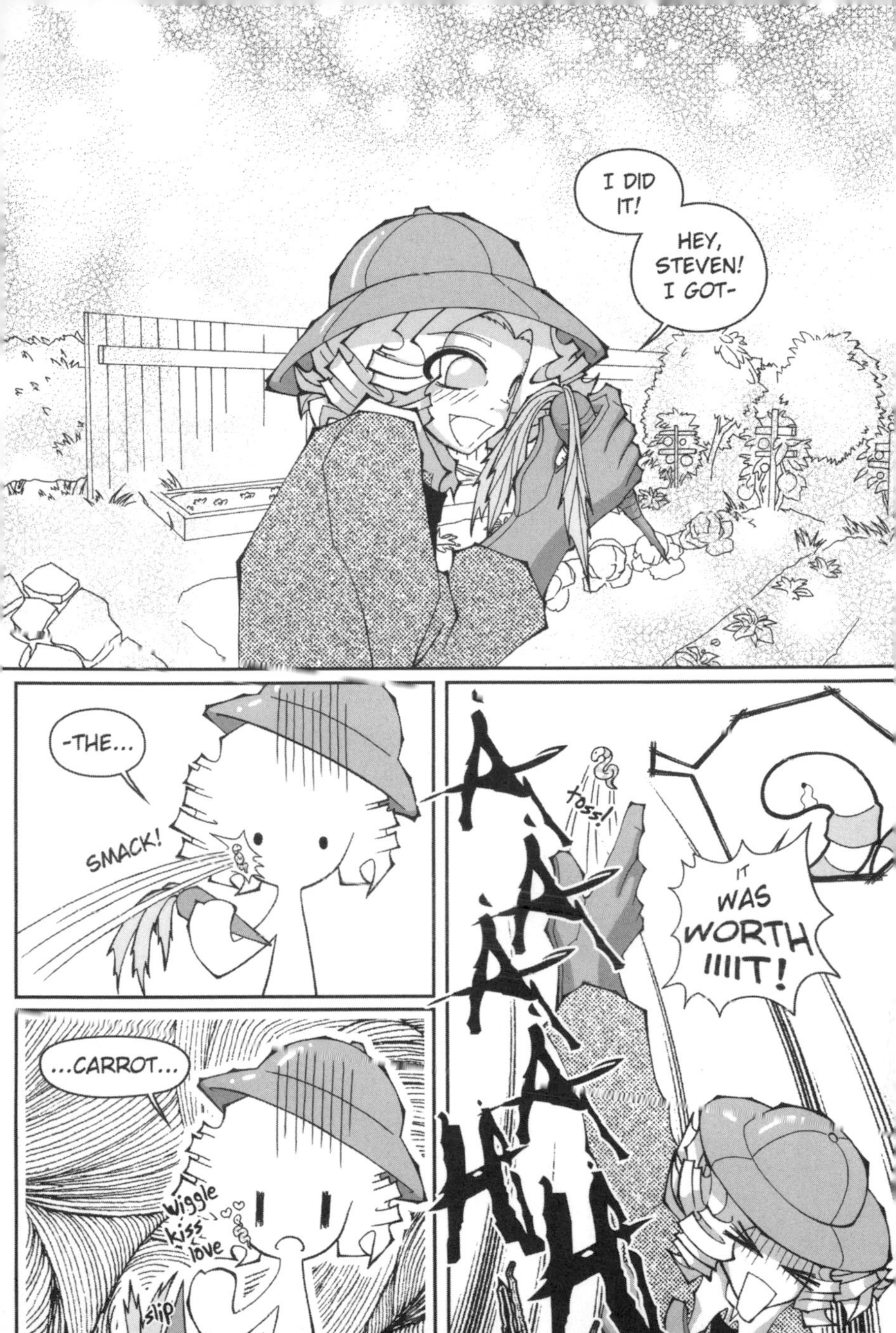
I DID IT!
HEY, STEVEN! I GOT-
-THE...
SMACK!
...CARROT...
wiggle
kiss
love
slip
AAAAAHHH
toss!
IT WAS WORTH IIIIT!

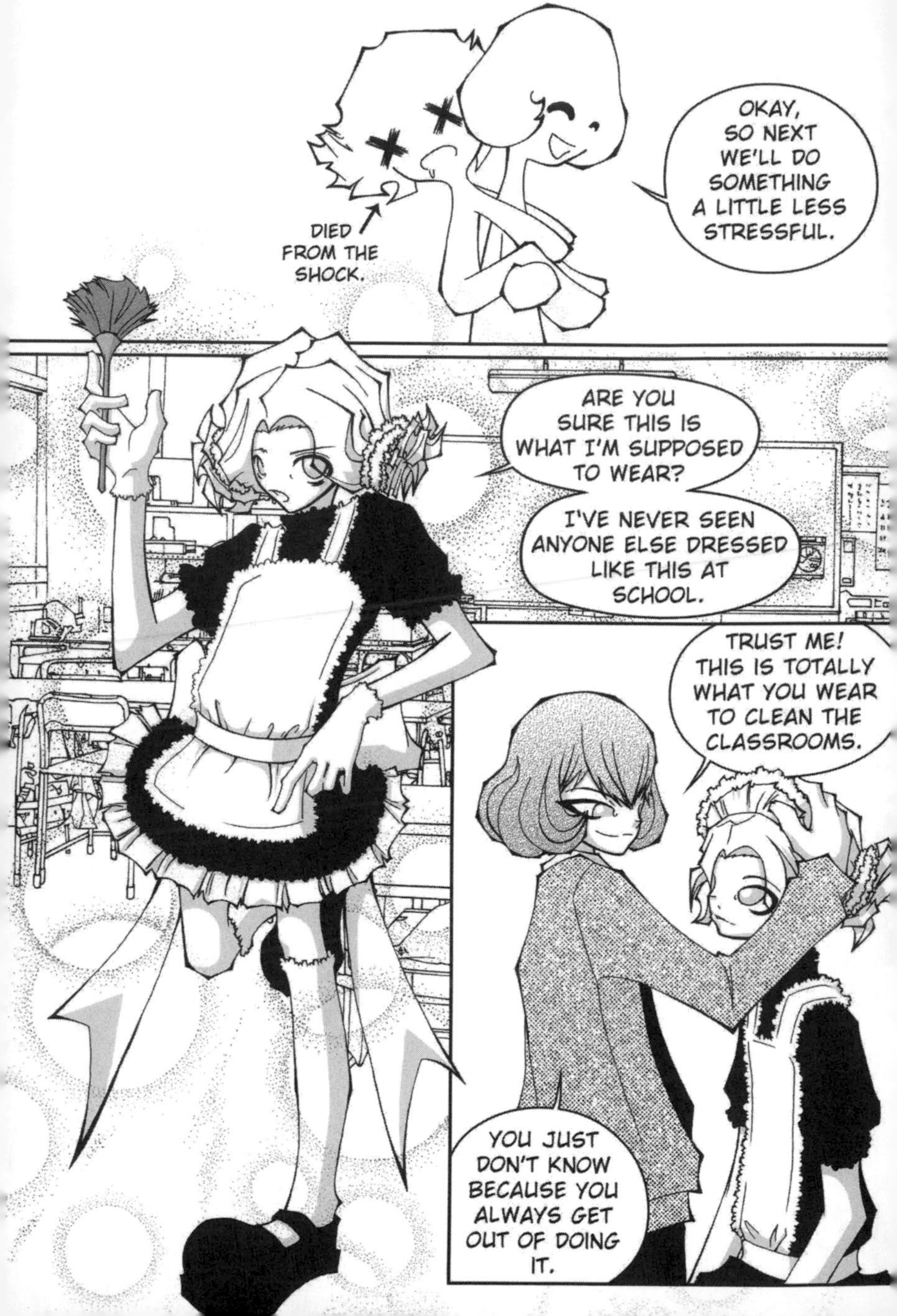
DIED FROM THE SHOCK.
OKAY, SO NEXT WE'LL DO SOMETHING A LITTLE LESS STRESSFUL.
ARE YOU SURE THIS IS WHAT I'M SUPPOSED TO WEAR?
I'VE NEVER SEEN ANYONE ELSE DRESSED LIKE THIS AT SCHOOL.
TRUST ME! THIS IS TOTALLY WHAT YOU WEAR TO CLEAN THE CLASSROOMS.
YOU JUST DON'T KNOW BECAUSE YOU ALWAYS GET OUT OF DOING IT.

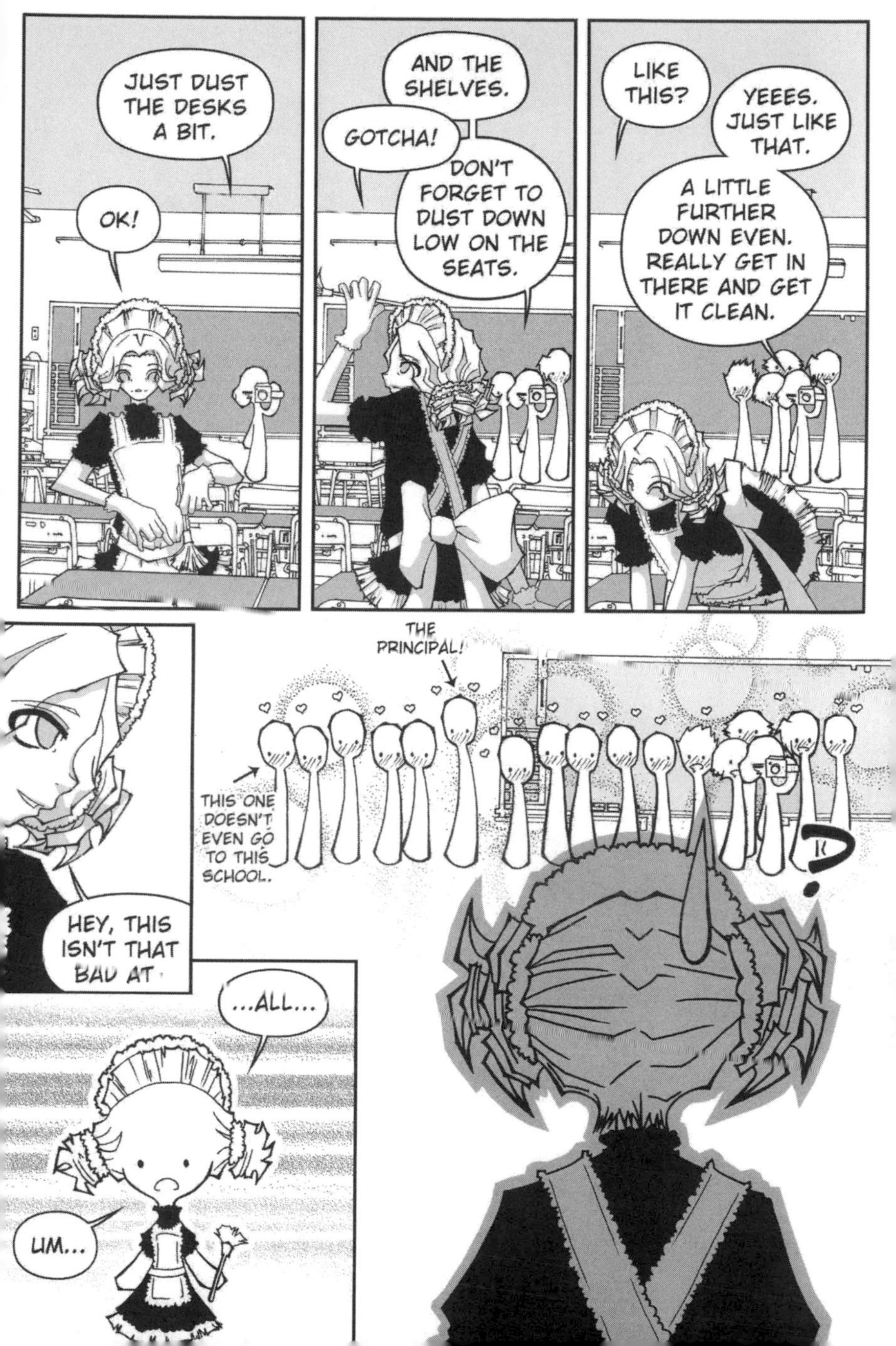
JUST DUST THE DESKS A BIT.
OK!
AND THE SHELVES.
GOTCHA!
DON'T FORGET TO DUST DOWN LOW ON THE SEATS.
LIKE THIS?
YEEES. JUST LIKE THAT.
A LITTLE FURTHER DOWN EVEN. REALLY GET IN THERE AND GET IT CLEAN.
HEY, THIS ISN'T THAT BAD AT
THE PRINCIPAL!
THIS ONE DOESN'T EVEN GO TO THIS SCHOOL.
...ALL...
UM...

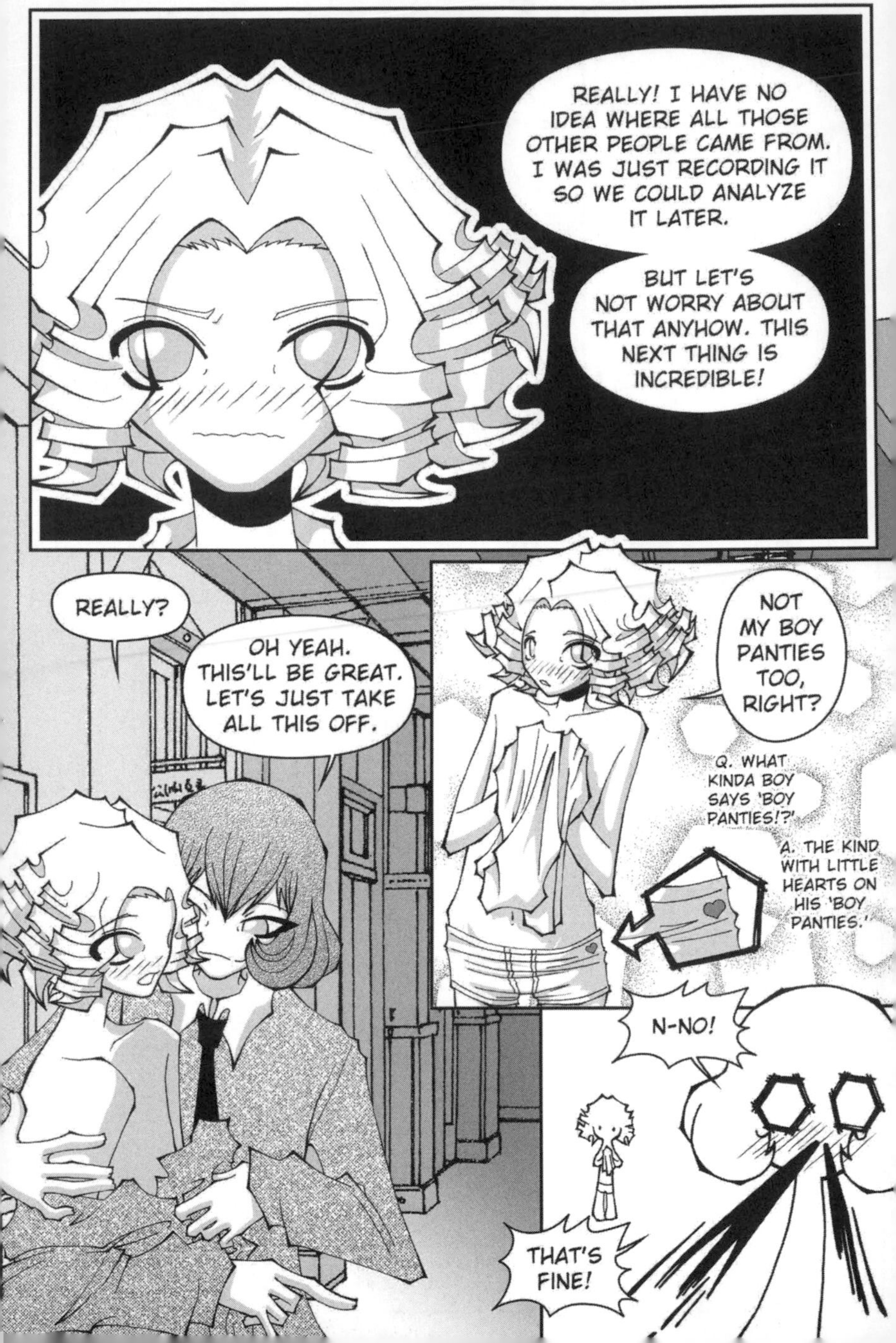
REALLY! I HAVE NO IDEA WHERE ALL THOSE OTHER PEOPLE CAME FROM. I WAS JUST RECORDING IT SO WE COULD ANALYZE IT LATER.
BUT LET'S NOT WORRY ABOUT THAT ANYHOW. THIS NEXT THING IS INCREDIBLE!
REALLY?
OH YEAH. THIS'LL BE GREAT. LET'S JUST TAKE ALL THIS OFF.
NOT MY BOY PANTIES TOO, RIGHT?
Q. WHAT KINDA BOY SAYS 'BOY PANTIES!?'
A. THE KIND WITH LITTLE HEARTS ON HIS 'BOY PANTIES.'
N-NO!
THAT'S FINE!

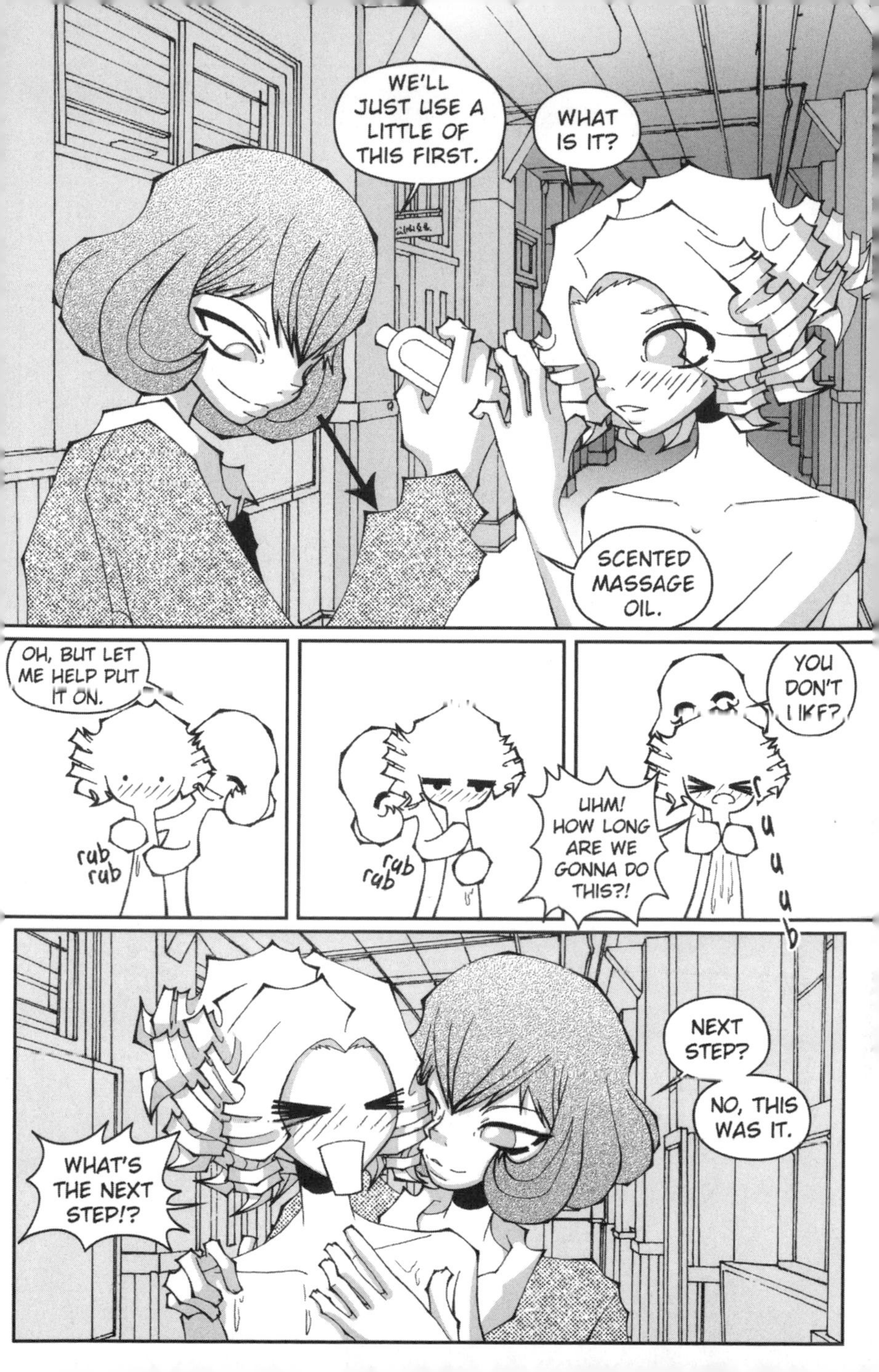
WE'LL JUST USE A LITTLE OF THIS FIRST.
WHAT IS IT?
SCENTED MASSAGE OIL.
OH, BUT LET ME HELP PUT IT ON.
rub rub
rub rub
UHM! HOW LONG ARE WE GONNA DO THIS?!
YOU DON'T LIKE?
uuub
NEXT STEP?
NO, THIS WAS IT.
WHAT'S THE NEXT STEP!?

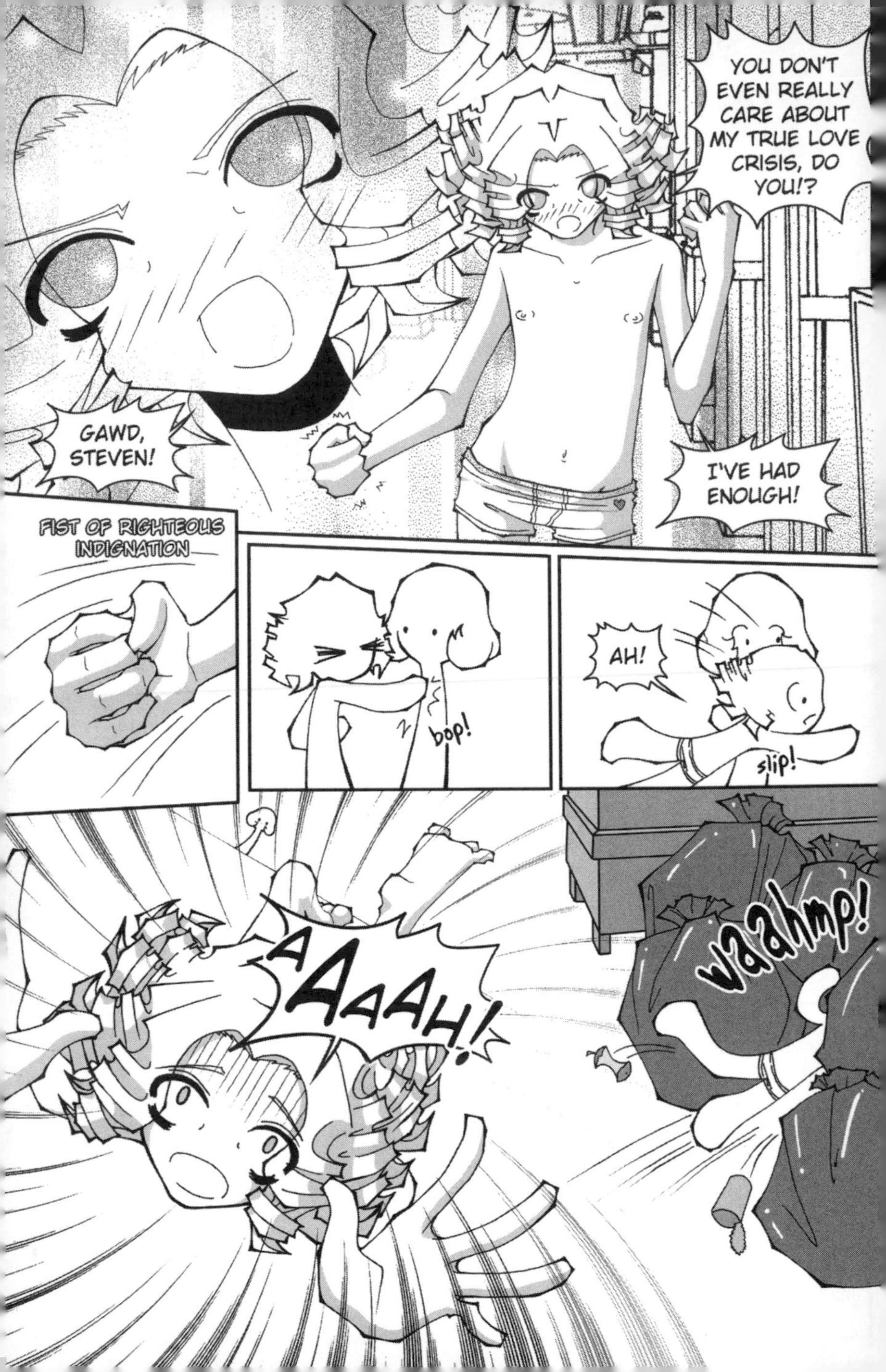
YOU DON'T EVEN REALLY CARE ABOUT MY TRUE LOVE CRISIS, DO YOU!?
GAWD, STEVEN!
I'VE HAD ENOUGH!
FIST OF RIGHTEOUS INDIGNATION
bop!
AH!
slip!
AAAAH!
vaahmp!

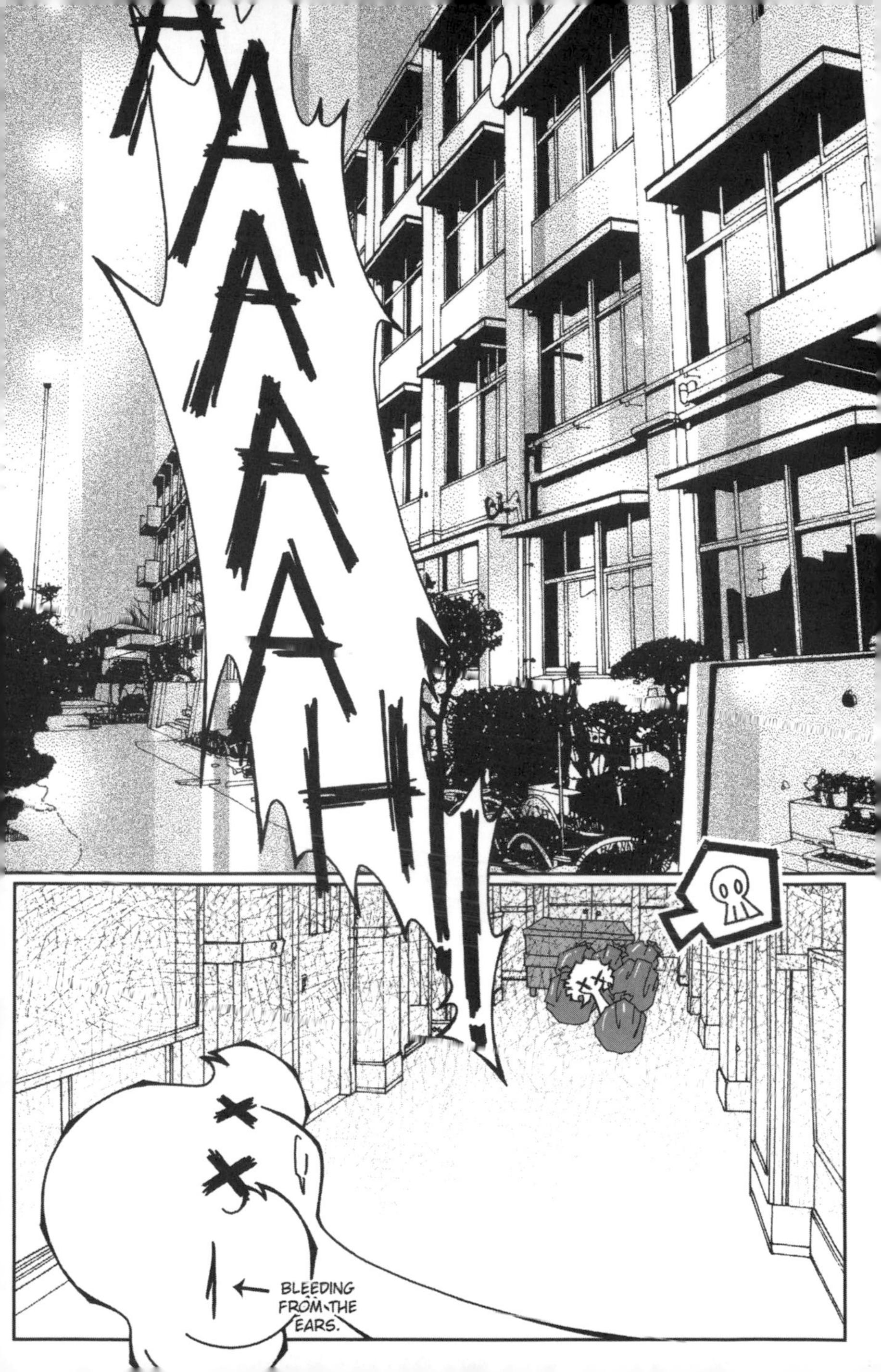
AAAAAAAH!!
BLEEDING FROM THE EARS.

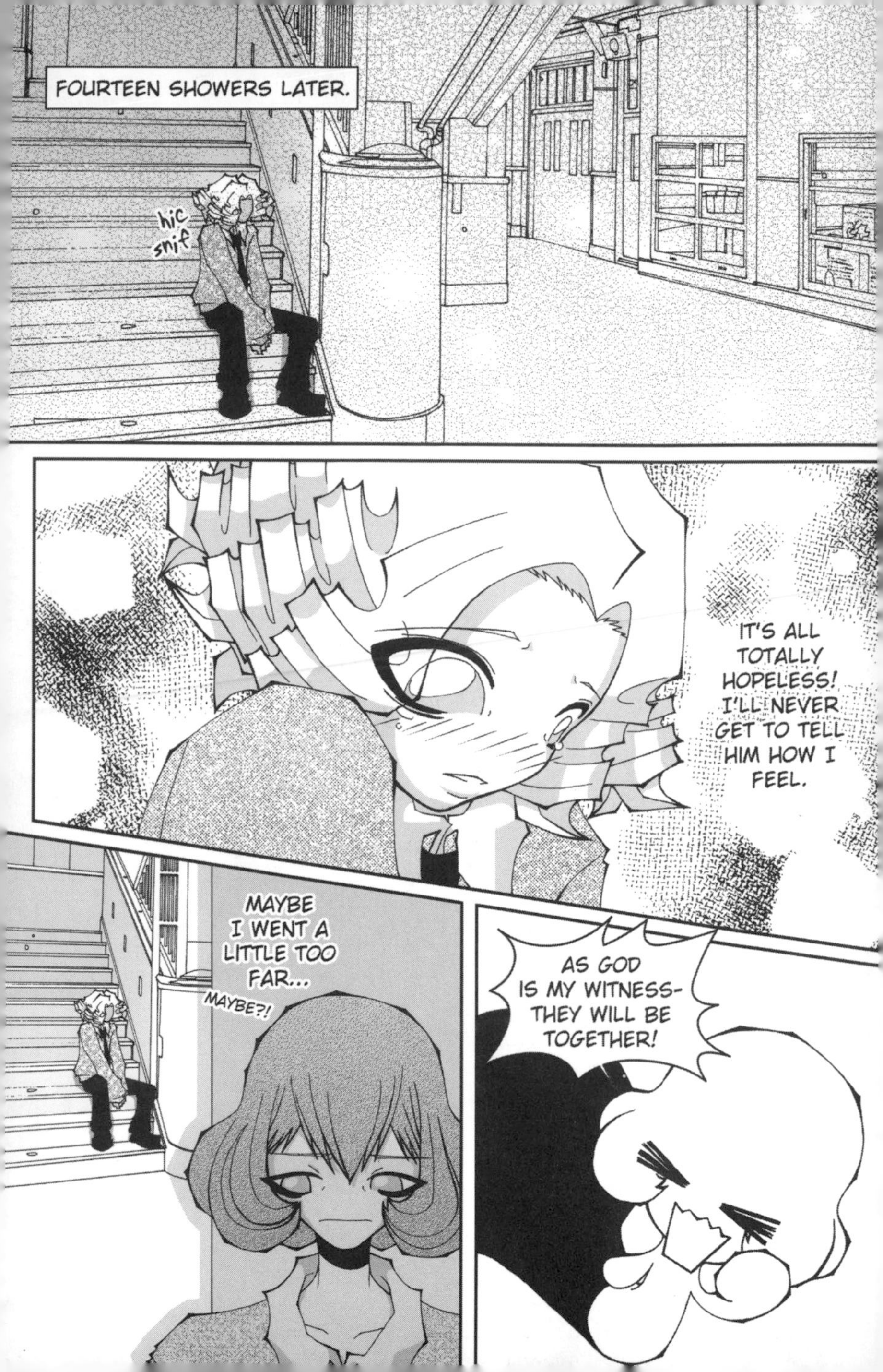
FOURTEEN SHOWERS LATER.
hic snif
IT'S ALL TOTALLY HOPELESS! I'LL NEVER GET TO TELL HIM HOW I FEEL.
AS GOD IS MY WITNESS- THEY WILL BE TOGETHER!
MAYBE I WENT A LITTLE TOO FAR...
MAYBE?!

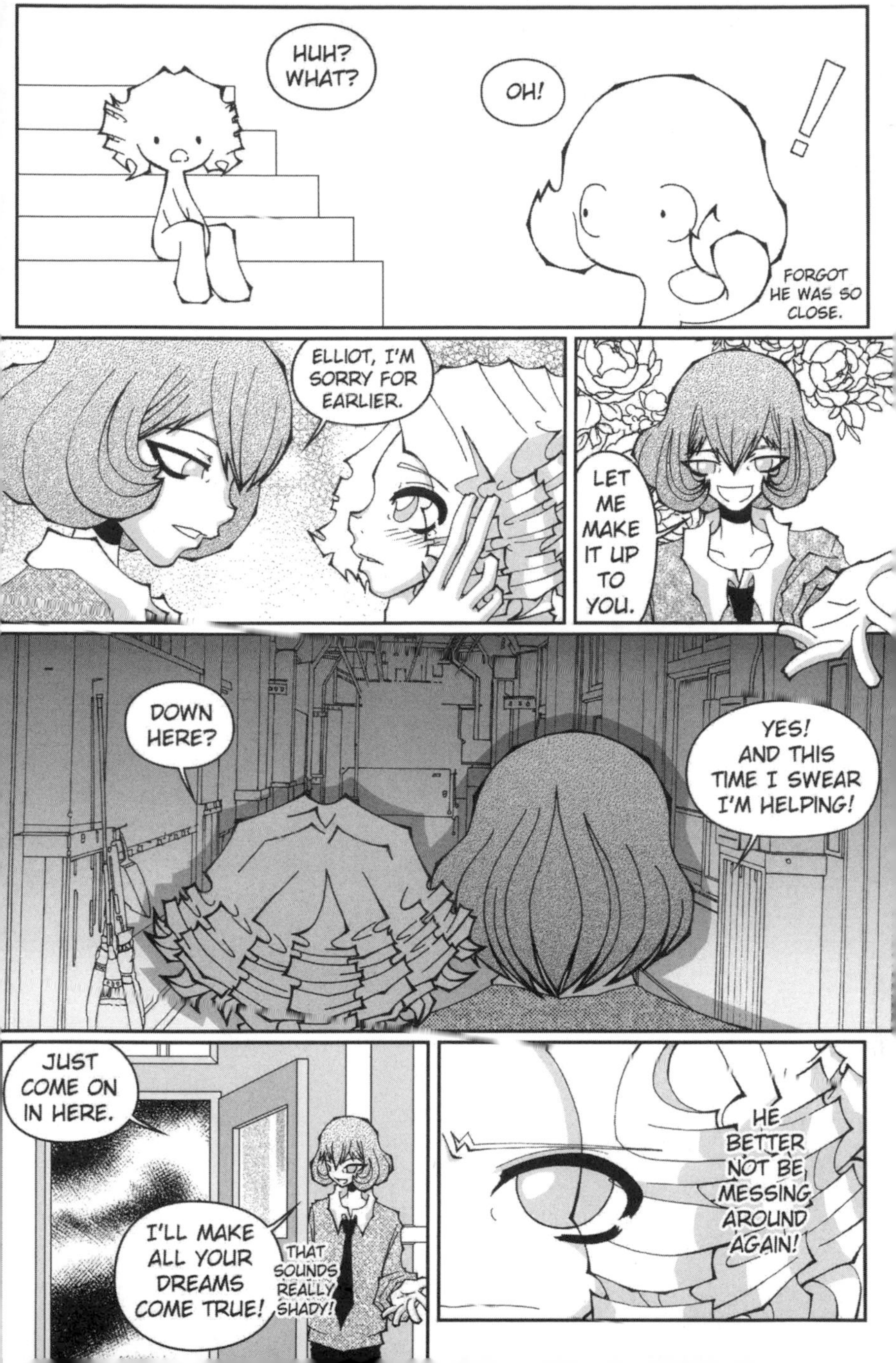
HUH? WHAT?
OH!
!
FORGOT HE WAS SO CLOSE.
ELLIOT, I'M SORRY FOR EARLIER.
LET ME MAKE IT UP TO YOU.
DOWN HERE?
YES! AND THIS TIME I SWEAR I'M HELPING!
JUST COME ON IN HERE.
I'LL MAKE ALL YOUR DREAMS COME TRUE!
THAT SOUNDS REALLY SHADY!
HE BETTER NOT BE MESSING AROUND AGAIN!

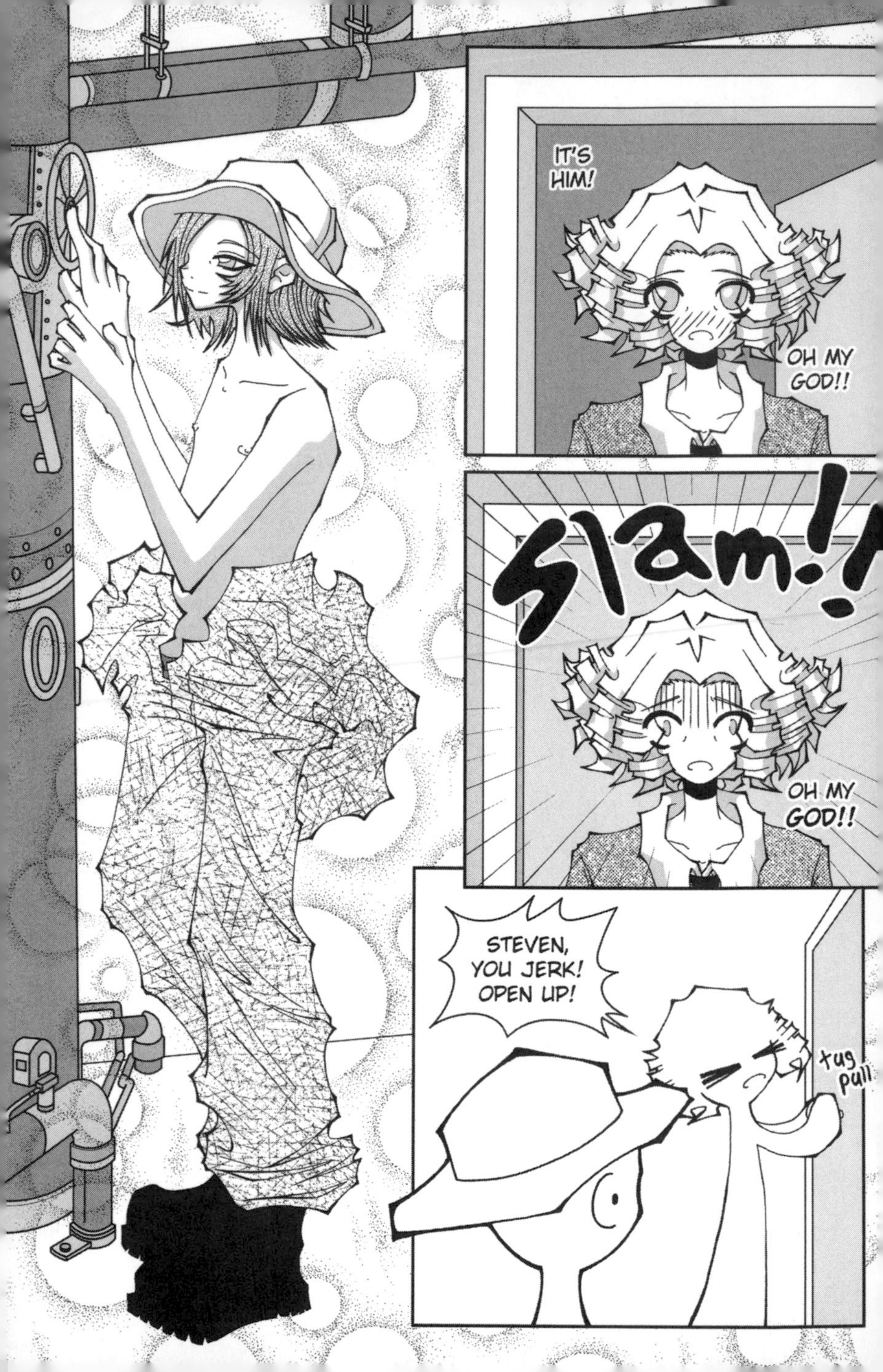
IT'S HIM!
OH MY GOD!!
SLAM!!
OH MY GOD!!
STEVEN, YOU JERK! OPEN UP!
tug
pull

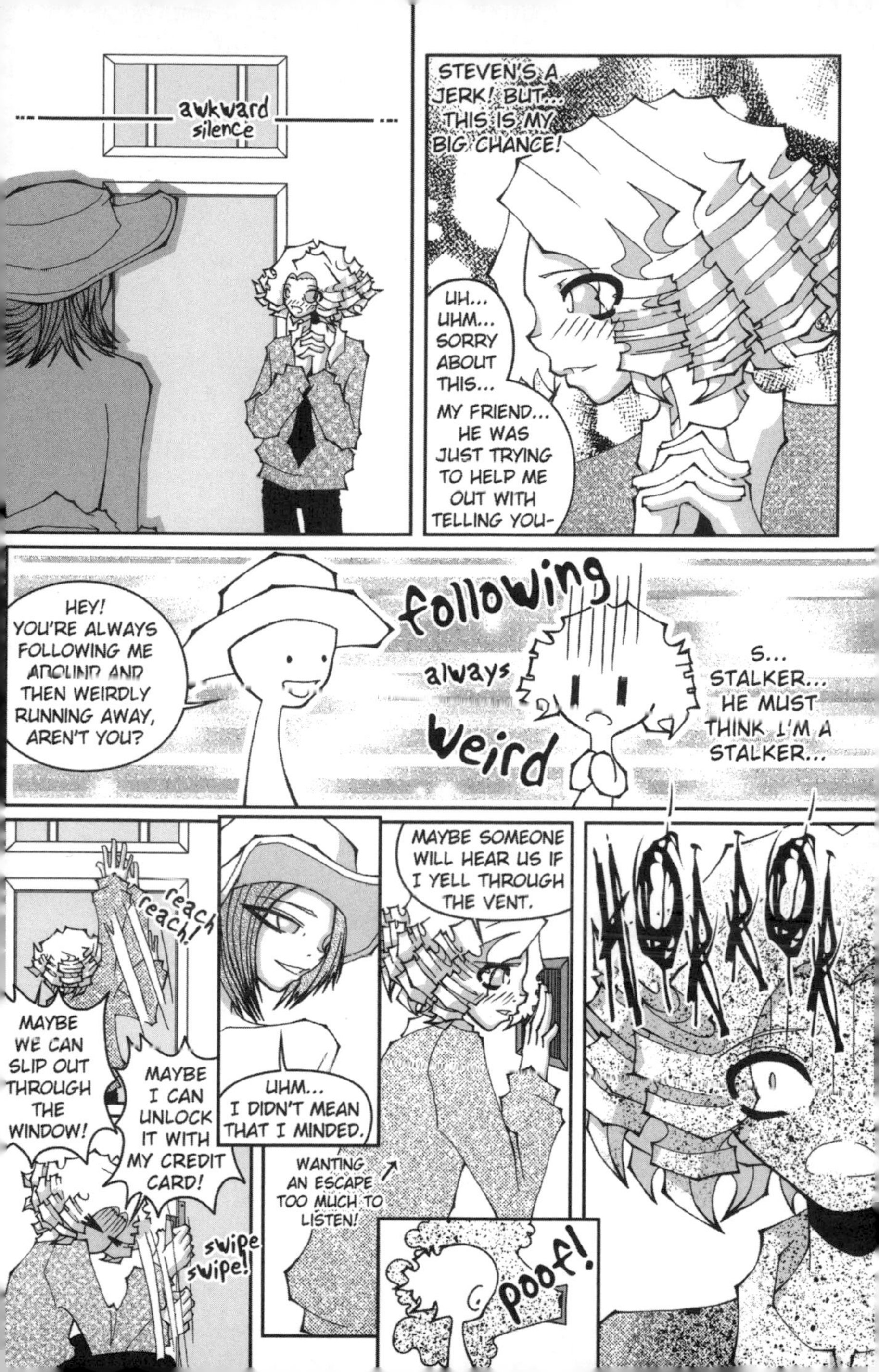
... awkward silence ...
STEVEN'S A JERK! BUT... THIS IS MY BIG CHANCE!
UH... UHM... SORRY ABOUT THIS...
MY FRIEND... HE WAS JUST TRYING TO HELP ME OUT WITH TELLING YOU-
HEY! YOU'RE ALWAYS FOLLOWING ME AROUND AND THEN WEIRDLY RUNNING AWAY, AREN'T YOU?
following
always
weird
S... STALKER... HE MUST THINK I'M A STALKER...
reach reach!
MAYBE WE CAN SLIP OUT THROUGH THE WINDOW!
MAYBE I CAN UNLOCK IT WITH MY CREDIT CARD!
swipe swipe!
UHM... I DIDN'T MEAN THAT I MINDED.
MAYBE SOMEONE WILL HEAR US IF I YELL THROUGH THE VENT.
WANTING AN ESCAPE TOO MUCH TO LISTEN!
poof!
HORROR

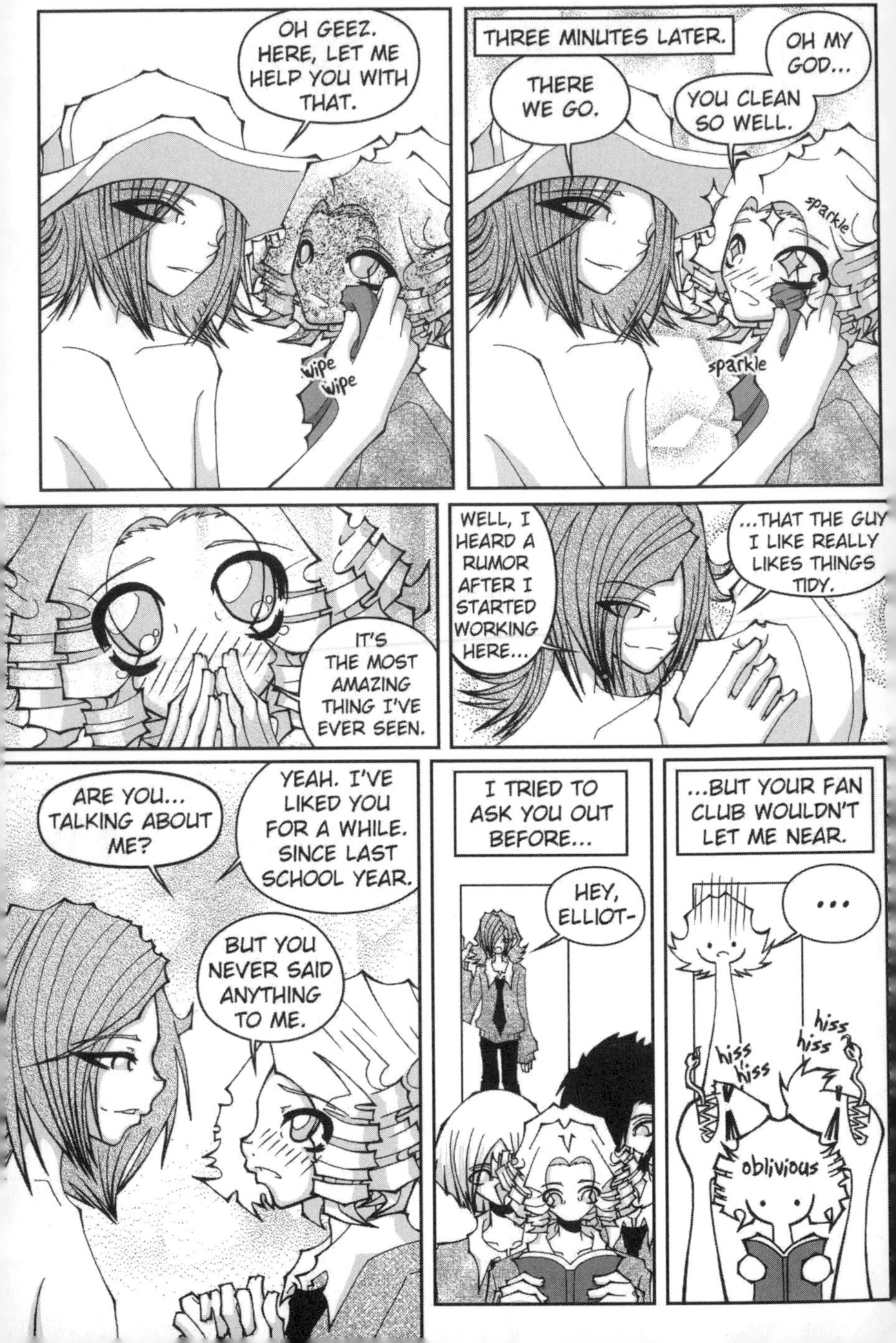
OH GEEZ. HERE, LET ME HELP YOU WITH THAT.
wipe wipe
THREE MINUTES LATER.
THERE WE GO.
OH MY GOD...
YOU CLEAN SO WELL.
sparkle
sparkle
IT'S THE MOST AMAZING THING I'VE EVER SEEN.
WELL, I HEARD A RUMOR AFTER I STARTED WORKING HERE...
...THAT THE GUY I LIKE REALLY LIKES THINGS TIDY.
ARE YOU... TALKING ABOUT ME?
YEAH. I'VE LIKED YOU FOR A WHILE. SINCE LAST SCHOOL YEAR.
BUT YOU NEVER SAID ANYTHING TO ME.
I TRIED TO ASK YOU OUT BEFORE...
HEY, ELLIOT-
...BUT YOUR FAN CLUB WOULDN'T LET ME NEAR.
...
hiss hiss
hiss hiss
oblivious

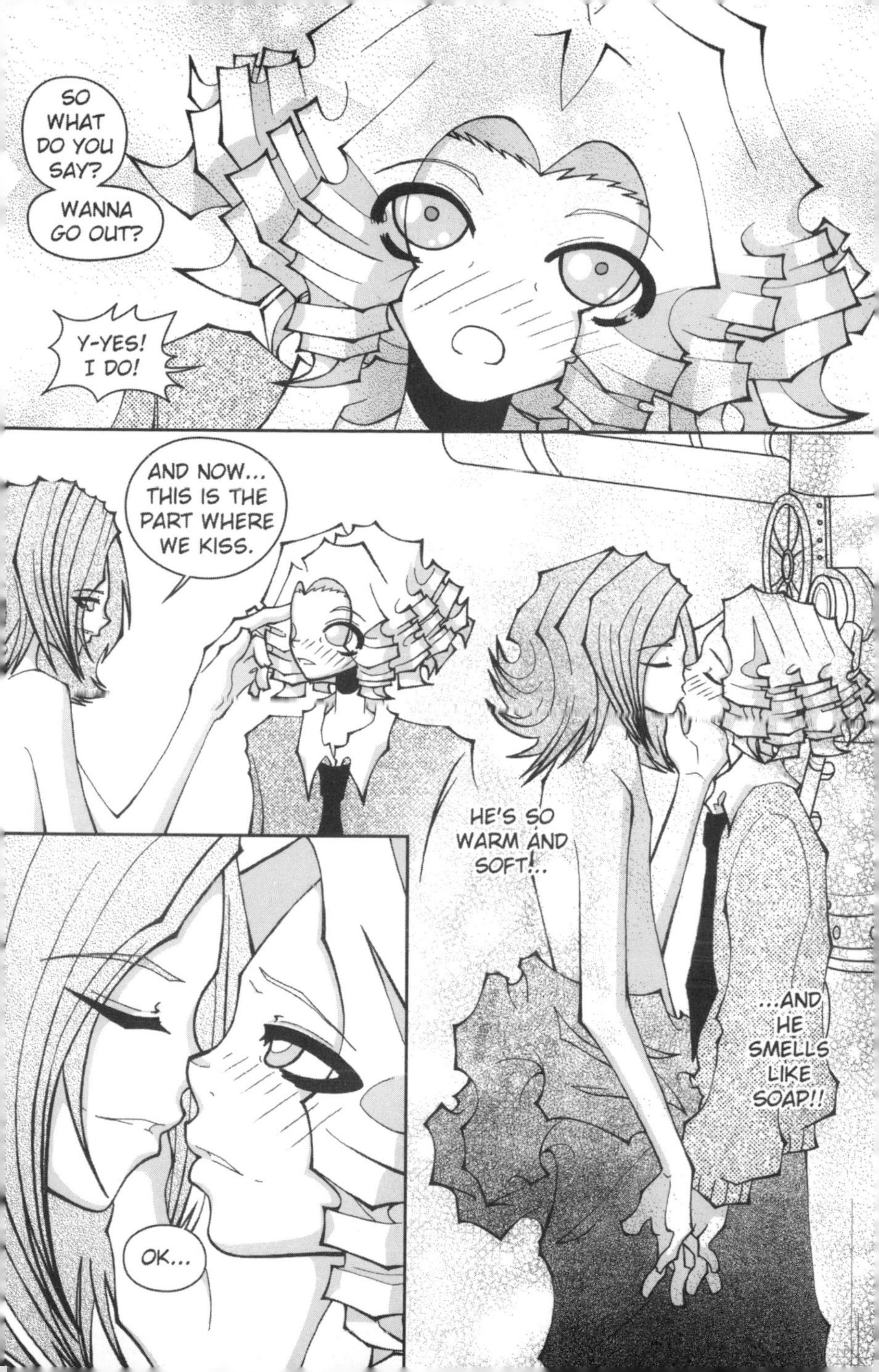
SO WHAT DO YOU SAY?
WANNA GO OUT?
Y-YES! I DO!
AND NOW... THIS IS THE PART WHERE WE KISS.
OK...
HE'S SO WARM AND SOFT!...
...AND HE SMELLS LIKE SOAP!!

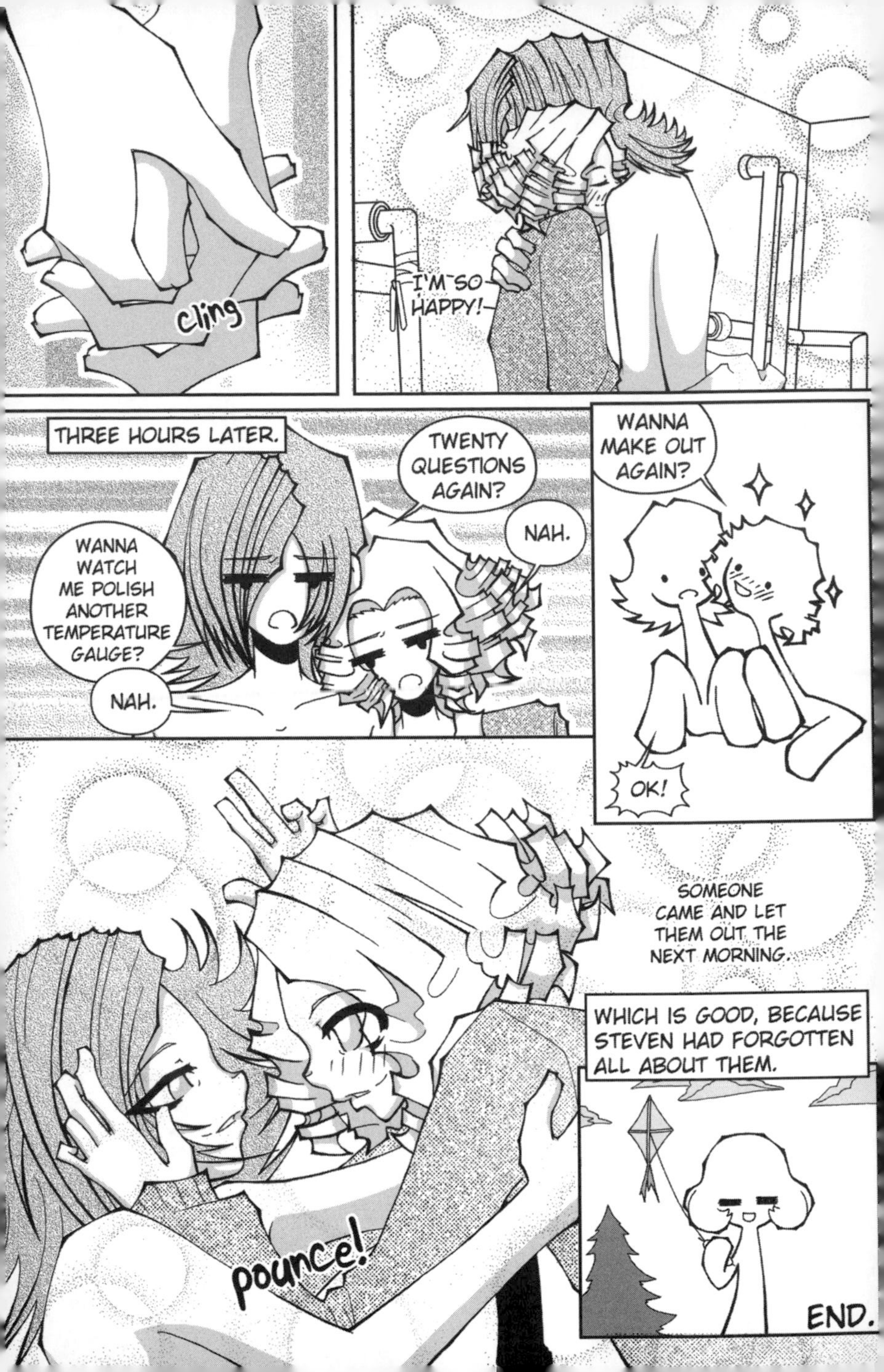
cling
I'M SO HAPPY!
THREE HOURS LATER.
TWENTY QUESTIONS AGAIN?
NAH.
WANNA WATCH ME POLISH ANOTHER TEMPERATURE GAUGE?
NAH.
WANNA MAKE OUT AGAIN?
OK!
pounce!
SOMEONE CAME AND LET THEM OUT THE NEXT MORNING.
WHICH IS GOOD, BECAUSE STEVEN HAD FORGOTTEN ALL ABOUT THEM.
END.

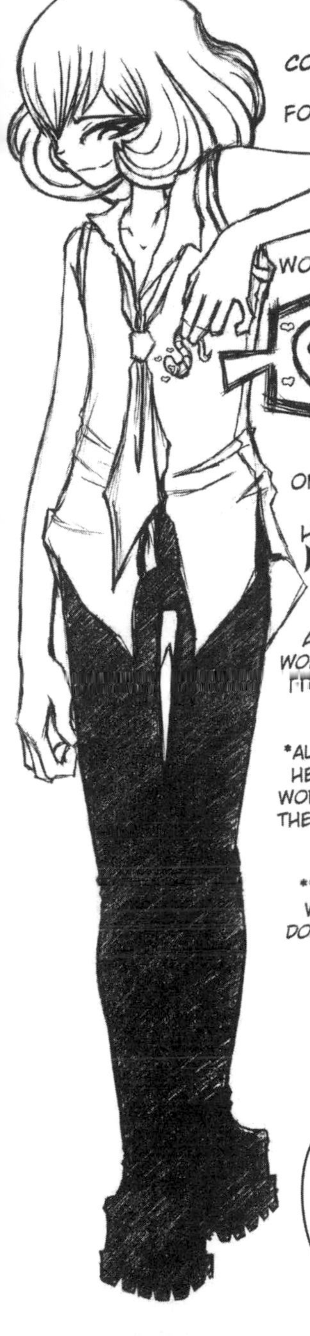

HELLO!

THIS IS LAILA, THE ARTIST FOR THE '***OBSESSIVE COMPULSIVE DESIRE***' STORY YOU HOPEFULLY JUST READ! IF YOU DON'T KNOW WHAT O.C.D. STANDS FOR, IT'S '*OBSESSIVE COMPULSIVE DISORDER.*' IT'S SORT OF LIKE WHEN YOU DO SOMETHING OBSESSIVELY AND REPEATEDLY AND IN THIS STORY'S CASE, ELLIOT IS A LITTLE OBSESSIVE COMPULSIVE WITH CLEANLINESS, HENCE THE PLAY ON THE TITLE! WOO, I HOPE THAT MAKES SENSE! I THOUGHT IT WAS FUNNY WHEN MY MANAGING EDITOR SUGGESTED THE NAME!!

I'VE DONE A FEW SHORT STORIES FOR YAOI PRESS LTD IN THE PAST BUT THIS IS MY FIRST COMEDY PIECE AND I'M SO HAPPY IT CAN BE IN SUCH A CUTE BOOK AS THIS ONE! I LOVE ALL THE OTHER STORIES IN HERE AND THE MAIN ONE, '***SURGE***' IS THE CUTEST THING! I HOPE YOU ALL ENJOY THIS BOOK AS MUCH AS I DO!

I DREW STEVEN AND THE WORM FOR THE EDITOR, XAVIERA! SHE SAW THE ROUGHS OF THE STORY AND ALL SHE KEPT SAYING WAS: "*BUT WHAT ABOUT THE POOR WORM!?*" AND ALSO SHE WAS SAD STEVEN DIDN'T GET A BOY-FRIEND, SO HERE YOU GO!! STEVEN AND THE WORM CAN BE-COME FRIENDS! <3

*ALSO, SPECIAL THANKS TO MY MANAGING EDITOR YAMILA FOR HELPING WITH MY BAD DIALOGUE BUT ALSO THE WONDERFUL WORM IDEA! THAT WAS TOTALLY HER GAG SO I TRIED TO MAKE THE WORM VERY FUNNY AND DREW A BEAUTIFUL AND DRAMATIC SPLASH PAGE JUST FOR HER!! <3<3

**ALSO LAST THANKS TO MY FRIENDS WHO HAD TO PUT UP WITH ME REPEATEDLY ASKING "*HEY, IS THIS FUNNY!? HEY DOES THIS MAKE SENSE!?*" THAT'S TO YOU, MY HONEY HONEY HONEY AND ALSO TO JI-GRANNY! <3

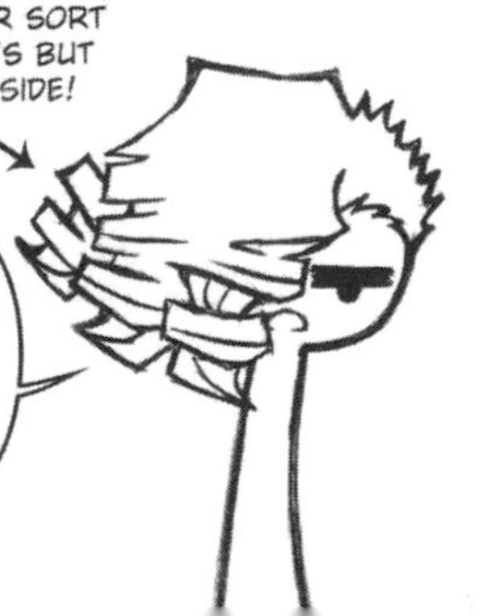
THIS IS SUPPOSED TO BE ME! I HAVE HAIR SORT OF LIKE ELLIOT'S BUT ONLY ON ONE SIDE!
I DID THIS STORY DURING A VERY BUSY TWO MONTH PERIOD FILLED WITH CONS AND TRIPS OUT OF STATE AND SO MUCH FLYING! I LOVED DOING IT BUT I'M SO GLAD TO BE DONE BECAUSE NOW I CAN GO FALL INTO A COMA FOR A DAY OR TWO!

Available Now!

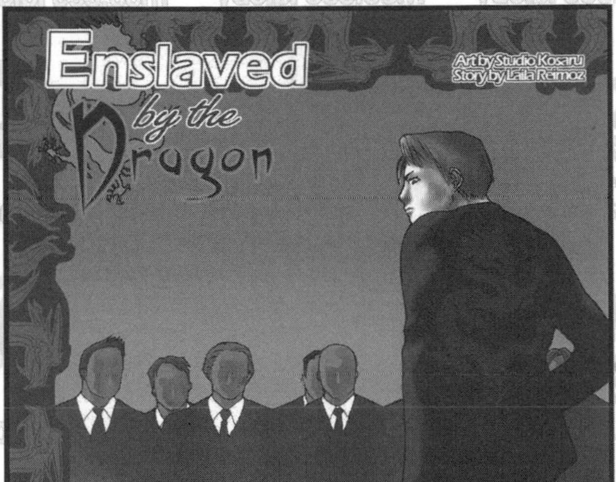
Enslaved
by the
Dragon
Art by Studio Kosaru
Story by Laila Reimoz
A YAOI MANGA

Enslaved by the Dragon

by Studio Kosaru and Laila Reimoz

The street punk Noah pick-pockets a crime lord right before he has a meeting with an embassy official. When crime lord Tokihiko can't produce his ID he misses the important meeting. Tokihiko captures Noah to torture him to death. When he sees how beautiful Noah is he makes him his slave instead.

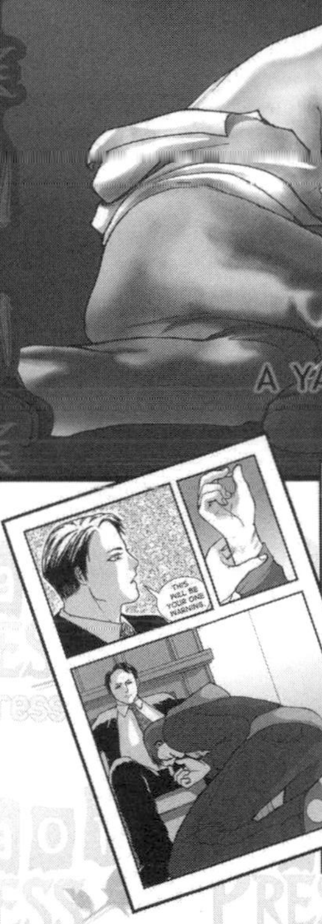
THIS WILL BE YOUR ONE WARNING.

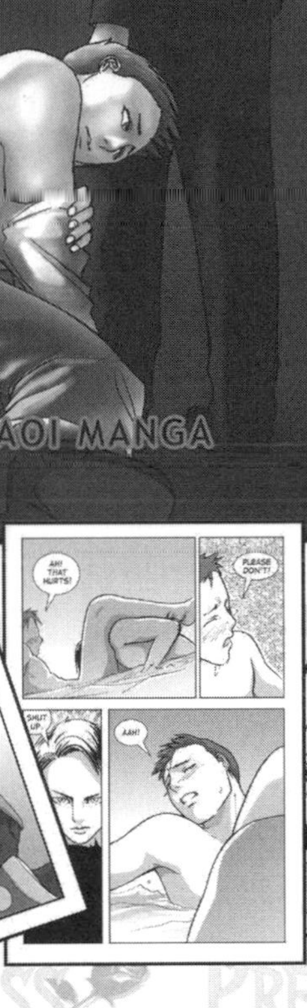
AH! THAT HURTS!
PLEASE DON'T!
SHUT UP.
AAH!

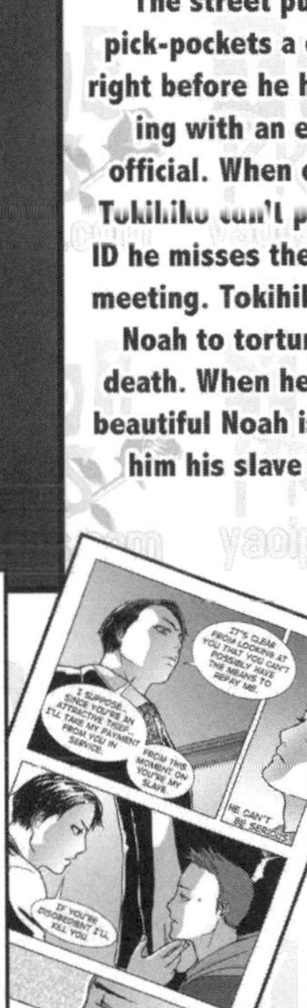
IT'S CLEAR FROM LOOKING AT YOU THAT YOU CAN'T POSSIBLY HAVE THE MEANS TO REPAY ME.
I SUPPOSE... SINCE YOU'RE AN ATTRACTIVE THIEF... I'LL TAKE MY PAYMENT FROM YOU IN SERVICE.
FROM THIS MOMENT ON YOU'RE MY SLAVE.
HE CAN'T BE SERIOUS.
IF YOU'RE DISOBEDIENT I'LL KILL YOU.

Available Now!

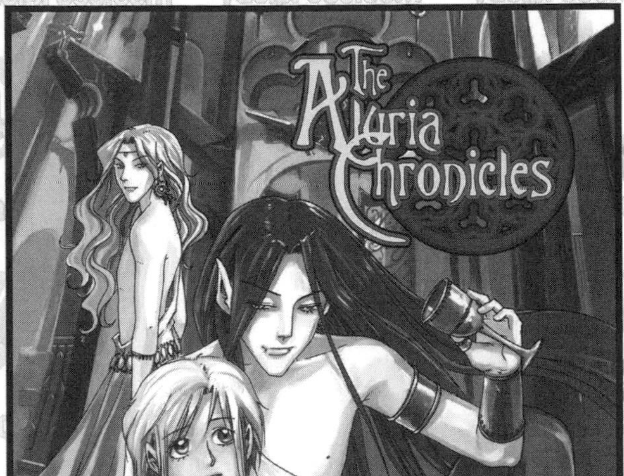
The Aluria Chronicles

The Aluria Chronicles

by Yishan Li and Calissa Leigh

Gin's an abused harem boy who gets sacrificed to a demon. The demon brings him to the mystical land of Aluria where two sexy vampires, one evil and one kind, decide they both want him as thier lover.

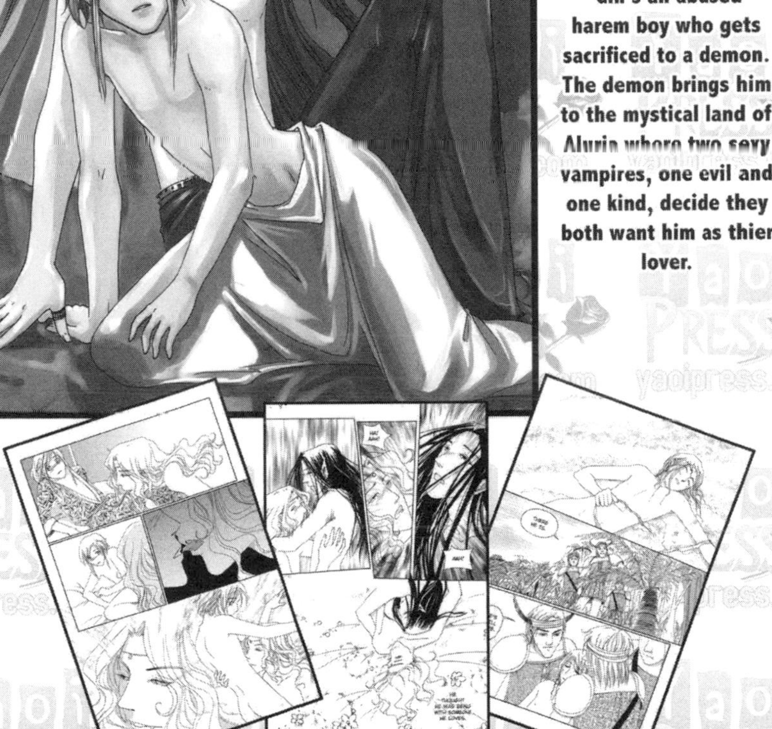

Schoolboy Crush

STORY BY YAMILA ABRAHAM
ART BY STUDIO KOSARU, LETTERS BY LAILA REIMOZ
EDITED BY XAVIERA PALLARS

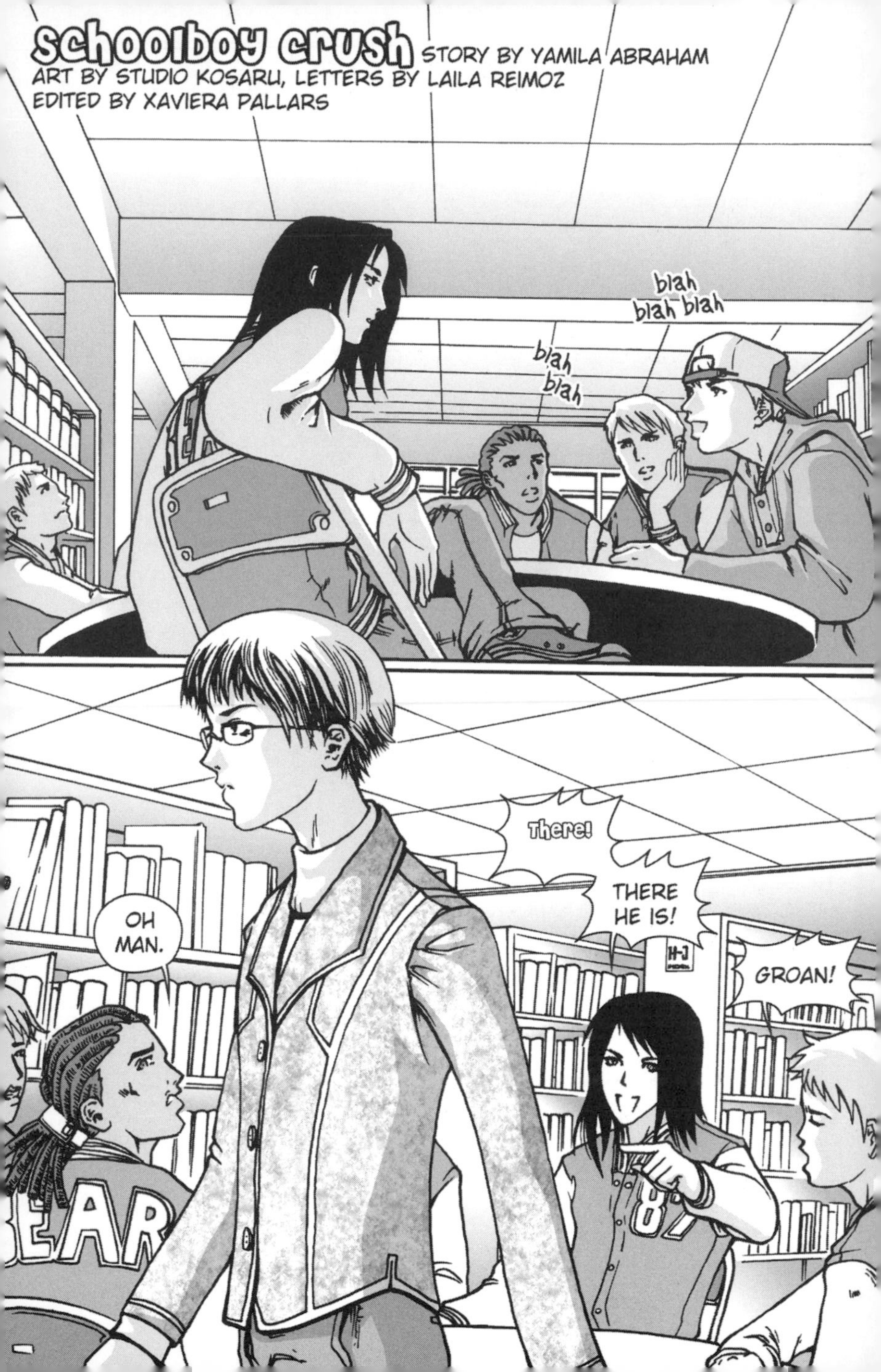
blah
blah
blah
blah blah
There!
THERE HE IS!
H-J
OH MAN.
GROAN!

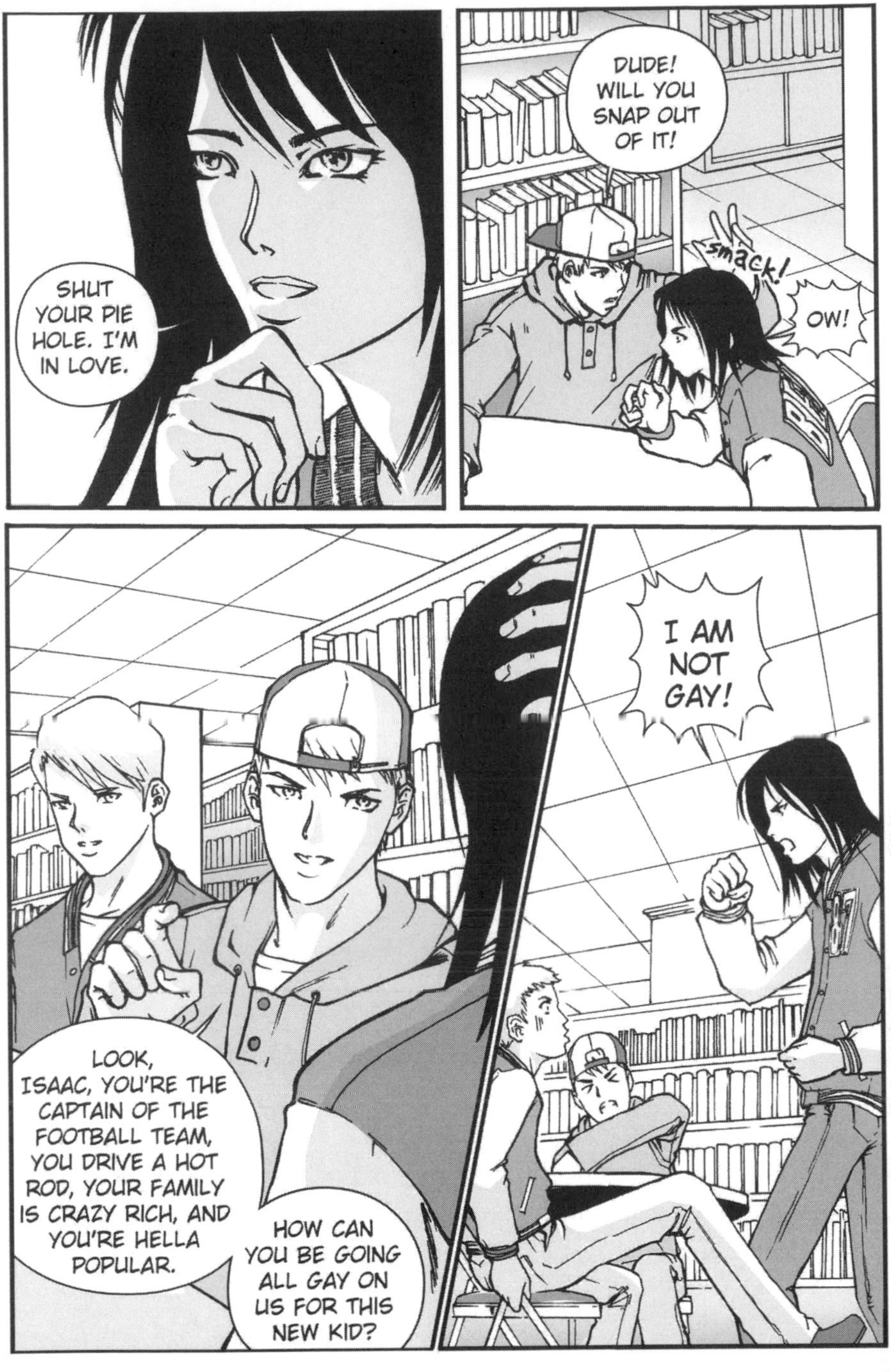
SHUT YOUR PIE HOLE. I'M IN LOVE.
DUDE! WILL YOU SNAP OUT OF IT!
smack!
OW!
LOOK, ISAAC, YOU'RE THE CAPTAIN OF THE FOOTBALL TEAM, YOU DRIVE A HOT ROD, YOUR FAMILY IS CRAZY RICH, AND YOU'RE HELLA POPULAR.
HOW CAN YOU BE GOING ALL GAY ON US FOR THIS NEW KID?
I AM NOT GAY!

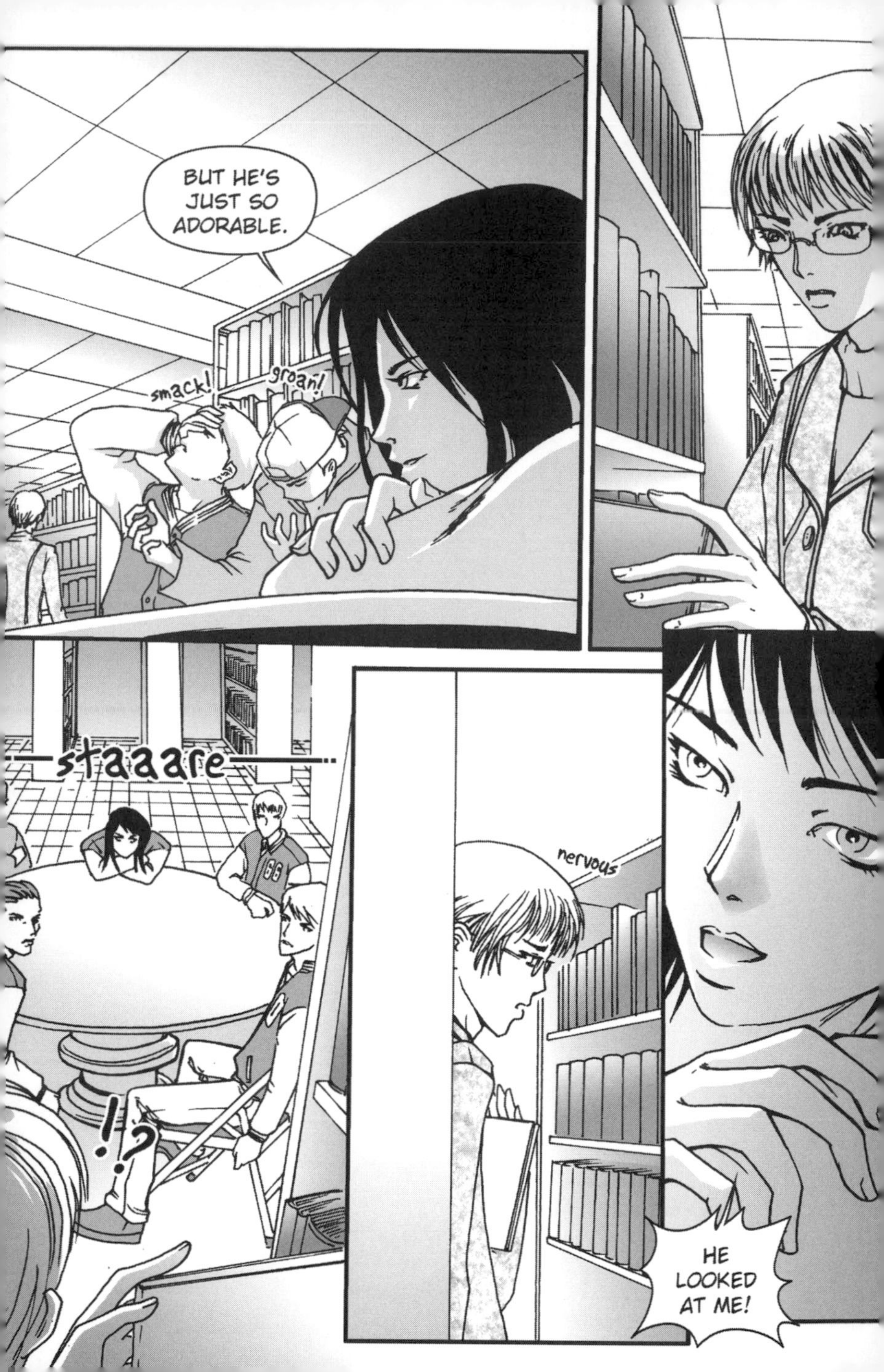
BUT HE'S JUST SO ADORABLE.
smack!
groan!
staaare
!?
nervous
HE LOOKED AT ME!

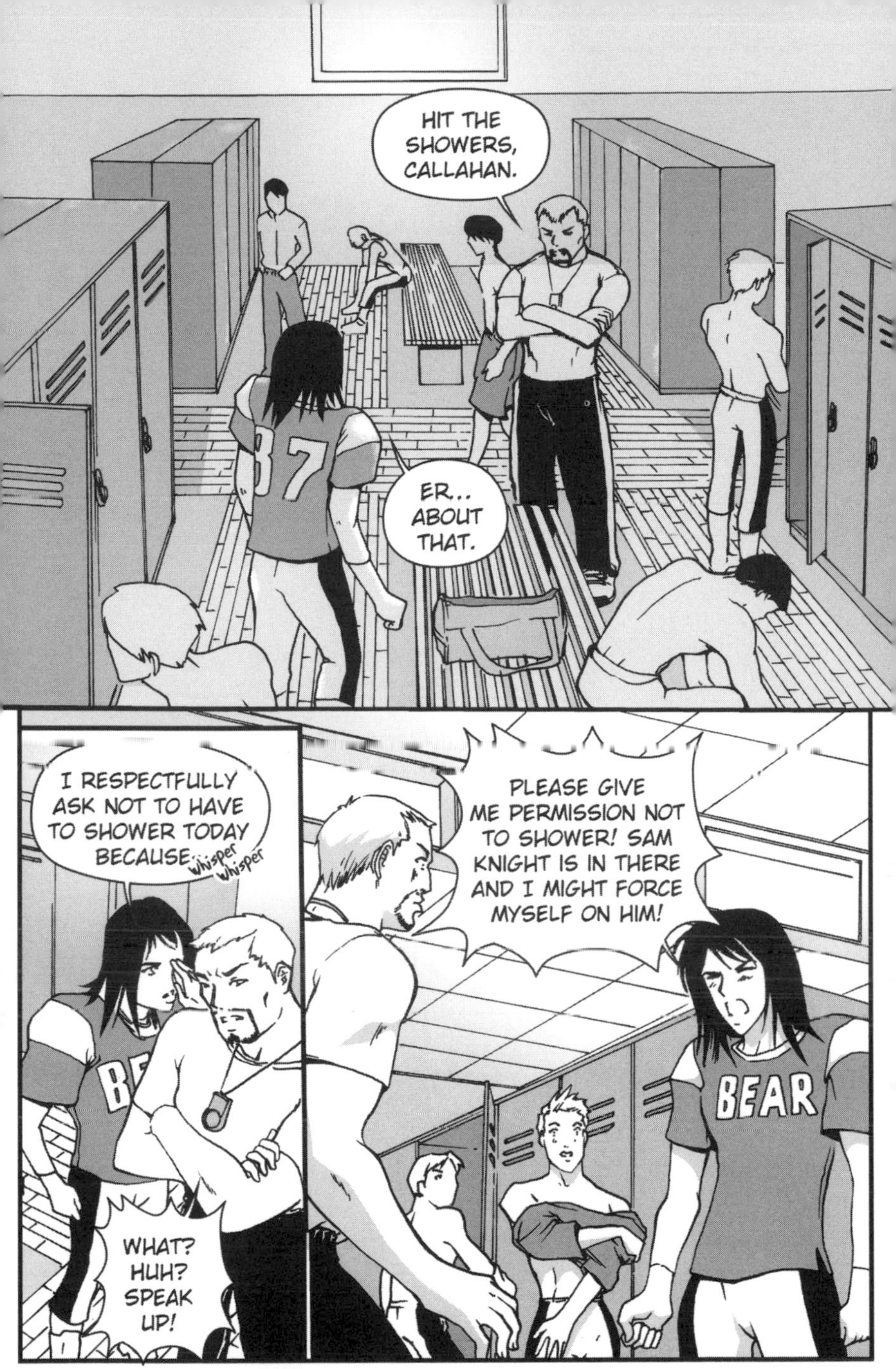
HIT THE SHOWERS, CALLAHAN.
ER... ABOUT THAT.
I RESPECTFULLY ASK NOT TO HAVE TO SHOWER TODAY BECAUSE...
whisper whisper
WHAT? HUH? SPEAK UP!
PLEASE GIVE ME PERMISSION NOT TO SHOWER! SAM KNIGHT IS IN THERE AND I MIGHT FORCE MYSELF ON HIM!
BEAR

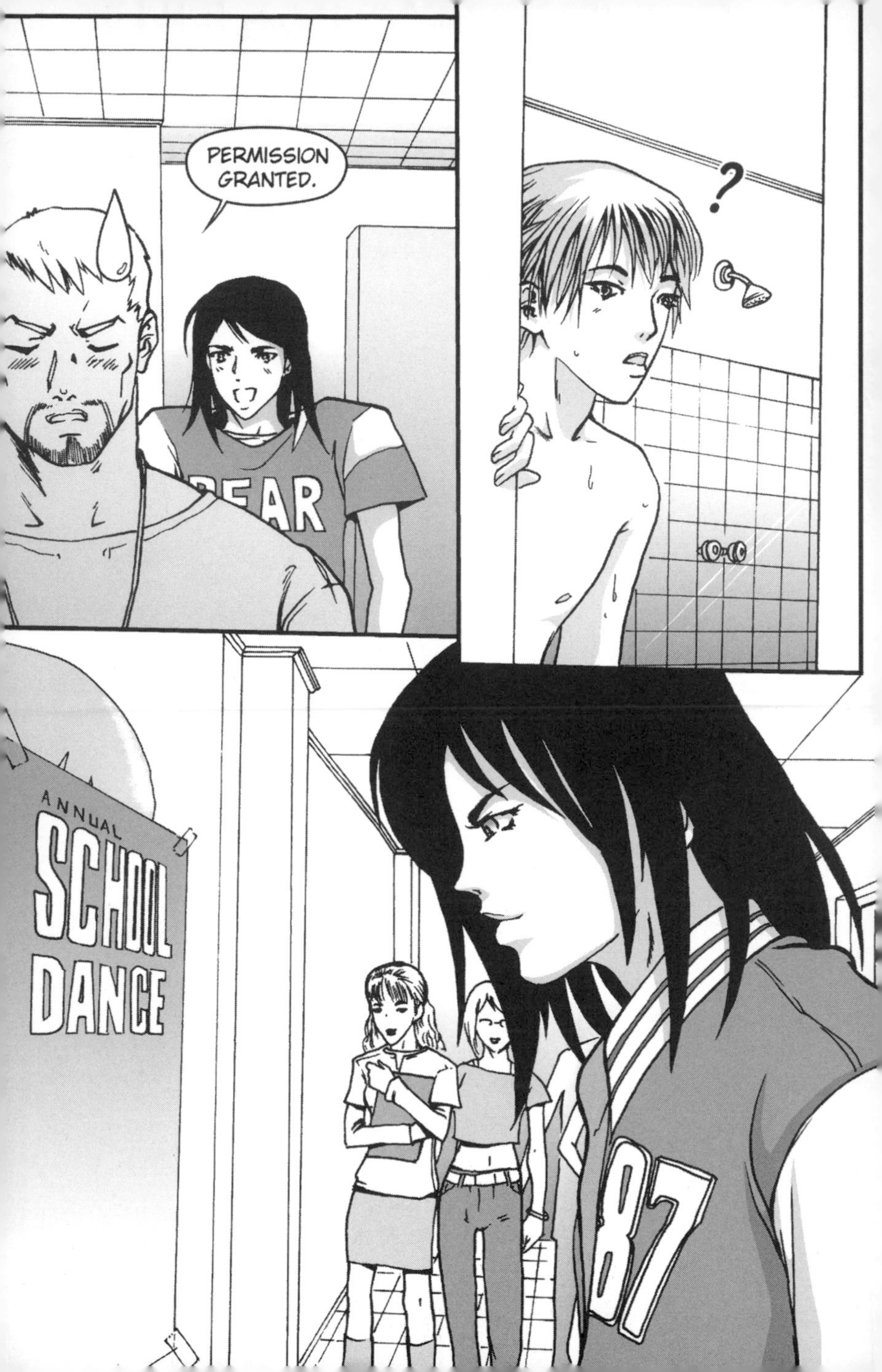
PERMISSION GRANTED.
?
BEAR
ANNUAL SCHOOL DANCE
87

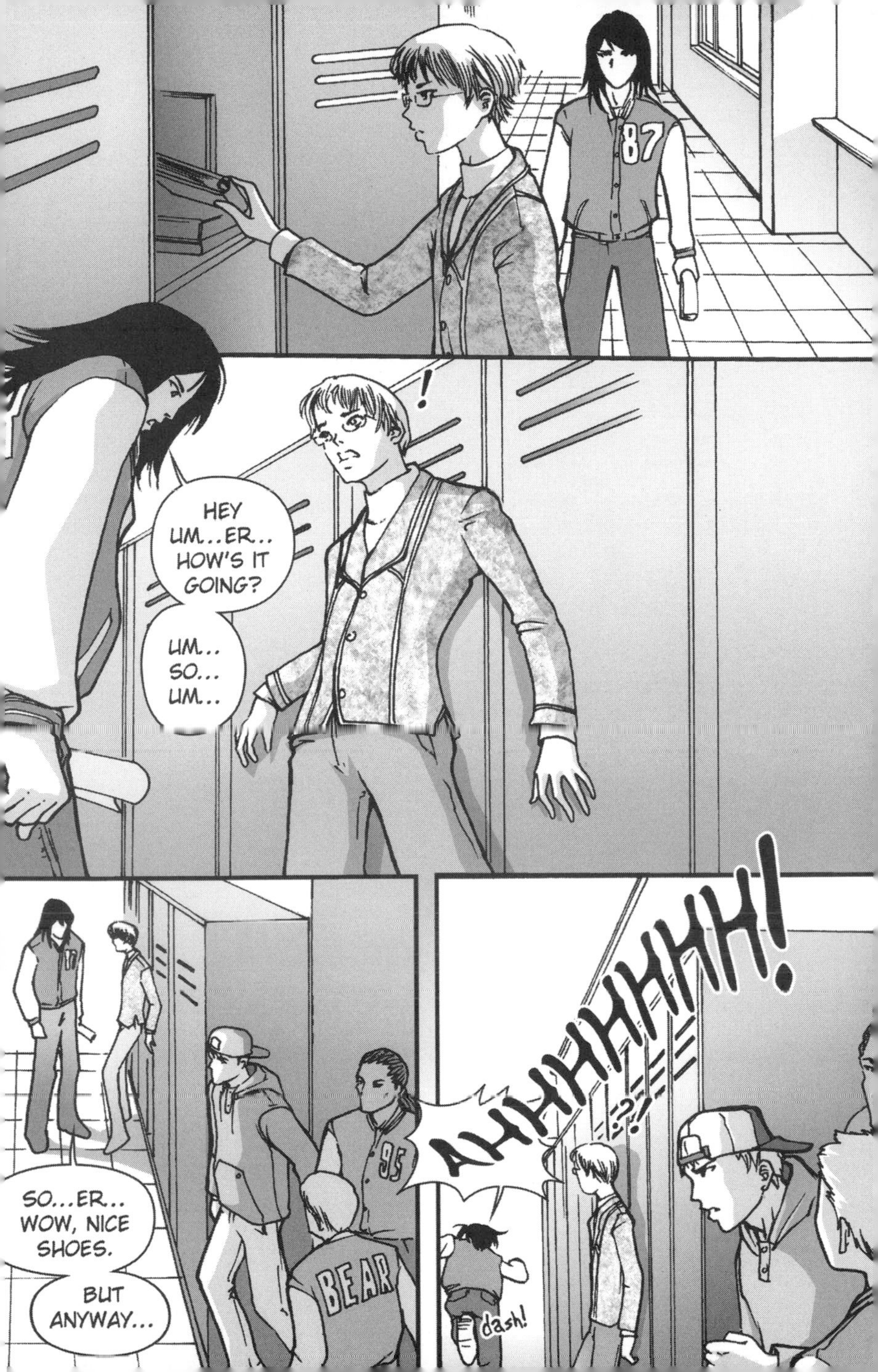

!
HEY UM...ER... HOW'S IT GOING?
UM.. SO... UM..
SO...ER... WOW, NICE SHOES.
BUT ANYWAY...
AHHHHHHHH!
?!
dash!

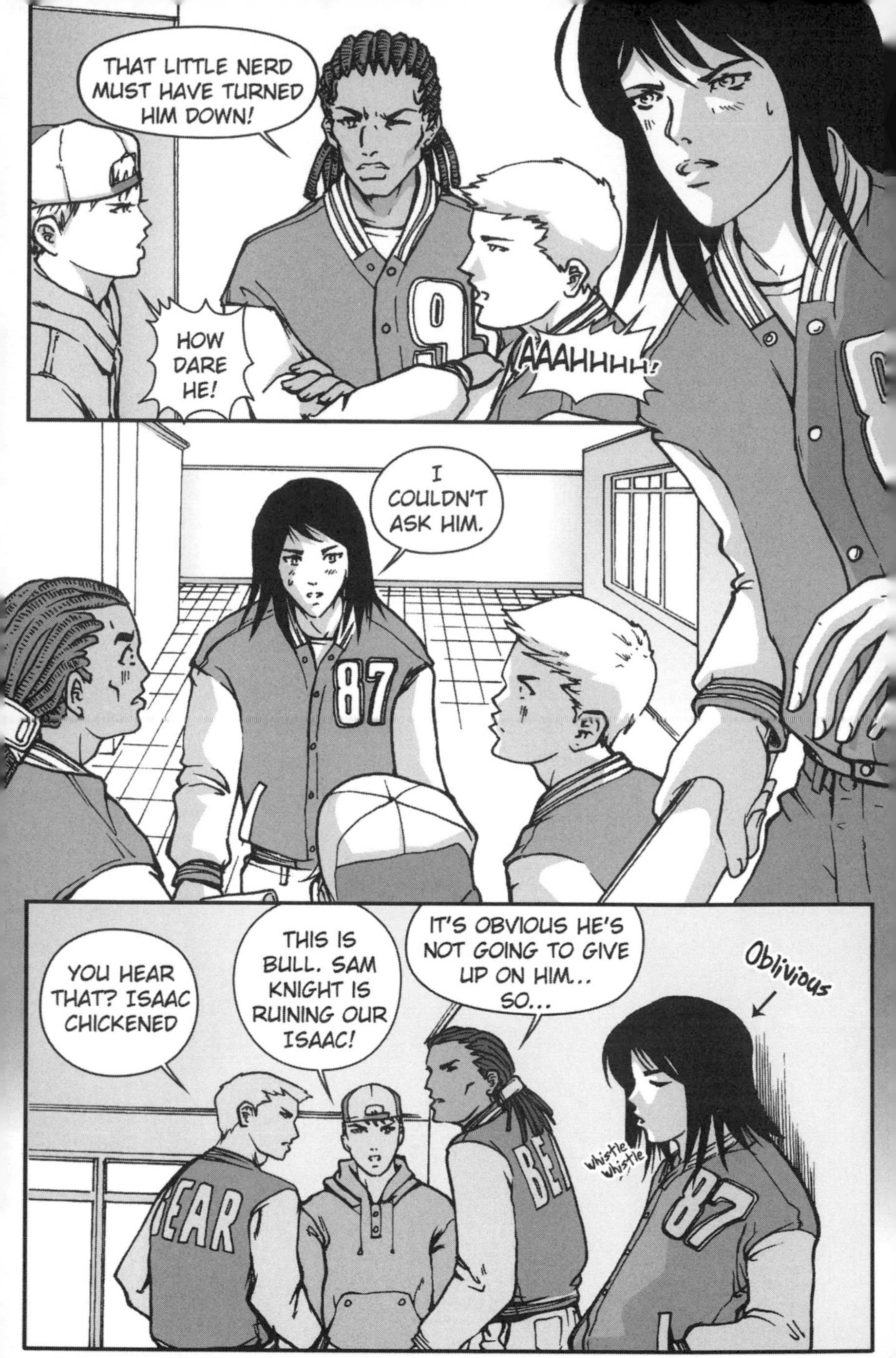
THAT LITTLE NERD MUST HAVE TURNED HIM DOWN!
HOW DARE HE!
AAAHHHH!
I COULDN'T ASK HIM.
YOU HEAR THAT? ISAAC CHICKENED
THIS IS BULL. SAM KNIGHT IS RUINING OUR ISAAC!
IT'S OBVIOUS HE'S NOT GOING TO GIVE UP ON HIM... SO...
Oblivious
whistle whistle

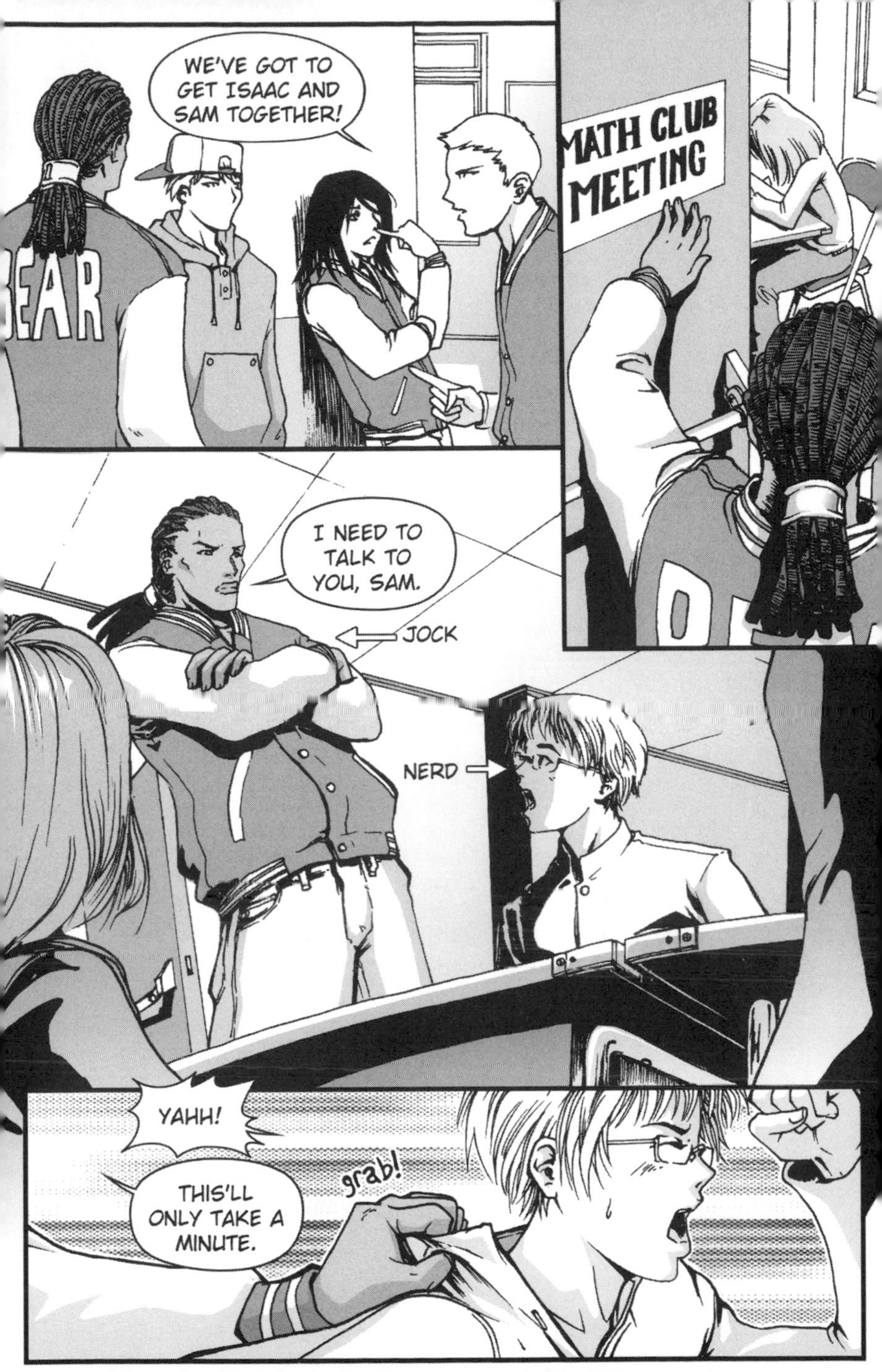
WE'VE GOT TO GET ISAAC AND SAM TOGETHER!
EAR
MATH CLUB MEETING
I NEED TO TALK TO YOU, SAM.
JOCK
NERD
YAHH!
THIS'LL ONLY TAKE A MINUTE.
grab!

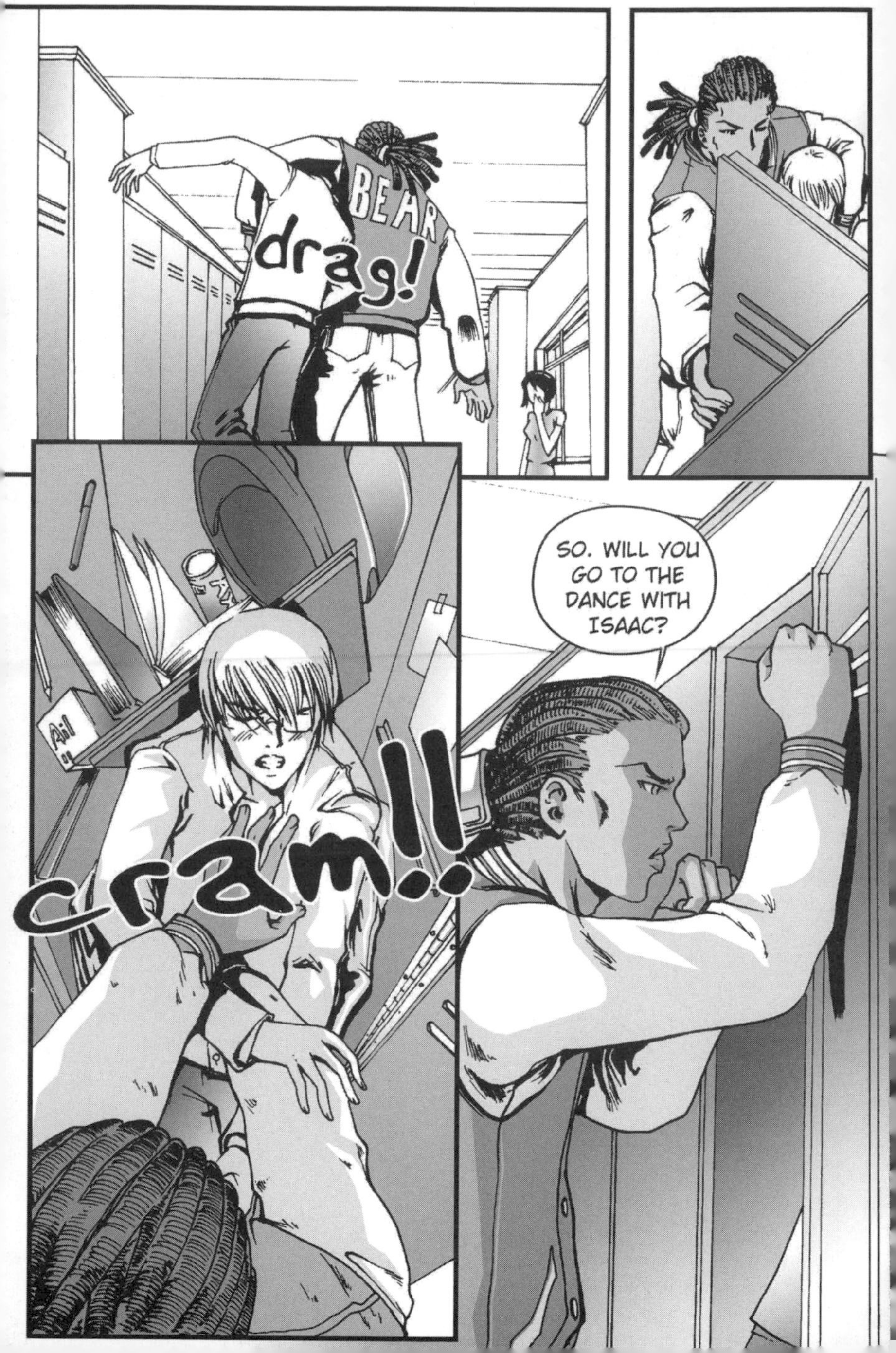
BEAR
drag!
SO. WILL YOU GO TO THE DANCE WITH ISAAC?
cram!!

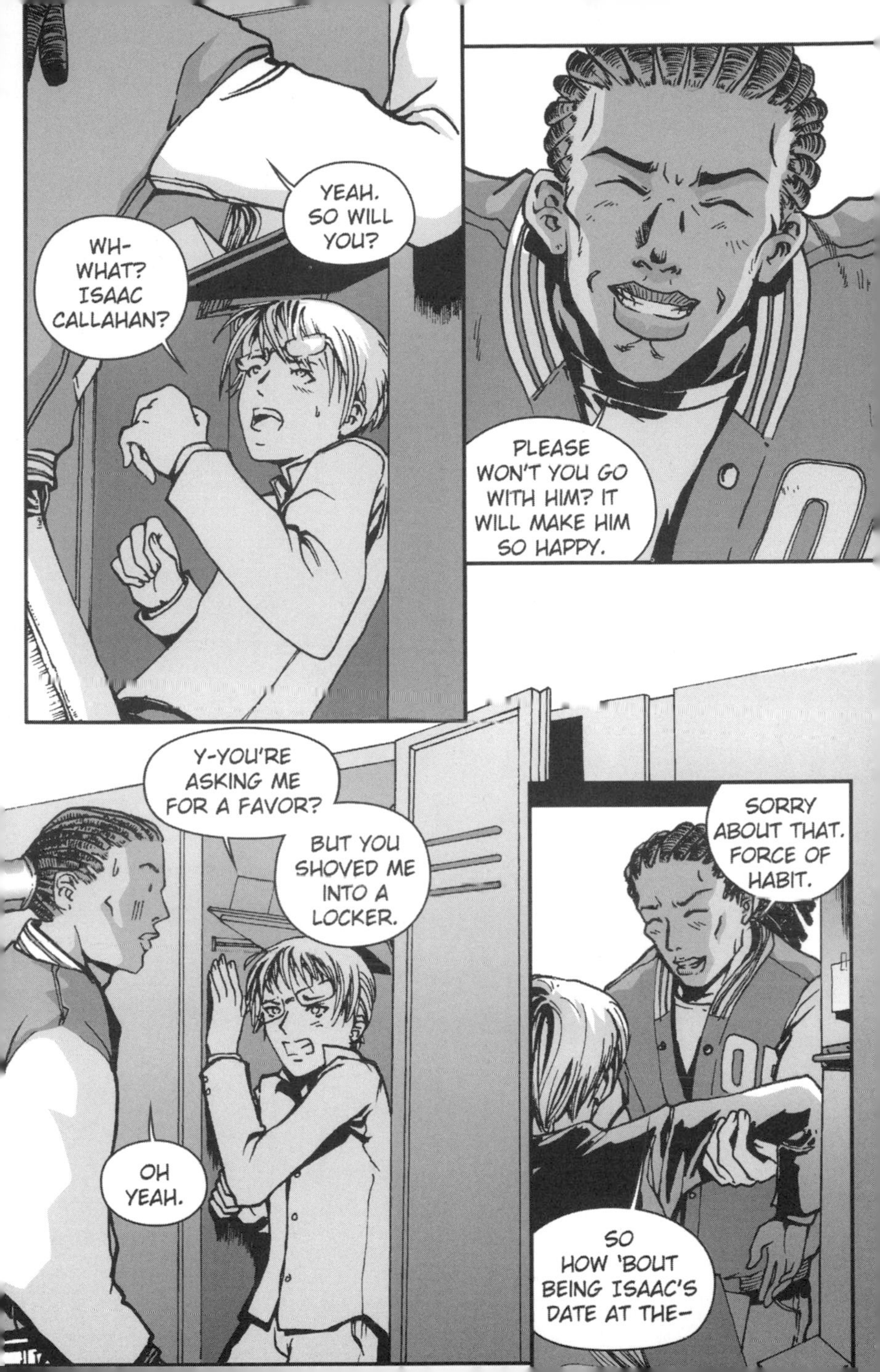
YEAH. SO WILL YOU?
WH- WHAT? ISAAC CALLAHAN?
PLEASE WON'T YOU GO WITH HIM? IT WILL MAKE HIM SO HAPPY.
Y-YOU'RE ASKING ME FOR A FAVOR?
BUT YOU SHOVED ME INTO A LOCKER.
OH YEAH.
SORRY ABOUT THAT. FORCE OF HABIT.
SO HOW 'BOUT BEING ISAAC'S DATE AT THE-

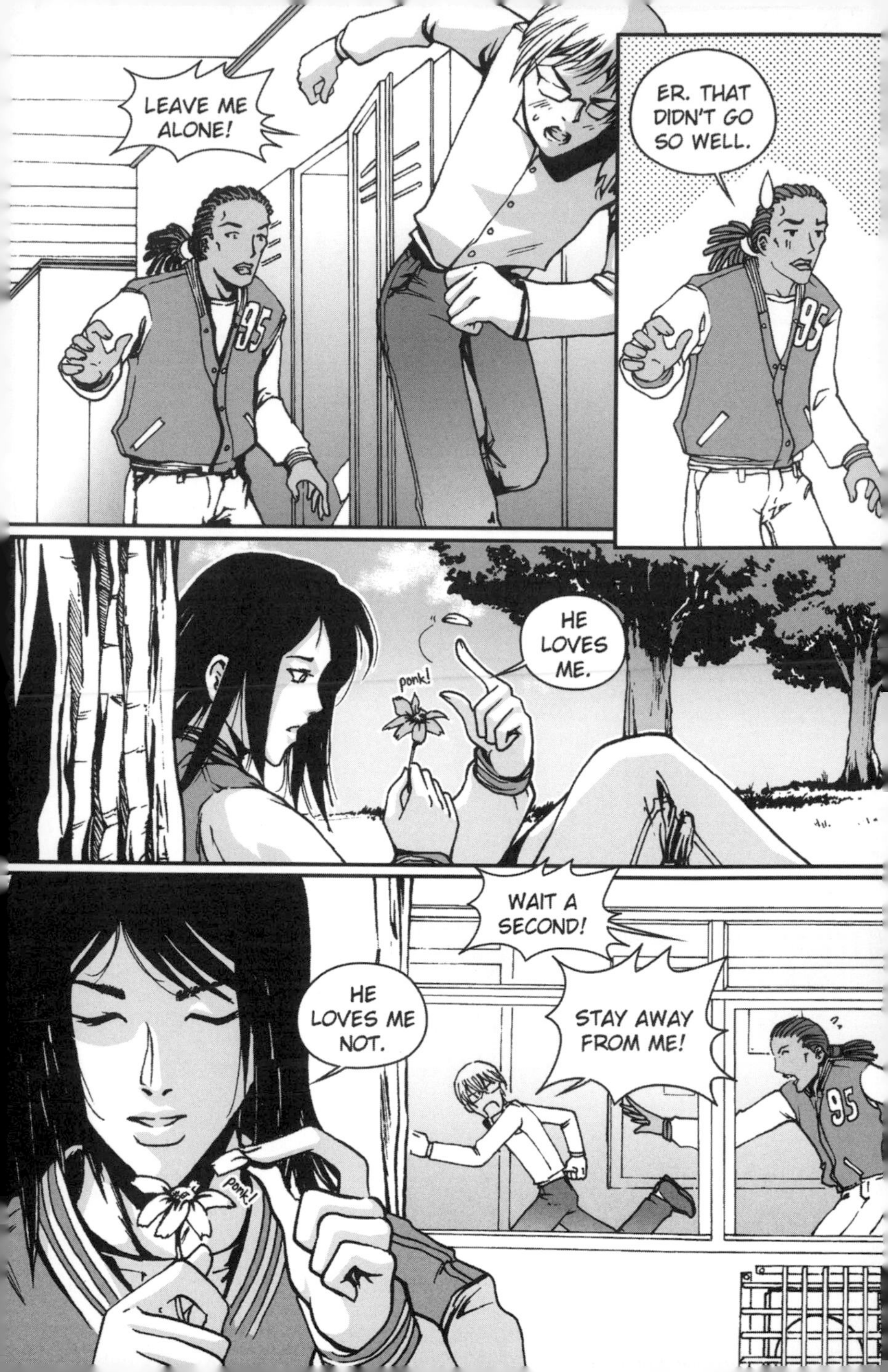
LEAVE ME ALONE!
ER. THAT DIDN'T GO SO WELL.
HE LOVES ME.
ponk!
HE LOVES ME NOT.
ponk!
WAIT A SECOND!
STAY AWAY FROM ME!

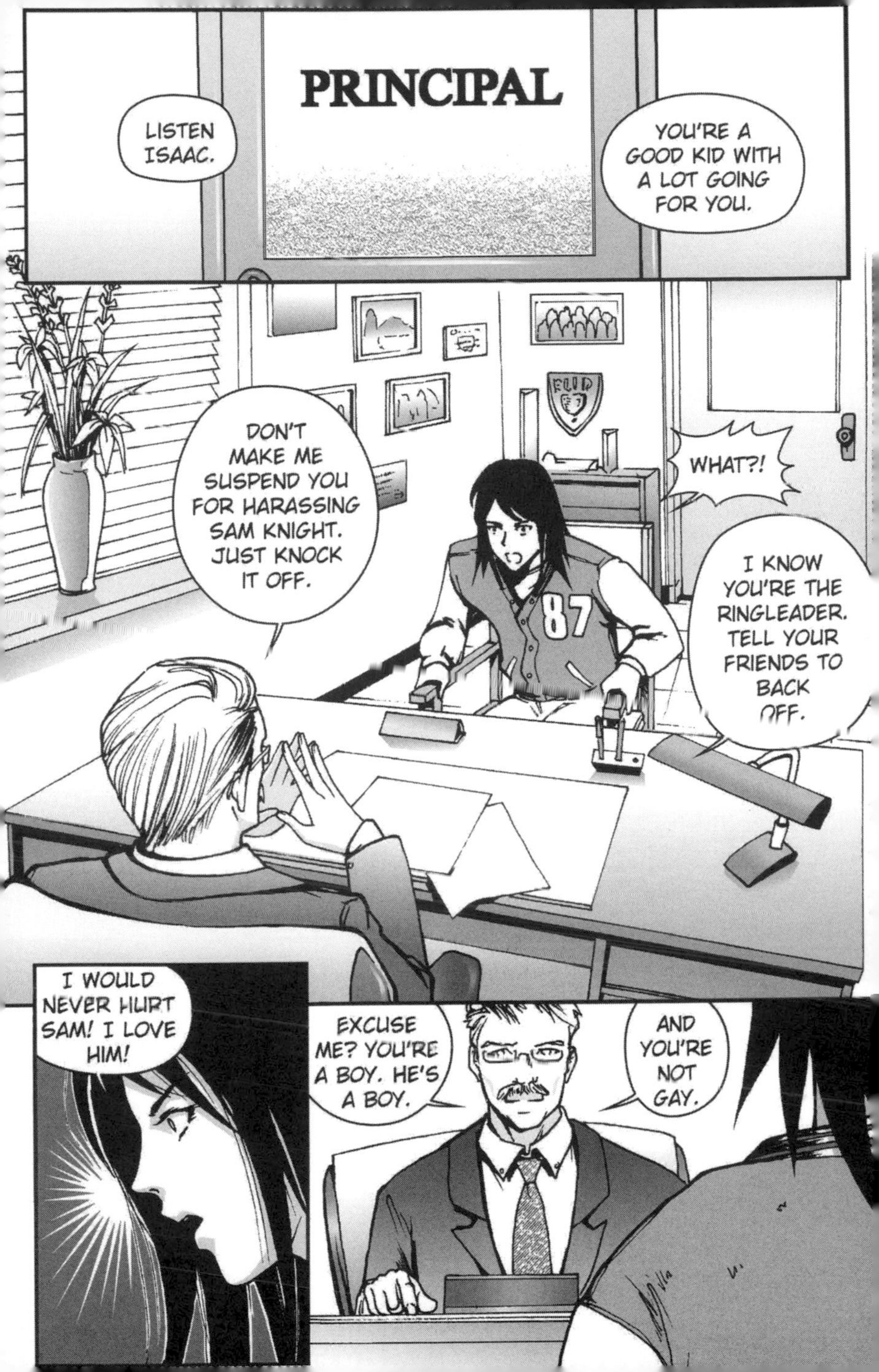
PRINCIPAL
LISTEN ISAAC.
YOU'RE A GOOD KID WITH A LOT GOING FOR YOU.
DON'T MAKE ME SUSPEND YOU FOR HARASSING SAM KNIGHT. JUST KNOCK IT OFF.
WHAT?!
I KNOW YOU'RE THE RINGLEADER. TELL YOUR FRIENDS TO BACK OFF.
87
I WOULD NEVER HURT SAM! I LOVE HIM!
EXCUSE ME? YOU'RE A BOY. HE'S A BOY.
AND YOU'RE NOT GAY.

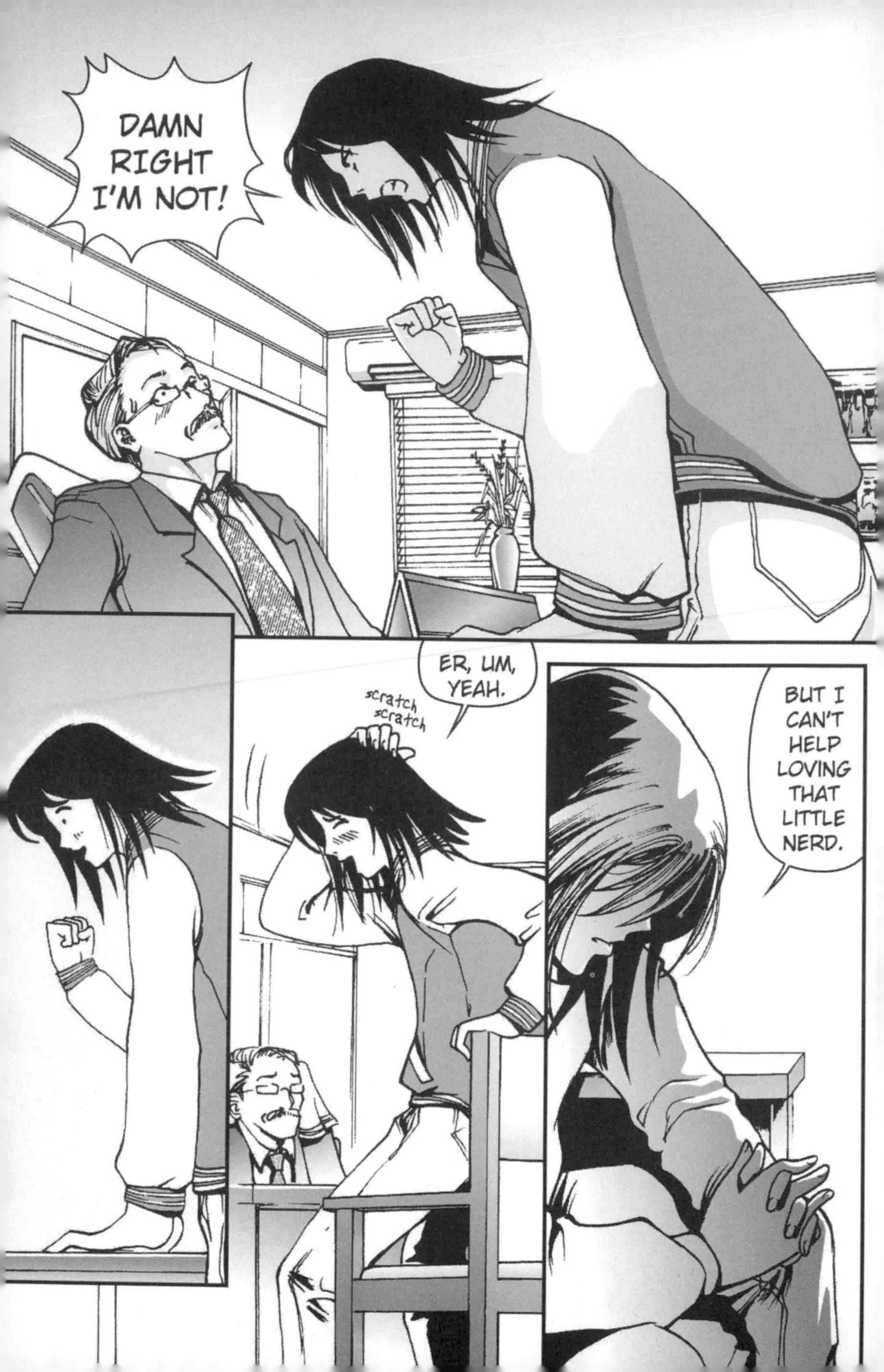
DAMN RIGHT I'M NOT!
ER, UM, YEAH.
scratch scratch
BUT I CAN'T HELP LOVING THAT LITTLE NERD.

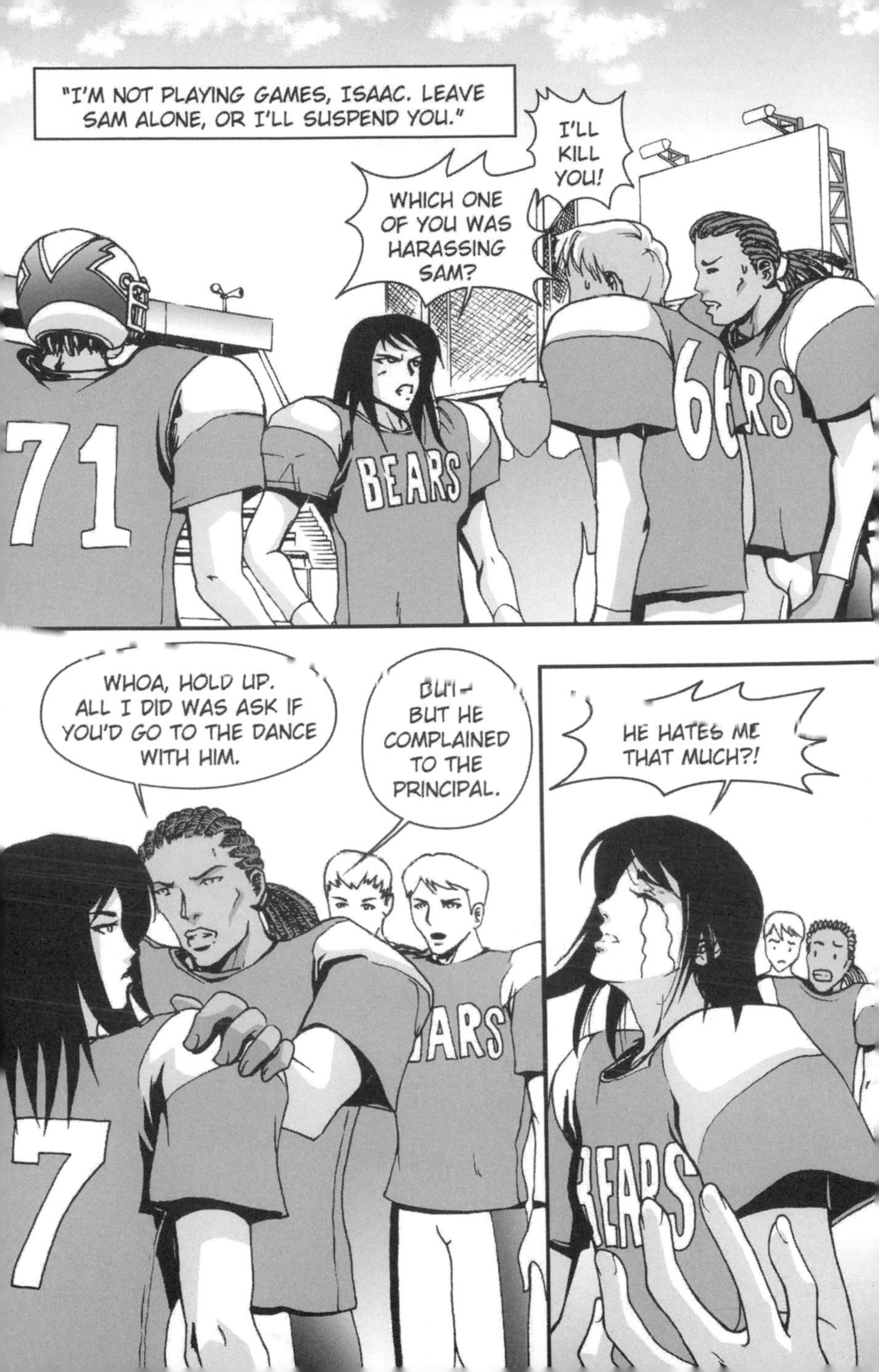
"I'M NOT PLAYING GAMES, ISAAC. LEAVE SAM ALONE, OR I'LL SUSPEND YOU."
WHICH ONE OF YOU WAS HARASSING SAM?
I'LL KILL YOU!
WHOA, HOLD UP. ALL I DID WAS ASK IF YOU'D GO TO THE DANCE WITH HIM.
BUT– BUT HE COMPLAINED TO THE PRINCIPAL.
HE HATES ME THAT MUCH?!

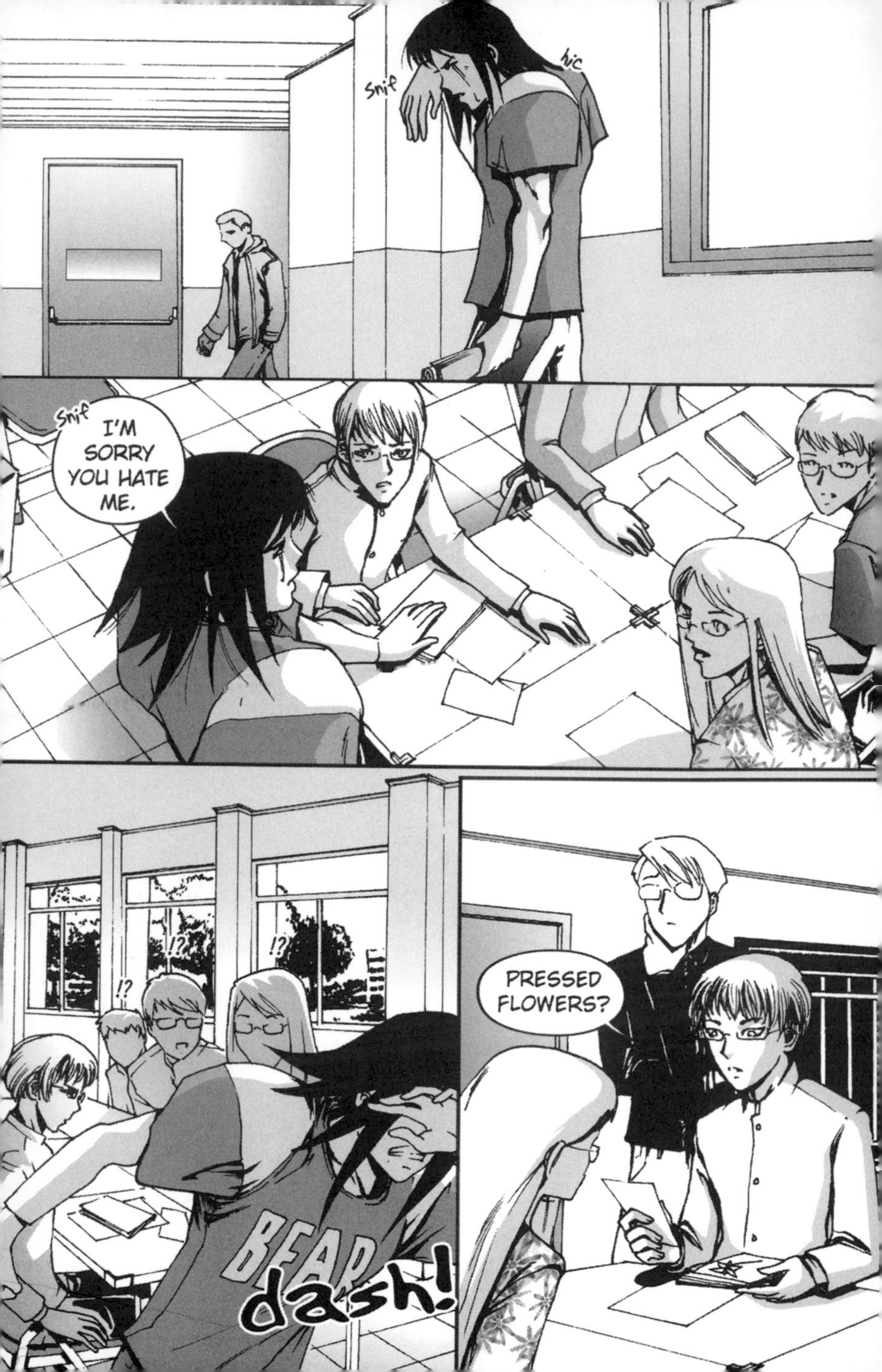
Snif
hic
Snif
I'M SORRY YOU HATE ME.
!?
!?
!?
BEAR
dash!
PRESSED FLOWERS?

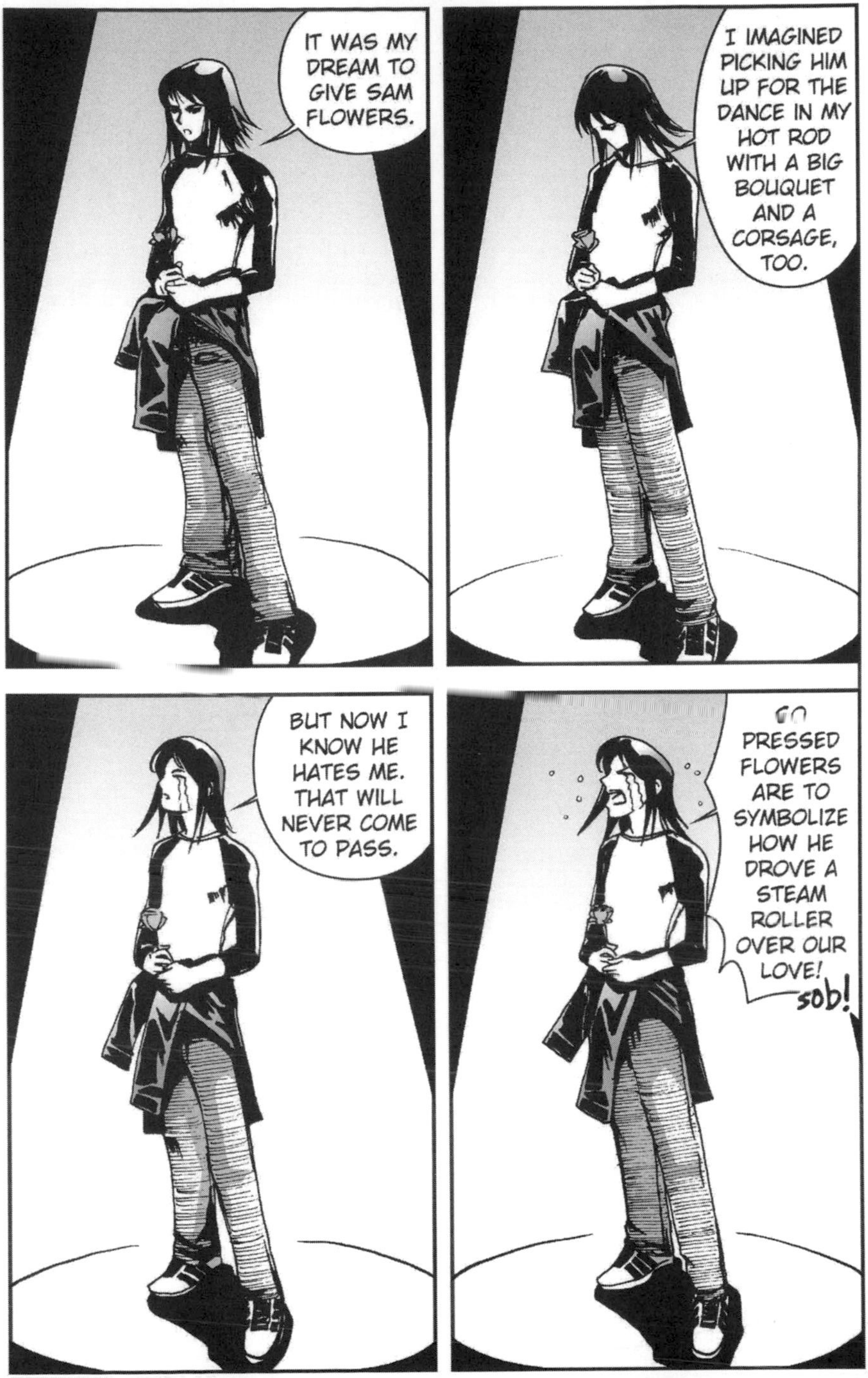
IT WAS MY DREAM TO GIVE SAM FLOWERS.
I IMAGINED PICKING HIM UP FOR THE DANCE IN MY HOT ROD WITH A BIG BOUQUET AND A CORSAGE, TOO.
BUT NOW I KNOW HE HATES ME. THAT WILL NEVER COME TO PASS.
PRESSED FLOWERS ARE TO SYMBOLIZE HOW HE DROVE A STEAM ROLLER OVER OUR LOVE!
sob!

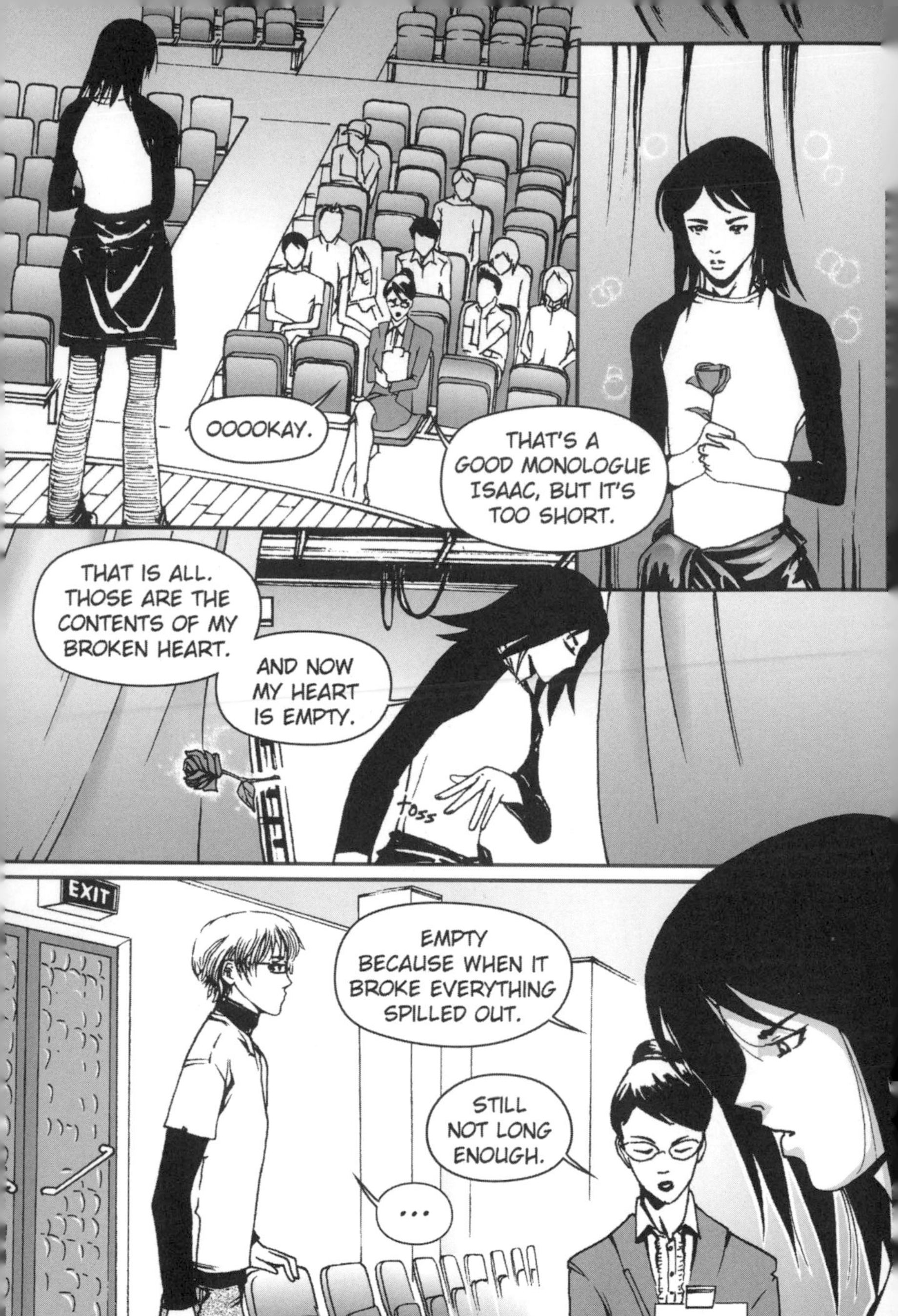
OOOOKAY.
THAT'S A GOOD MONOLOGUE ISAAC, BUT IT'S TOO SHORT.
THAT IS ALL. THOSE ARE THE CONTENTS OF MY BROKEN HEART.
AND NOW MY HEART IS EMPTY.
TOSS
EXIT
EMPTY BECAUSE WHEN IT BROKE EVERYTHING SPILLED OUT.
STILL NOT LONG ENOUGH.
...

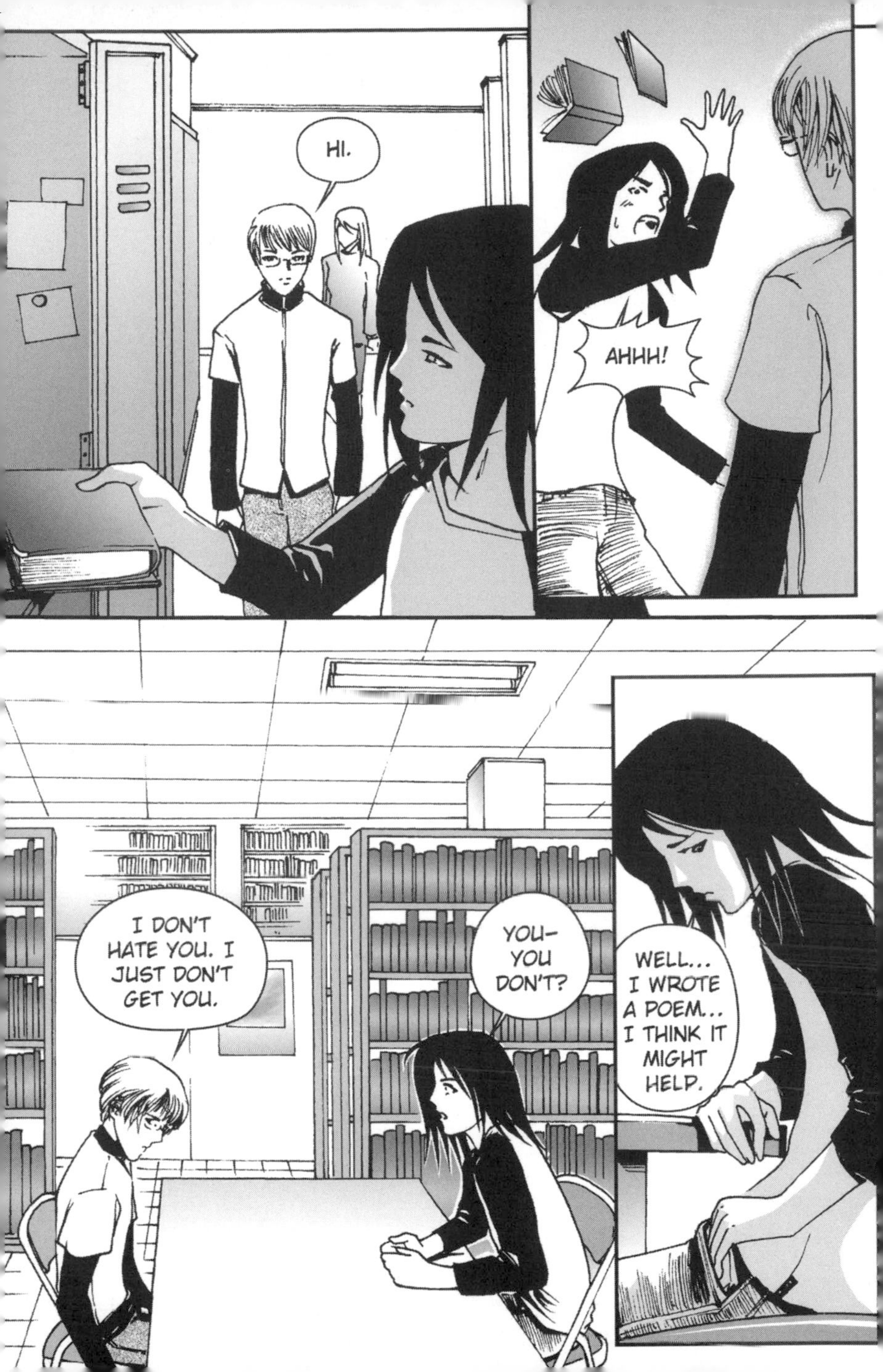
HI.
AHHH!
I DON'T HATE YOU. I JUST DON'T GET YOU.
YOU— YOU DON'T?
WELL... I WROTE A POEM... I THINK IT MIGHT HELP.

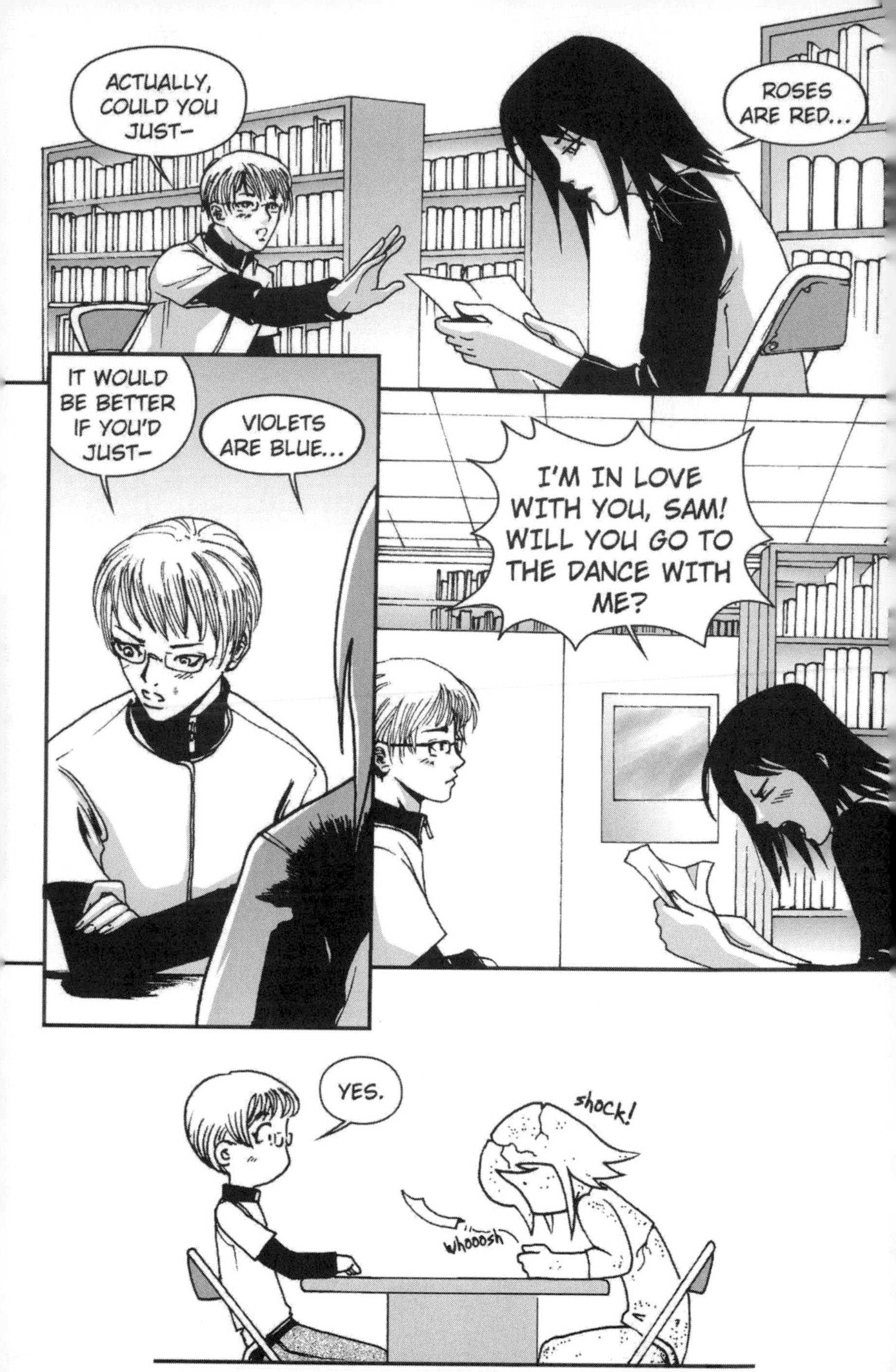
ACTUALLY, COULD YOU JUST-
ROSES ARE RED...
IT WOULD BE BETTER IF YOU'D JUST-
VIOLETS ARE BLUE...
I'M IN LOVE WITH YOU, SAM! WILL YOU GO TO THE DANCE WITH ME?
YES.
shock!
whooosh

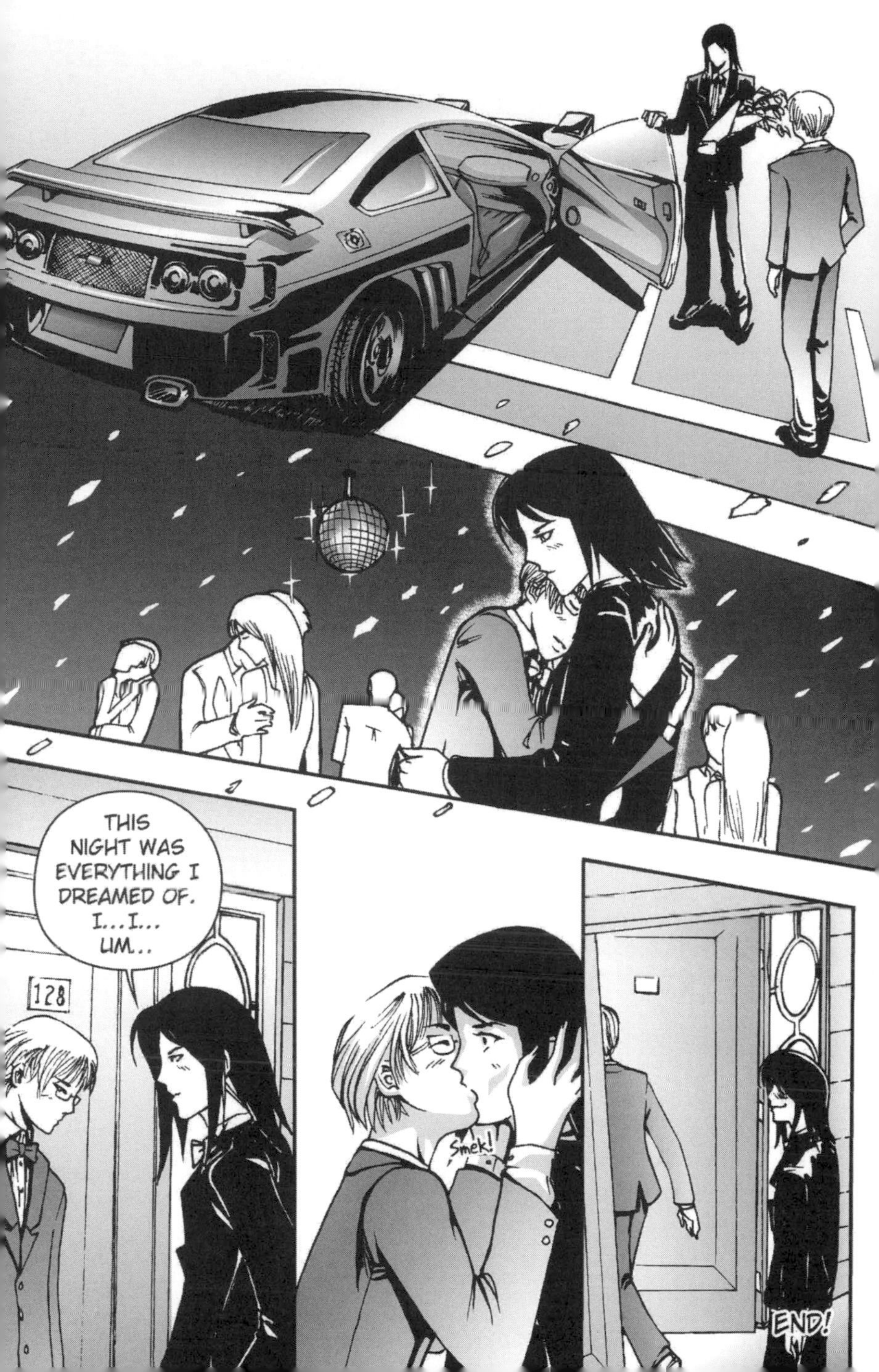
THIS NIGHT WAS EVERYTHING I DREAMED OF. I...I... UM..
Smek!
END!

Coming Jan. 2007!

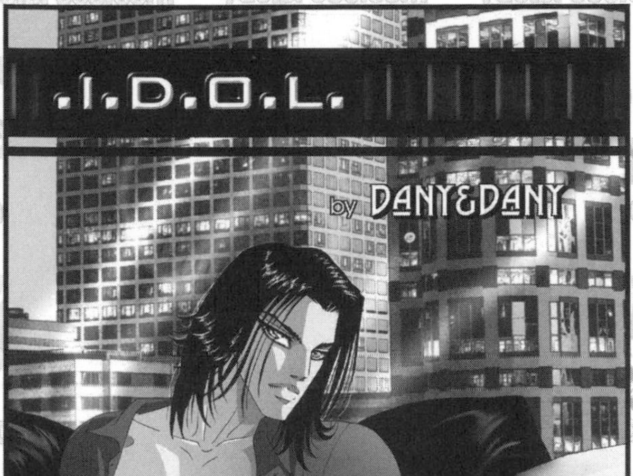
.I.D.O.L.
by DANY&DANY

Idol

by Dany&Dany

The jaded artist David hires the hustler Adam as an art model. This painting finally conveys the passion in David's heart. His model stirs passions of another kind. Acting on these feelings draws David into Adam's dark world of dangerous liaisons and jealous lovers.

THE ENGLISH LANGUAGE DEBUT OF THE RENOWNED ITALIAN YAOI STUDIO DANY&DANY!

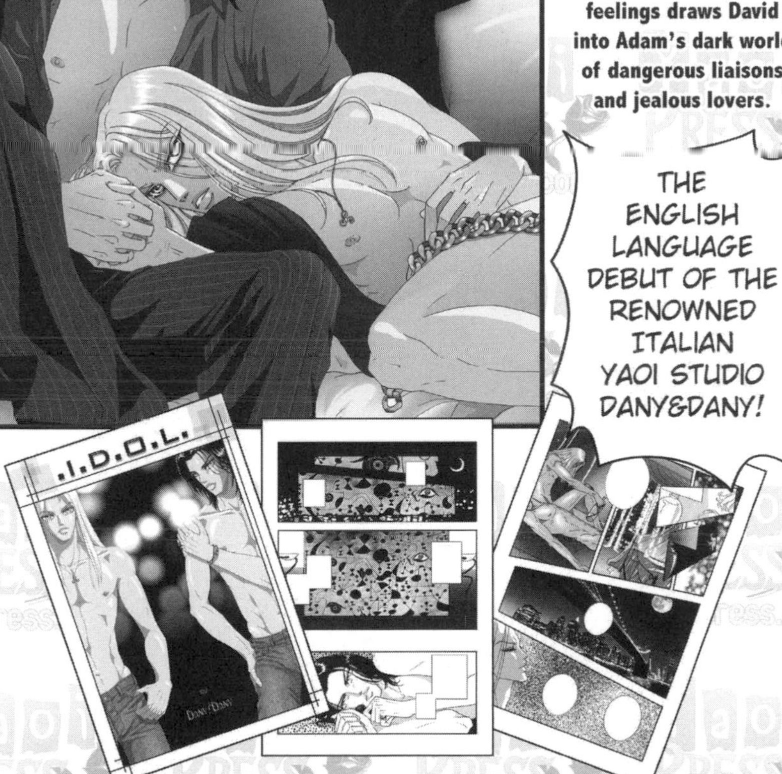
.I.D.O.L.
DANY&DANY

Coming Feb. 2007!

Yaoi Vol.1
Various Artists

Yaoi anthology of three heart wrenching love stories. First theres romance between prisoners of a medieval circus, then between members of rival Tokyo gangs, and finally, between a cop and a young man who escapes two sadistic hillbilly captors.

Available Now!

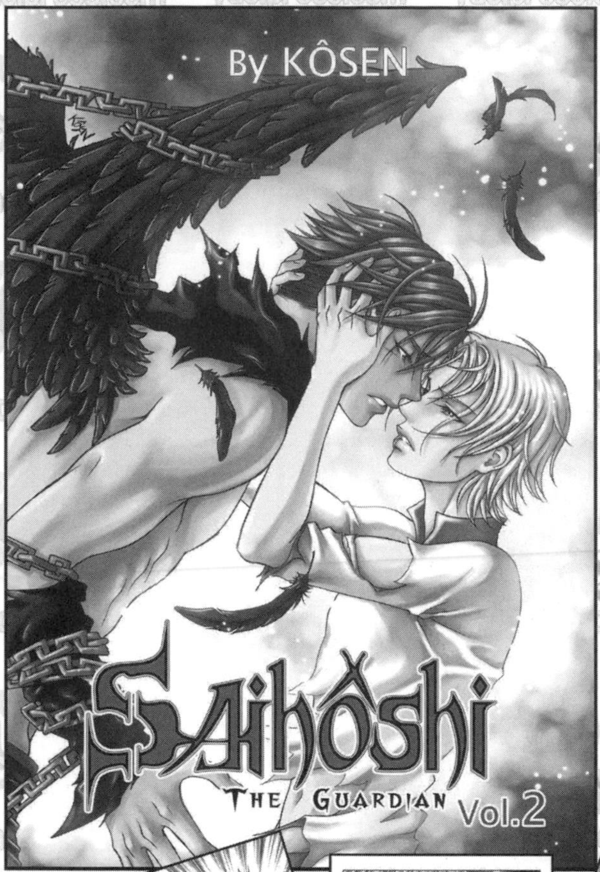
By KÔSEN
Saihôshi
THE GUARDIAN Vol.2

Saihôshi the Guardian Vol 2

by KÔSEN

The second and final volume of the smash hit series. If the guardian Sastre wants to avoid a death sentence he must rescue Prince Anel, defeat his rival Riot, and prevail against a rogue guardian. That leaves little time to protect Anel's decoy, who he's fallen in love with.

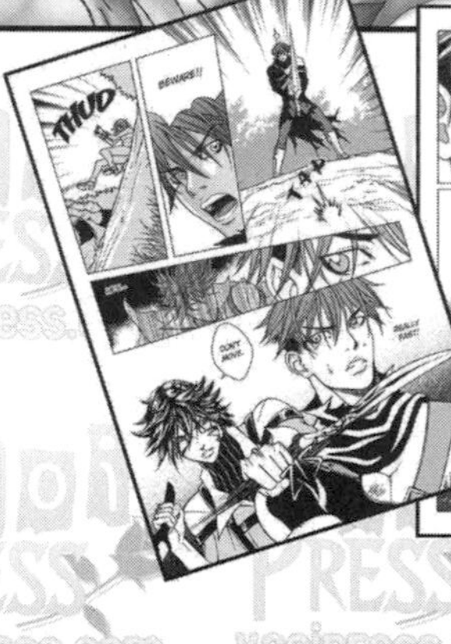

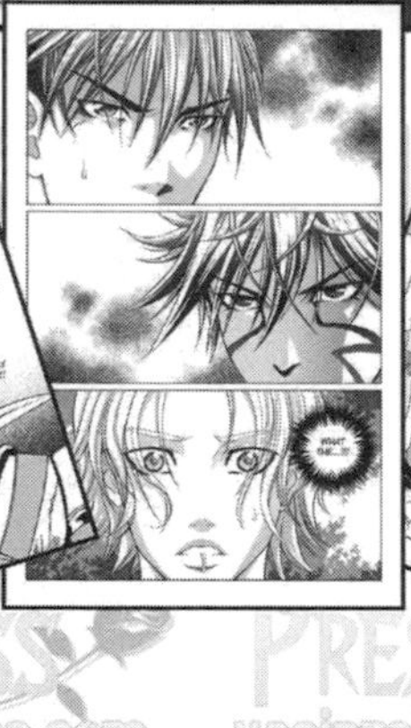

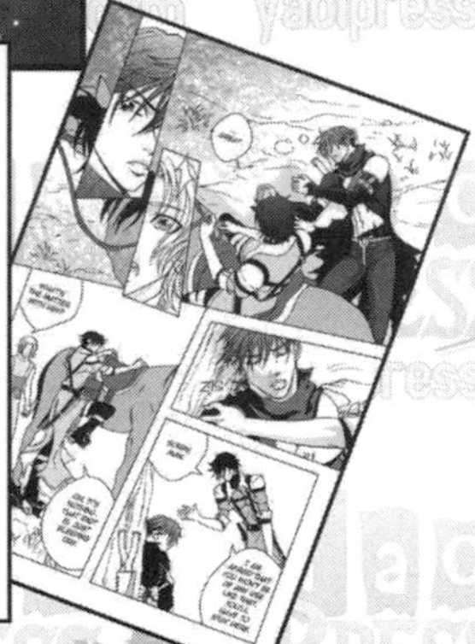

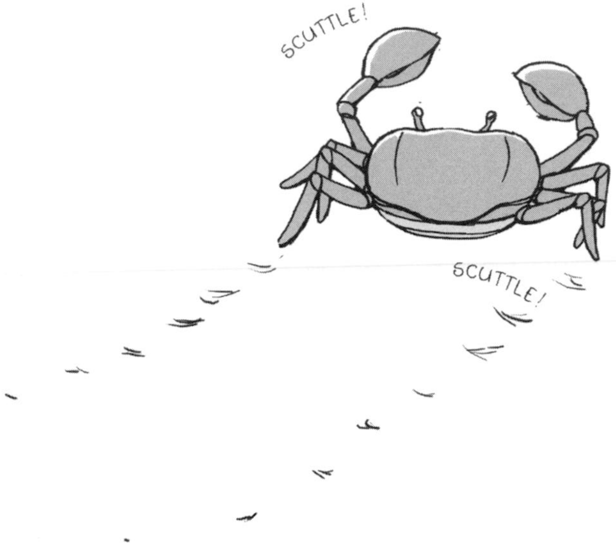
SCUTTLE!
SCUTTLE!